BROTHER
LOVE

BROTHER
LOVE

Murder, Money, and a Messiah

Sydney P. Freedberg

Pantheon Books, *New York*

A cataloging-in-publication record has been prepared for
this title by the Library of Congress.

ISBN: 0-679-42015-0
LC: 94-4606

BOOK DESIGN BY LAURA HOUGH

MANUFACTURED IN THE UNITED STATES OF AMERICA
FIRST EDITION
9 8 7 6 5 4 3 2 1

To Ira, Lucille, Robin and Ali

Contents

Who's Who
ix

Part I Autumn of Terror
1

Part II Divine Calling
35

Part III Heaven on Earth
87

Part IV Operation Jericho
257

Source Notes
317

Who's Who

The Principal:

Hulon Mitchell, Jr., also known as Hulon X, also known as Hulon Shah, also known as Father Michel, also known as Brother Love, also known as Moses Israel, also known as Ock Moshe Israel, also known as Emmanuel, also known as Yahshua the messiah, also known as Yahweh the messiah, also known as Yahweh Ben Yahweh

Supporting Characters:

Father: Hulon Mitchell, Sr.—reverend in the Church of God In Christ

Mother: Pearl Olive Mitchell—nurse, pianist, singer, inspiration for her fifteen children

Pre-Yahweh wives: the former Nodie Mae Chiles and the former Chloe Hight

Sister: Palmor Jean Mitchell Solomon, also known as Deborah Vashti Israel—Mitchell child number six, a temple teacher and chef

Nephew: Anthony Solomon, also known as Joshua Israel—Jean Solomon's son, a temple doctor-in-training

Cousin: Carter Cornelius, also known as Gideon Israel—a popular singer and temple elder

Son: Hulon Mitchell III, also known as Zedekiah Israel—the youngest of Yahweh Ben Yahweh's four biological children and a bodyguard for his father

Who's Who

Temple Dissidents:

Eric Burke, also known as Yakim Israel—an air-conditioning mechanic

Carlton Carey, also known as Mishael Israel—an accountant

Aston Green, also known as Elijah Israel—Carlton Carey's Jamaican-born roommate

Mildred Banks, also known as Danielle Israel—Carlton's temple wife, a postal worker

A man known only as Melchizedek, the boyfriend of a temple member

Leonard Dupree, also known as Azariah Israel—a karate black belt from New Orleans

Other Key Characters:

Linda Gaines, also known as Judith Israel—number-two person in the temple

Linda's children—Freddie, Jr., also known as Solomon Israel; Kelly, also known as Jeremiah Israel; Lydia, also known as Sarah Israel

Lloyd Clark, also known as Yehudah Israel—a onetime temple elder, member of the dance troupe

Ricardo Woodside, also known as Zerubbabel Israel—Lloyd Clark's best friend, an elder in Jacksonville

John Foster, also known as Enoch Israel—head of the temple's Circle of Ten security force

Richard Ingraham, also known as Job Israel—the temple's hairstylist, one of Yahweh's most devoted followers

Patricia Albert, also known as Sherah Israel—a girl from Enid, Oklahoma, one of Yahweh Ben Yahweh's alleged wives

Jeffrey Glover, also known as Abyah Israel—Pat's stepfather, a onetime elder

Michael Mathis, also known as Aushalom Israel—Pat Albert's husband, a member of the Circle of Ten

Walter Lightburn, also known as Amri Israel—a temple electrician, karate expert, and onetime elder

Robert Beasley, Jr., also known as Dan Israel—Atlanta elder

Sharon Saunders, also known as Sharon Israel—one of Robert Beasley's wives

Ernest Lee James, Jr., also known as Ahinadab Israel—a county water worker

Robert Rozier, Jr., also known as Neariah Israel—a onetime elder, temple strongman

Broderick McKinney, also known as Uriah David Israel—an Atlanta hotel manager, the temple's national ambassador

Key Establishment Supporters:

Xavier Suarez, Miami mayor
Arthur Teele, Dade County commissioner
Ellis Rubin, temple house counsel
David Lazarus, temple civil lawyer

Lawmen:

John King, Metro-Dade County homicide detective
Rex Remley, Metro-Dade County homicide detective
Herbert Cousins, Jr., FBI special agent
Richard Scruggs, assistant U.S. attorney
Gertrude Novicki, assistant Dade County state attorney
Janet Reno, Dade County state attorney

Who's Who

Non-Member Murders That Investigators Suspect Are Connected to Followers of Yahweh:

Attilio Scalo, an intoxicated person in his fifties from Newark

Ricardo McGee, a man looking for a job in Broward County

Harold Barnett, an elderly man who drank vodka and slept near temple property

Glendell Fowler, a hospital technician

Kurt Doerr, a waiter

Michael Mahaven, a credit manager living with his grandmother in Pittsburgh

Clair Walters, a Vietnam veteran squatting in an abandoned motel in Miami

James Lee Myers, an unemployed maintenance man from Indiana walking along Biscayne Boulevard in Miami

Elizabeth Schwark, a San Francisco woman in her forties who worked as a waitress and was trying to "find herself" in Miami

Luis Llerena, a man with a professionally done tattoo on his right arm depicting a casket with flowers and a cross

Lyle Bellinger, a street-corner preacher wearing a Star of David T-shirt

Raymond Kelley, a master mechanic

Cecil Branch, a county garbageman who had a confrontation with a Yahweh woman

Harry Byers, an elderly man sleeping on a park bench

Reinaldo Echevarria, a onetime bank clerk from Cuba

Rudolph Broussard, an unemployed man with a broken arm living near his sister in an Opa-locka housing project

Anthony Brown, a friend of Rudolph Broussard's who blasphemed Yahweh

Part I

Autumn of Terror

1

Eric Burke cranked shut the windows in his apartment. The lights were off. It was Wednesday, November 11, 2 A.M. He pulled over a chair to the living-room window and peered through a corner of the flowered curtains. He loaded his blue-steel .357 Magnum. Then he waited for the killers to come.

A sliver of yellow light from a small bulb, tacked to the side of the gray stucco building, shone into Eric's apartment, number 1. His corner, one-bedroom walkup was clean but sparsely furnished. A broken TV, a frayed sofa, and a few chairs and tables were arranged to hide the dirty green carpet.

A paperback, *You Are Not a Nigger! Our True History, the World's Best-Kept Secret: Yahweh God of Gods*, topped a stack of papers and pamphlets neatly organized on a table.

Eric angled his eyes toward Northwest Sixty-second Street. He couldn't see anything. The odor of acrid free-base cocaine sometimes filtered through the neighborhood. Transformers hummed, punctuated by an occasional siren, a motorcycle howl, or a fast pop-pop that no one in Miami's Liberty City ever mistook for a car backfiring.

About four miles north of the glass-and-steel skyscrapers, Armani suits, and black Porsches of downtown Miami, Liberty City is a neighborhood of neat, Easter egg–colored houses, crowded apartments, and bars, mixed haphazardly with small grocery shops and churches. The neighborhood was constructed in the 1930s to relieve overcrowding in nearby "Colored Town." Ever since, Liberty City has been notorious for race riots prompted by the periodic killing of black men by the police.

Eric's apartment, situated next to a church and across the street from a coin laundry, wasn't far from where the big 1980 riot started. It erupted after a jury acquitted four white policemen in the beating death of Arthur McDuffie, a black insurance man. The medical examiner testified that they cracked McDuffie's skull "like an eggshell." But the facts were so hard to figure out, the jury simply let everyone off. From his second-floor window, Eric heard the gunshots, got his bites of tear gas, and watched as a marauding gang of teenagers torched the tire store next door. He knew his building would be next because his landlord was Cuban. He tried to get the police to help, but they were nowhere in sight. They stood outside the "riot zone," skittishly agreeing to let black people blow off steam as long as they did it in their own neighborhood. Eric reached for his pistol, ran downstairs, and scared off the armed arsonists. He saved his building, became a neighborhood hero, and wore his McDuffie T-shirt with pride. That was seventeen months earlier.

Now, Eric thumbed the safety catch on his Magnum to off. He tried to decide from which direction the killers might come. He figured they would approach from the east, following a narrow path through a vacant lot below his window. They would climb the flight of stairs outside the building.

Framed by a rattling, wrought-iron handrail, the staircase led directly to his apartment. The twenty concrete steps were littered with scraps of trash. At the base of the stairwell was an overflowing garbage can and some old appliances—toaster ovens and air conditioners Eric had been meaning to fix.

He never got to it. His fear, escalating for about a month, had wreaked havoc on his schedule. He thought he was being watched, but if they made a move, he knew he had the guts to blow them away. "Bunch of fuckin' faggots," Eric fumed.

A short, slender man with coffee-colored skin, small braids, and a goatee, Eric liked to stand up against things most men wouldn't dream of standing up against. He had no tolerance for con men of any type—dope dealers, prostitutes, pimps, dirty cops, preachers, faith healers, all the money-mad demagogues robbing the people of the few pennies they had. Eric Lorenzo Burke seemed to find them wherever he went.

Born in the Panama Canal Zone on May 17, 1937, he went to school through the twelfth grade and learned how to hustle for a buck. He could fix anything that was broken, but he specialized in air conditioner repairs. Eric lived in New York for a while, but finding it too big and too cold, he fled to the Magic City. The pace of the South seemed to suit him better. He spoke perfect Spanish, and his friends thought he was part Spanish, part West Indian, and part indigenous Indian. But Eric didn't play the skin-color game. As far as he was concerned, he wasn't mixed blood—black, colored, Negro, nigger, coon, spade, African-American, or any other label the world pinned on him. He was a Hebrew Israelite, and for two years he had studied with a group of people who traced their lineage to the biblical Tribe of Judah. They discussed the world situation together and called the big white building where they met the Yahweh temple, or the Temple of Love. It was just a few blocks from Eric Burke's apartment. He had found the people warm and caring, not like some blindly ignorant Christians swaying in their seats and bursting into hallelujahs. They didn't believe the meek would inherit the earth. They thought that by standing up for themselves, they would. For a long time Eric believed he had found heaven on earth. But by Tuesday night, November 10, he had become absolutely disillusioned. He feared that the very people he had turned to for salvation were about to do him in.

At 11 P.M., a few hours before he stood guard at the window, someone knocked on Eric's door.

He peeked out. It was Brother Samuel, a talented artist who had once attended Hebrew classes with Eric. Why was Samuel coming here so late, Eric wondered. Suspicious, he picked up the telephone and called his friend Horace. Eric quietly asked Horace to call back. Eric would just let the phone ring. That way, Samuel, assuming no one was home, would go away.

The phone rang in Eric's apartment. When he stole a look outside, Samuel was still standing there. He wasn't holding a gun, a knife, or anything Eric could see, but Samuel wasn't leaving, either. When the telephone stopped ringing, Eric drew back and dialed Horace's number again.

Eric whispered that Samuel was still prowling around outside.

5

Again, Horace called Eric's apartment. The phone kept ringing. Five minutes went by. The phone stopped. Ten minutes. Samuel just stood there. Fifteen minutes passed. Eric had three options: call the cops, get killed, or kick Samuel's butt. Eric didn't trust the police. If he dialed 911, they'd probably start asking about his past—about the time he ripped off a guy or the time he smacked his girlfriend around. Or worse. His skin crawled whenever he saw a cop in Liberty City beat people upside the head with a flashlight. Eric decided to help himself.

As it turned out, he didn't have to. Twenty minutes after arriving, Samuel walked down the stairs, his figure retreating in the dim light.

Eric suspected he knew who was behind Samuel's visit. Just a few weeks before, intruders had broken into Eric's apartment. It was a warning, he had told a neighbor. If they came twice, they might come a third time.

A few minutes later Eric heard another knock on the door. When he looked through the window, he saw a silhouette—a tall, lanky man with a pistol in his hand. Eric looked closer, finally realizing who it was: his friend Horace, a fellow Hebrew Israelite. The two men had once passed the Word together, distributing leaflets about their religion to their brothers and sisters floundering in darkness.

Eric unbolted the door and joined his buddy outside. Horace said he was uneasy. Did Eric need help? Eric said he felt certain Samuel had been sent as a lookout. Eric was fed up. He didn't care what it took to deal with the problem. He didn't know, didn't really care, whether it was truly evil people who were after him or good people who just did bad things. Maybe they didn't want to kill him. Maybe they simply wanted to warn him or to shock him into doing something silly, like coming after them with a gun. Whatever their intentions, Eric told Horace, he could handle it alone. Horace handed him a gun and left.

Before going inside, Eric sprinkled broken glass on the steps leading to his dark apartment. If someone came back, he would hear them, even if he didn't see them. Eric walked inside and secured the door bolt. He slouched in a living-room chair and dozed off.

It was Wednesday, November 11, 3 A.M. A guard dog named Flipper was chained to the garage door of Eric's building. For some reason, the dog hadn't warded off Samuel earlier that night. A white German shepherd, Flipper had bitten twenty-eight would-be muggers in the past, sometimes injuring them severely. But something was wrong tonight. Flipper wasn't barking.

Suddenly, Eric woke up to the sound of crackling glass. He fumbled for his gun, tried to stay composed.

He heard a scraping, scratching at the lock on his front door. Someone was trying to get in. Eric edged toward the door. Then he darted to the window and saw two, three, or possibly four black men. One looked familiar.

"Get him!" Eric heard someone say.

Someone hurled himself against the door. And again. The door held. Eric aimed the gun and sent a slug or two out the window.

People heard the cracks from a distance. No one came to help. In Liberty City, not many people do; trouble finds the innocent fast enough.

After a few seconds, the noise died down. Eric opened the front door. The intruders were taking off in different directions. They wore dark clothes and knit caps.

Eric bolted downstairs, careful not to touch the handrail. Preserve the fingerprints. Call the police. Two ten-inch kitchen knives glinted at the base of the stairwell. The knives looked familiar. One had a black handle, the other a brown one. They weren't there before. Had he seen them in the kitchen of the Temple of Love? Next to the knives was a wooden club.

Eric banged on a neighbor's door, which was dented and scratched from attempted break-ins. The neighbor stumbled out of bed, and the two men ran upstairs to Eric's apartment. He didn't have a choice. He knew he had to call the cops. He picked up the telephone. The line was dead. Eric and his neighbor checked the overhead wire outside the door. The would-be killers had cut it.

From the neighbor's apartment, Eric dialed 911. The call came in at 3:11 A.M., the 387,250th emergency call of 1981 in Dade County, Florida. "They cut the telephone lines," Eric said, "and when I made known to them . . ."

The 911 operator logged the complaint routinely. Code 26. Burglary. Just another attempted break-in in Liberty City. In Miami, where people are strangled with dead snakes and motorists are shot for making a left turn too slowly, burglaries are too frequent to get excited about.

Patrolman Timothy Wiseman, badge number 2089, was cruising the streets of the Central District when he got the call from the dispatcher. The night had been relatively peaceful, and the officer pulled to the curb in minutes. As Wiseman shone his flashlight, Eric sputtered about what had happened. The officer jotted down a few particulars: "Victim advised that he was a former member of the Yahweh temple and that the other members are trying to get back at him."

Officer Wiseman, a baby on the midnight shift, was hired four months after the McDuffie riot. He observed the cut black telephone wire, collected the knives for the property room, and at 4:20 A.M. handed Eric a case number. Wiseman didn't interview any neighbors "due to time of day." No one dusted for fingerprints. "No scene to process," he wrote in his report.

After telling Eric a detective would be in touch, Officer Wiseman left the scene. He began cruising the streets for muggers and killers he could see.

2

Paul Addison backed his truck up to a dirt road on the edge of the Everglades. He needed to check on heavy equipment at a rock pit. As he made a broken U-turn, he looked to the right, then straight ahead. He noticed the red blanket.

It was Friday, November 13, about 11:30 A.M. Paul had already been on the job four and a half hours. A superintendent for Capeletti Brothers, Inc., a paving contractor that dug rock, sand, and black muck from the ground, Paul supervised production at three rock pits. He also was in charge of the expensive machinery used in the dredging operations.

Paul's crew had left a bulldozer and other heavy equipment unsecured overnight, on the south side of Capeletti's pit number nine. Though he had checked the equipment twice before that morning, Paul was still worried about it. If anything happened to that equipment, his boss might make him pay. An old special forces soldier, Paul had once served as General Maxwell Taylor's personal bodyguard. He knew about chains of command.

In the old days, the construction equipment, no matter how expensive, would have been completely safe. The rock pits used to be practically impossible to find. No street signs, no houses, just centuries-old grass, bearded live oaks, black-water canals, and here and there a snake or a panther lurking in the undergrowth.

In 1981, however, the east Everglades were hardly bucolic. Organized criminals were exploiting the land for any possible profit. Though still wooded and undeveloped, the Glades had become a gathering spot for soldiers of fortune, veterans of the Bay of Pigs, and anti-Sandinista rebels training to kill dictators back home. American mobsters and cocaine cowboys from the emerging Colombian cartels dumped corpses there. More amateurish criminals, petty vandals, and high school thrill seekers used the land for target practice. They liked to take shots at soda and beer cans, empty packs of cigarettes, and heavy construction equipment. Paul remembered the time they'd shelled a Capeletti bulldozer. The replacement parts had cost thousands of dollars.

As he headed to pit number nine, Paul spotted a medium-size truck with tinted windows. He didn't recognize it. He stopped his three-quarter-ton Chevy near a dirt road, beneath some high-tension utility wires. The road was blocked by a long plastic pipe, strung between two wooden posts. Paul did a double take on that red blanket. It was lying atop tall, saw-toothed grass, just a couple of feet from the road. Paul hadn't noticed the blanket the other times he had checked on the equipment that morning.

He climbed from his truck to investigate, and as he got closer, he thought he saw something underneath the blanket.

Paul circled, stopping near a utility pole, a few feet from the roadblock. Something was under the blanket. He bent over and peeked. A dead person. Blood was dripping from the body. No, Paul thought, it can't be a person.

"My God!" he said to himself. "A neck. No head. . . . Did this just happen?"

Paul knew the best thing to do was to get the hell out of there. As he turned to go back to his truck, he noticed a melaleuca tree, about seven feet tall, to the right of the body. Blood was splattered on its leaves.

He ran to his truck, so scared he didn't know what to do. He had seen some horrible things in his life, but never anything like this. He reached for the truck radio to call his office. "Get security out," he shrieked.

Minutes later, or perhaps minutes before, a jogger running along the road came upon the same gruesome sight. The jogger hailed a worker driving through the area. He radioed the police. The jogger kept running.

The police finally dispatched units at 12:50 P.M.: An apparent "deceased person" in two parts at about Northwest 136th Avenue and Twenty-fifth Street, about five miles west of Miami's sprawling international airport. The second homicide of the day, the 530th homicide in what would be Dade County's banner murder year.

In Little Havana's La Esquina de Tejas restaurant, where Ronald Reagan would one day eat lunch, Detectives John King and Randy Baker were checking out the customers as they sipped café Cubano from thimble cups. The waitress had just set down King's arroz con pollo when he got a call on his radio. Call homicide.

At 2 P.M., when the detectives arrived at the crime scene, it was already swarming with squad cars, Capeletti security trucks, Florida Power & Light linemen, passersby, and rubberneckers. King walked over to the headless torso for a quick inspection: the victim was a black male, lying on his back near a drainage stream. The body seemed to have been positioned as though for burial: left leg crossed over right, arms crossed over the chest. The red blanket was beside it. That wasn't the way the body looked when Paul found it. Evidently, some curious bystander had already messed with the scene, removing the torso from the blanket and flipping it on its back.

The victim was fully clothed. The collar and shoulder portion of his white T-shirt, bearing a green logo with the words *Florida Atlantic University*, was stained with blood. His cloth belt had red, yellow, and green stripes, the colors of the Ethiopian flag, sometimes worn to symbolize the battle for Pan-African independence. Maybe a Jamaican doper, the detectives surmised, possibly a Rastafarian. The cops had had trouble with a few Rastas. They were muscling in on Miami's marijuana market, starting to control distribution all the way down to retail dealerships in inner-city neighborhoods. Collectively, they were sometimes called posses. One was called the Shower Posse, because its men liked to shower their victims with bullets. The detectives recalled a case where a posse dismembered a defiant dealer and delivered his body parts to his mother in Kingston.

Detective King reached into the pocket of the dead man's blue jeans, checking for valuables or identification. There were none. No papers, no wallet, no ID. Just five keys on a ring. King put the keys in his pocket and began following a blood trail. Just west of the victim's shoulders was a large coral rock with a circular blood spot, four inches in diameter.

The trail ended at the bank of the drainage stream, three feet and eight inches from the torso. At the edge of the stream was the severed head. It was wrapped in a white sheet and bound with surgical tape. The killers had taped a scrap of green carpet, about eight inches square, to the top of the head. "Unusual," King thought. "A horrible way to die."

For homicide detectives in Miami, the macabre was routine. They had turned up body parts floating in Biscayne Bay and the Miami River. Once, they found a rotten finger, compressed in an inmate's Bible. They told tales of Colombians hacking off arms or ears as a warning to other cocaine smugglers. They even arrested a berserk naked man who cut off his girlfriend's head, carried it through a quiet neighborhood, and finally hurled it to an alarmed patrolman on busy U.S. 1.

What made this decapitated corpse a tad unusual was that the head was so close to the torso. Usually, when a beheading occurred, it was done for the express purpose of confusing authorities as to the victim's identity: the killer would hide the torso in one place; the head would be concealed in a separate burial ground. This homicide was different. It seemed as if the killers wanted the whole world to know what they had done.

The detectives itched to unwrap the white bindings from the victim's head. But the procedure had to be performed by the medical examiner. By midafternoon, a dozen cops waiting for the M.E. were busying themselves at the scene. They measured the body: with the head in its normal position, the victim was about five feet ten inches. The police photographed tire tracks along the dirt road. They dusted the scene for latents—on the blanket, the bushes, anything near the victim that might yield a fingerprint. They impounded a branch of the melaleuca, about five feet from the victim's torso, with a speck of blood on it. They checked the blood spatter in the area. The blood looked pretty fresh and appeared to have originated on the coral rock, spreading outward onto bushes, shrubs, and the plastic-pipe roadblock.

12

The pattern suggested the victim's chest had been placed on top of the rock to extend his neck. Apparently, the killers had severed his head on the rock.

Otherwise, there didn't seem much in the way of clues. More than a few homicides in Dade County were victims disposed of in the Everglades. Some were never solved. In fact, a few victims were never identified.

Dr. Charles Wetli, Dade County's deputy chief medical examiner, finally arrived at the scene. He was easy to spot. He drove up in a 1977 Checker, the kind of vehicle usually seen taxiing passengers around New York City. He lifted the victim's head, unswirled the adhesive tape, and unwrapped the sheet. The dead man's hair was long and nappy, but didn't look like the dreadlocks usually worn by Rastas. The Rastas tried to make their locks resemble a lion's mane. "Maybe they're changing their hairstyle," the pathologist commented.

The police deferred to Wetli. He had done 5,300 autopsies and specialized in ritual homicide. In the past, he had encountered human bones encased in wax and chicken feathers. He had seen a variety of tattoos on Miami homicide victims—from dragons and arrows to patron saints and cult deities to religious death messages, usually etched in black ink. *Hoy soy víctima; mañana seré verdugo,* said one. (Today I am the victim; tomorrow I will be the executioner.) Wetli kept a small collection of skulls, both artificial and real, at the office. The police had found one skull with three pennies and a nickel in the eye socket. They had discovered another atop an iron cauldron filled with dirt, railroad spikes, machetes, and dead goats.

To Wetli, this "decap scene" was probably the most dreadful homicide sight he had ever observed. His eyes glanced away from the severed head. "This is horrible," he said. He requested color photographs of the victim from special angles. "Just because you find a head with a torso does not necessarily mean they go together," the pathologist explained.

He checked the head for injuries. The victim had traumatic, yellowed wounds: a broken tooth, a bloody mouth, a blackened left eye swollen shut, bruises on his cheek, a bloody nose, cuts on his lower and upper jaw, puncture wounds inside his mouth, a half-inch cut just below his hairline, and a big bump on his scalp.

A tough homicide, no way to fix the time of death. But clearly, the man had been struck with some type of object before the decapitation. "It would probably be some instrument such as a stick, steel pipe, or something like that," Wetli said.

On the torso was more evidence of a beating: ligature marks on the victim's wrists; "typical," the pathologist noted, "for someone who was struggling while their wrists were bound, handcuffed, what have you." What's more, Wetli observed patterns on the chest, consistent with sneaker prints. He concluded, "Someone was jumping on the body."

The cuts on the back of the victim's neck and torso suggested the killer or killers hesitated about precisely where to sever the head. Wetli suspected some sort of "chopping, hacking procedure, possibly from a dull machete blade."

The pathologist examined the blood-spray on the foliage. "There isn't an awful lot of blood around," he noted. If the victim had been fully alive at the time of the beheading, Wetli would have expected to find more blood.

As police took two sets of fingerprints and other measurements needed for an ID, Wetli reported his preliminary findings to Detective King: The victim had been gagged, beaten severely, then beheaded from the back. "I don't think he was quite dead," the pathologist said, "but he was probably in the process of dying at the time the decapitation took place."

On Saturday morning, November 14, 1981, Charles Wetli confirmed his initial observations through the official autopsy. There were no identifying marks, no birthmarks. No alcohol on the victim, no drugs. Police technicians checked to see if the man's fingerprints matched any exemplars on file with the FBI's national computer bank. They generated a match from a rap sheet. The cops in neighboring Broward County had taken the victim's prints twice, most recently after a nighttime arrest on October 4, 1980. He had been driving a green Opel without a license plate when the police stopped him. He didn't have a license, a registration, or an ID, so they searched his car and discovered a bag of marijuana.

The FBI called Detective King to report the positive identification. The headless man in the east Everglades, the bureau said, was Aston Vassel Green. A check of Dade County intelligence files revealed he was a Hebrew Israelite.

3

Mama, they found Aston's body," said one of Louretta Green's sons on the telephone. "His head was cut off."

With those ten words, Mrs. Green, a mother of eight, started to die a little bit inside. Her youngest child, a twin, had passed suddenly at less than a week old. Aston was her oldest, and the second to die.

On Saturday, November 14, at 11:30 A.M., Louretta Green, a nurse, was at work when she got the call. She and her husband, Arthur, a mason, lived in a stucco house with burglar bars, on a typical south Florida street lined with palm trees.

A friend drove Mrs. Green home that Saturday morning. John King and Randy Baker were waiting for her. They had already told her husband in general terms about Aston's death. Mrs. Green wanted so much to know what really happened. How? Did he suffer long? Where did it happen? Where were Aston's things?

The detectives didn't know much, and what they knew, they wouldn't say. They tried to get Mrs. Green to tell them why Aston was killed. She didn't know. The six-foot Aston was such a happy person, an extrovert with a booming voice that made his friends laugh. Generous to a fault, he gave them free ginger beer. Mrs. Green insisted her son was no druggie. He made an honest living as an auto mechanic, and he believed in God. What kind of God? the detectives asked. A black God, Mrs. Green replied. He was no Rastaman.

Louretta Green was a small woman who wore no makeup. She believed deeply in a Christian God. She spoke with a musical, lilting accent. Just like her son. Born in Kingston, Jamaica, Aston Vassel Green had been a Church of God Sunday school teacher before coming to America on August 8, 1976. He had long eyelashes and dark eyes that twinkled with good humor. Aston was a month shy of his twenty-sixth birthday. In the weeks before his decapitation, he had been trying to grow a beard.

16

"He was me first child in me life," Mrs. Green said, wiping tears. "Brute, brute killin'. Young mon, young mon, dey beat him, beat him, chop him . . ."

The Greens said they didn't know exactly where Aston lived. He had left home going on nine months, but usually he dropped by his parents' house on Saturday night or Sunday afternoon. On occasion, he would take off for a week or so, then show up. The detectives pressed the Greens for names of the people Aston lived with. His parents didn't know.

When Mrs. Green last saw her son, two weeks earlier, he never mentioned he was in any kind of danger. He was wearing a watch with a black band and a gold neck chain with some sort of pendant on it. His mother prepared a special meal for him. Aston had recently become a strict vegetarian, in keeping with his Hebrew religion. Mrs. Green explained that he was deeply involved in classes at the Yahweh temple in Liberty City. He had pleaded with his parents to join. "Mama," Aston would say of his dynamic teacher, "he's a man of God for the black race. Come and look. See what me talkin' about."

Aston's father wouldn't go. But Mrs. Green, a daughter, and a church sister didn't see any harm in taking a drive south to Miami to see what it was all about. During the prayer session, Aston sat away from his mother, on the other side of the large auditorium. She waited for him outside after the service. "This is not my society," she told him.

"But, Mama," Aston said, "they give me food and everything."

"Me love you, honey," the mother said, "but I have to go my own way."

Just a few days before the body was discovered, Mrs. Green had a premonition something was wrong. Aston missed her birthday party, and he was just too good a son to do that.

Louretta Green started rummaging through her pocketbook. Aston, she told the detectives, had given her a telephone number where he could be reached. Whenever she dialed the number, someone else answered and called her son to the phone. She took out a slip of paper with the number—625-2493—and handed it to Detective King.

He thanked her, saying he'd be in touch. The detectives climbed into King's beat-up Plymouth, radioed the station house, and asked for a check of the phone number. They traced it to 2936 Northwest 192nd Lane, an address in Carol City, due west of the soon-to-be-built Miami Dolphins stadium.

It was about 4 P.M. After calling for backup squad cars, King and Baker decided to go there. Carol City is a tree-shaded neighborhood about twelve miles north of downtown Miami. Waterways wind through it, and similar-looking, single-story town houses are built on cul-de-sacs. The detectives finally found the right circular street, Northwest 192nd Lane, one block west of a main thoroughfare. They pulled to the curb and walked through a walled patio to the front door of the house. It was an aluminum-frame ranch with jalousie windows, an enclosed front patio, a double driveway, and a sliding door off the den. The curtains were drawn. In the driveway were two cars: a red Datsun station wagon with the Florida tag SPY 783 and another Datsun with no tag. Parked in the center of the cul-de-sac was a third car, a green Opel bearing an expired Florida tag, TMW 376. Above the tag was a decal with a Star of David and the word Israel printed above it.

The patio floor was littered with junk: a suitcase, a couple of lawn mowers, some auto parts, a pile of gold-colored shag carpet. At the top of the front door, in gold-colored letters, was the word YAHWEH. The black rubber doormat said Welcome.

King knocked several times. No one answered. He looked through the window, then reached into his pocket for the keys he found in Aston Green's blue jeans. Sure enough, one of the keys fit the door. King and three other officers entered the house.

On the living-room floor was a machete with a black handle. A sheath lay beside it. King picked up the knife and checked for blood. There was none. The detectives cautiously proceeded through the house. On the dining-room table was a King James Bible. In both bedrooms, the den, and the living room, the detectives eyed messy stacks of paper—accounting reports and fliers about the He-

18

brew Israelite religion. Just inside the front door was a note on yellow legal-size paper.

"Ock Yakim," it said. "Down the street. 621–0203."

The detectives checked the telephone number. It traced to an address about two and a half miles away. About 6 P.M., they went over and rang the doorbell.

A woman in her twenties answered. She was a little hesitant but polite. She introduced herself as Sonia. Her husband called himself Maurice, a banker from Jamaica. They invited the detectives inside.

"Aston Green was murdered yesterday," King said.

The couple went stone-cold silent. After a short pause, Sonia admitted she knew Aston. She didn't want to say anything until she and Maurice had a chance to talk to some other people. They asked the detectives to wait.

About fifteen minutes later, five or six people drove up to the house. The men wore turbans. The women had on long skirts. They were all nervous. They seemed to know about Aston Green's murder even before Detective King told them.

He asked what they saw or heard. Finally, one brash man stepped forward. "My name is Eric L. Burke," he said. He also called himself Yakim Israel. Everybody who joined the Hebrew religion took a new name, he explained. Eric said he was a self-employed mechanic specializing in air conditioners.

"What is the name of the God that you worship?" King asked.

"The name of the God I worship is Yahweh," Eric said. "We are the true Hebrew Israelites of a Tribe of Judah." All the people at Maurice's house had the last name Israel.

Detective King, an intense, former navy man, was a bit perplexed. Before joining homicide, he had worked at the enforcement of law in Liberty City, where he observed high priests in fezzes, voodoo medicine men, and Rastafarian healers. But the Tribe of Judah was a new experience for King, a born-again skeptic from Lynn, Massachusetts.

Eric went on heatedly. They knew Aston from the Yahweh

temple, headquarters for a group variously known as Yahweh, Hebrew Israelites, Followers of Yahweh, the Children of Yahweh, the Children of Israel, the Nation of Israel, the Tribe of Judah, and the Nation of Yahweh.

None of the people in the room, Eric said, had anything to do with the beheading. He said all their lives were in danger. For the third time in three days, he related to the cops his close call: how knife-wielding intruders had tried to make their way into his apartment. He thought he'd recognized one of them, a stocky light-skinned man named Zedekiah Israel. It was no burglary, Eric insisted. It was an attempted murder.

Eric gave the officers names of nine "potential victims" who might have information about Aston's murder. He introduced one, the man standing next to him. He was a compact, dark-skinned man in a green turban, with plaited hair, a beard and mustache, and a few missing teeth, but he still managed to be handsome. He called himself Carlton Carey. While the forty-four-year-old Eric seemed bold and self-assured, Carlton, ten years younger, sounded over-cautious and looked frightened. He wouldn't reveal much about himself, other than to say he was an accountant and community activist, born in Poughkeepsie, New York. He once taught basic English grammar to poor children. He rented the house on Northwest 192nd Lane, where the detectives had gone earlier.

Aston Green, Carlton finally confessed, was his roommate. They lived with Carlton's wife, Mildred Banks. He introduced her. The detectives took notice of her soft smile and sexy figure. Eric said she was also known as Danielle Israel. Carlton said his religious name was Mishael Israel.

Carlton eyed the detectives grimly. At 10:30 A.M. Thursday, he said, Aston had borrowed his car, a Datsun 610 station wagon, color beige. Aston said he was going to look for a job and waved good-bye. That was the last time Carlton and Mildred saw their roommate. "I don't know if anybody saw him after I did," Carlton said.

"No one has told you that they've seen him since then?" Detective Baker persisted.

20

"No."

The detectives kept quiet, but they wondered why Carlton Carey kept a machete in his house. They didn't have any reason to arrest him, but King asked if the men would come to the homicide office to give sworn statements voluntarily. Probably, they replied. The cops handed Eric and Carlton cards, jotted down a few notes, and went back to headquarters.

The people at Maurice's house debated strategy. They were bitter and scared, didn't want to get involved. They had already spoken to the police at least four times about threats against them. Busy desk officers stuck their complaints in file drawers. Some of the people thought it would be better to remain anonymous and erase the violent memories from their minds.

The group turned to Carlton Carey for advice. He was a savvy businessman, a Scripture scholar who always brought a high level of spirituality to their discussions. In Carlton's opinion, they needed the cops. No matter how scared they were, they couldn't submit to fear. Eric and Carlton, it was agreed, would give statements with two other men. Carlton's wife, Mildred, would wait at Maurice's house with Maurice, his wife, and Eric's friend Horace.

Carlton borrowed Maurice's machete. Just for safety. Just in case. He kissed Mildred good-bye, and the four men made the twenty-minute drive to the Metro-Dade Police Department head-quarters. Miami's expensive, high-rise skyline loomed to the right. The station house was in a neighborhood where derelicts hustled and thieves hung out, but when they arrived about 8 P.M., the build-ing was eerily empty. Many detectives had already gone home for the weekend. The cops called headquarters the dungeon, because it was so dull and dingy inside, with gun-metal desks and drab filing cabinets. Whenever it rained, water leaked through the roof into the fifth-floor crime labs.

Detective King came to escort the four witnesses upstairs. As they walked through a narrow corridor to the end of the hall, King observed the raw fear etched on their faces. The men about to testify suspected there were moles in the station house who might leak details of their statements to the press. Their reputations could be ruined. Or worse.

Eric, Carlton, and their two friends talked informally with the detectives for two hours. About 10 P.M., Eric took a seat in the lieutenant's office, across the desk from Detective King. Stenographer Charlotte Stempel entered with a recording device, and for twenty minutes, Eric spontaneously related a story about the curious state of affairs in the Yahweh temple and why he thought Aston might have been killed. Eric didn't know whether the cops believed him. "Are you currently under the influence of any intoxicating beverage or drug?" Detective King asked.

"No sir," Eric replied. "I do not take any type of drugs, pills, or anything of that nature."

"Do you have a mental condition?"

"No sir, I do not."

Next, at 11:05 P.M., Detective Randy Baker began the interview with Carlton Carey, seated submissively and wearing wrinkled gray and white striped pants and a sweaty black turtleneck. Carlton tried to keep his voice matter-of-fact, but it quivered a little as the stenographer took down what he said.

Aston had been having problems at home and with the law. After Carlton introduced him to the Hebrew classes a year before his death, things went smoothly for a few months. Aston took the biblical name Elijah. He found a job, moved into Carlton's house, and started dating a young mother of twins. Aston was very secretive about their relationship. The girl's name was Joann. Carlton wasn't sure how to reach her, but he said she had called the house just two hours before Aston's headless body was discovered. A short time later, Carlton had tried to make a telephone call, but the line was dead. He couldn't understand why. He'd paid the bill.

As the interview drew to a close, Carlton's voice suddenly went to pieces. "I'm in dire fear for my life and my family's life because of open threats being made," he said.

The tired cops checked their watches. It was 11:15 P.M., and they agreed to call it quits for the night. They asked the two witnesses waiting to give statements to come back. After assuring the police that another time was fine, the four men turned around to leave. They went out of the dingy station house the same way they had come in.

4

Carlton Carey shuffled to the car in his brown sandals, haggard and apprehensive. It was Saturday, November 14, about 11:30 P.M., and Miami's expressways were crowded with party traffic going in all directions. There was a special music to the streets—the scream of sirens, the whine of car alarms, and the thud-thud-thud from helicopters, constant, inescapable. Radio news blared the latest in what the cops called "typical citizen outrage" against the city's crime wave. An outraged homeowner, already the victim of three break-ins, had gone after burglars with an ax. They shot him dead. The man's frightened neighbors told reporters they planned to arm themselves with guns.

As Carlton drove to Carol City, he suspected he was being followed. He had Maurice's machete, though. A machete was part of the citizens' growing arsenal in 1981 Miami, a weapon of choice, especially for exiles who had survived the brutal sugar fields of Central America. Carlton couldn't forget the moment three days before, when machete-wielding men stalked him and his wife, Millie.

Now the trusting Aston Green was dead. It hurt to think about it. Aston and Carlton had been like blood brothers for three years. Carlton's family, like Aston's, came from Jamaica, but they met on a soccer field in south Florida. Their friendship deepened. After Aston was in a serious car wreck, his mind became confused, fuzzy. Carlton began to feel responsible for him in every way. When Carlton counseled his roommate to take precautions against the threat of violence, Aston insisted he had things under control. He was even warning others of danger. Just four days before his headless corpse was found, Aston telephoned a popular WMBM-AM talk-show host named Robert Hall. Aston said there was a contract on the radio man's life. The two men agreed to meet, but they never got the chance.

Carlton pulled up to Maurice's house, where Millie Banks was on edge, waiting anxiously for her husband. The pressure of the threats had begun to unnerve her. A thirty-year-old postal clerk, Millie had been married to Carlton for only six months. Tonight she needed him more than ever. He got out of the car, walked to Maurice's front door, and joined her and the other people in the house. After reporting briefly on the interviews that he and Eric had had with the police, Carlton said he wanted to get Millie home. He couldn't hang around. She picked up her purse and said good night to Maurice and his wife.

It was Sunday, November 15, about 12:20 A.M. The couple climbed into Millie's light-blue BMW 320. The car had a Florida tag, MILLIE C, and an Israel decal affixed to the trunk.

They approached the house about ten minutes later. Carlton felt uneasy about what they would find inside. He wasn't sure he had done the right thing by going home. He circled the block several times, looking for strange cars. He didn't see anything, but Millie had a funny feeling in her gut. As they pulled into the driveway, she noticed the light was on in Aston's bedroom. That's odd, she thought. They had left so early in the morning. Why would they leave the lights on?

"Did you leave the lights on?" she asked Carlton. No, he said, but the detectives who had been there earlier probably had.

Carlton turned off the engine, reached for Maurice's machete, and locked the car doors. He started walking toward the house, leaving his brown briefcase on the sidewalk. Mildred hesitated for a second, ambling to the mailbox. Some junk mail was waiting, an ad for a sale at the Red and White Thrift Store. Millie picked up Carlton's briefcase. It contained many important papers about the Hebrew Israelites.

When she got to the front door, Carlton was already inside. The house needed a thorough cleaning. There were dirty dishes in the sink, and Carlton's desk was cluttered. Aston's bedroom was a mess. He never made his bed. His clothes were strewn all over.

The accountant checked the laundry room to make sure no one was there. Millie came inside. She locked the door and put down

Carlton's briefcase. She started thinking about Aston. She had better bolt the door, she said to herself. They never double-locked the door, but she figured she had better tonight. Just for safety. Just in case.

Carlton walked from the kitchen, pausing for a moment before crossing the living room. Then, as he headed for the den, he froze. Millie saw him hesitate. Her eyes and mouth opened in terror. Two hooded gunmen burst from the den.

"Get out!" she screamed.

One of the killers stepped forward, pausing for a second after pointing the muzzle of the gun close to Carlton's neck. The killer fired. Carlton staggered.

Millie tried to get out of the house, but she couldn't. She realized she had double-bolted the door. As she hesitated, an assassin pointed the gun and pulled the trigger.

"I think they shot me," Millie thought, sinking against the door. The first shot seemed louder than the second, but it was hard to know for sure because everything happened so quickly.

Carlton stumbled to the back door, blood leaking from his neck at every heartbeat. A third shot rang out. Then a fourth, a fifth, a sixth, a seventh.

Millie's vision blurred. She felt a burning sensation in her forehead and breast. She realized that someone had opened the door, and as she tried to get out, she sensed someone climbing over her. Holding her by the shoulder, he slit her throat. A golden Star of David necklace slipped off her neck.

A few minutes passed. Mildred opened her eyes and tried to figure out how badly she was hurt. She thought about Aston's head being cut off. They were going to do the same thing to her and Carlton. Where was Carlton? Maybe they had dragged him from the house. Maybe he'd gotten away. Call the cops, Millie said to herself. She couldn't. She remembered their phone was down. Knowing she needed to get help, she started crawling, clinging to the wall as she prayed to God for strength.

Millie lifted herself up and stumbled to the house next door. She rang the doorbell time and again, leaving a print of her bloody right hand over the bell. Nobody answered. She took off her right brown sandal, and used it to bang on the living-room window. She pounded on the window, screaming for help, and shattered four panes. Still no answer. As she grasped any object she could, she smeared blood on the wall of the house, and along the window frame and the cement sill below it. She staggered to the back of the house and knocked and knocked. Why didn't they answer? Where were the people? Partying, probably. It was Saturday night, and Miami always partied on Saturdays.

Leaving her sandal behind in a pile of broken glass, Millie crawled through the backyard to the next house. She pounded on the bathroom window, then on the sliding glass patio door. Nobody answered there, either. She banged on another window. An elderly woman was inside with her husband. The woman got up and looked out a glass door, but she couldn't see anything, or so she told herself. People in Miami instinctively knew what not to see. The elderly woman went back to sleep.

Millie stumbled to the patio of another house. The left side of the awning windows was open at a forty-five-degree angle. A thirty-eight-year-old woman heard the knocking and screaming. Millie broke another windowpane, and finally the woman inside turned on a fluorescent porch light. She opened the glass slats of the jalousie and looked outside.

A trembling woman, framed in darkness, stared into the window and made a colossal effort to stand up and speak. Blood dripped from her forehead and her neck as her closed lips suddenly opened.

"Help me!" Mildred Banks cried. "I've been shot!" She collapsed in her neighbor's flower bed.

5

Mildred Ilene Banks never saw her husband lying ten feet from her, in a batch of lilies. Carlton Barrington Carey had staggered to the nearby backyard, and died. On a glass window awning above his body was Millie's bloody palm print.

It was Sunday, November 15, 1:02 A.M. The flashing blue lights of a police squad car sliced the blackness of the night. It screeched to a stop at the scene of the attack. A frightened neighbor directed Police Officer Charles Triana to Carlton's body. The barefoot accountant was slumped against the east wall of the house, head lolling to one side, blood still trickling from his nose. His legs were spread straight out, with a broad-leaf cactus plant between his knees. His green turban lay beside him.

Nearby, in a bed of bark chips, Millie Banks was lying on her back, breathing shallowly. As paramedics placed her body flat on the ground, they could see the life draining from her fast. They cut off her blue wrap skirt and worked furiously to stop the flow of blood spurting from her neck, her forehead, and under her left breast. The medics dressed a bone-deep, five-inch slit on the left side of her neck and inserted a chest tube and an IV. They lifted her onto a stretcher and placed her in the back of the rescue truck for a siren-screeching trip to Miami International Hospital. The rescue workers didn't think Millie Banks would make it through the night, but they had to try to save her.

The scene in Carol City was bustling with patrolmen, detectives, lab technicians, and personnel from the medical examiner's office. It was 2:50 A.M. The pathologist pronounced Carlton Carey DOS, dead on the scene. There were three bullet holes: a fatal, front-to-back wound in the middle of his neck, angling horizontally through the carotid artery and exiting the right upper back; a second through-and-through wound in the lower right back, tunneling down and out, and a third wound, also back-to-front, apparently leaving a

28

projectile lodged in the top of Carlton's left arm. The pathologist hoped to recover bullet fragments embedded in the arm muscle. He logged the victim's personal property, a twenty-dollar bill and his Star of David necklace, and ordered the body removed for autopsy.

As the cops sealed the circular street, residents in the quiet neighborhood turned on their porch lights and gathered in their pajamas. Patrolmen approached them one by one and asked if anyone saw anything.

Nobody saw a thing. Seven shots pierced the darkness, but nobody was peeking out until the shooting stopped.

At 2:55 A.M., detectives began following two blood trails, Millie's and Carlton's. On the door stoop, by the overturned welcome mat, they found her broken Star of David necklace and what they believed was a blood-stained machete. On the bottom of the opened front door, an officer saw traced in blood what appeared to be the vague outline of a face—where Millie had fallen.

When Detective Ronald Cooksley picked up the telephone in the living room, he discovered the line was dead. He checked the metal junction box outside, fixed to the east wall. Two telephone wires, one red, the other green, had been cut. Inside the house, police observed a second machete, near the living-room sofa. They found casings, bullet fragments, and projectile holes, suggesting two guns had been used in the ambush. One most likely was a .22-caliber Ruger semiautomatic pistol, the other, a .32-caliber H&R revolver, sometimes known as a Saturday night special. The cops flipped through Carlton Carey's accounting papers. They collected tape recordings of Hebrew Israelite meetings and a voluminous trunk of recollections about the past few years. They shot 126 color photos and dusted for fingerprints, lifting 110 latents from the tampered telephone box, the bloody door, and the machetes.

Not one print could be linked to a suspect, and the only promising eyewitness was too scared to cooperate. She confided to a neighbor that she thought she got a look at a killer pulling a hood off his face. He climbed into the back of a getaway car, possibly a blue Catalina, with two men in the front seat.

With no witnesses and no suspects, Detective Steve Roadruck

felt a new urgency to talk to Mildred Banks. A handsome, easygoing officer fairly new to homicide, Roadruck had been assigned as the lead investigator. He raced to the hospital, hoping to get there for Mildred's deathbed declaration. When he arrived in the emergency room, she was hooked to a respirator, bleeding profusely.

Hospital personnel had administered four pints of blood, inserting chest tubes to open her air passages. Millie Banks's faith in God had always helped her through bad times, but now the hospital gave her only a 20 percent chance.

At 3:15 A.M., Detective Roadruck pulled a chair next to her in the emergency room, bending his head close so he could hear her. No, she whispered, she hadn't seen the killers' faces. There were two, she thought. Both wore ski masks with red or orange around the eyes. She couldn't remember whether they were wearing gloves. She seemed to recall black sweaters. She hadn't noticed any accents.

Millie gave Roadruck the names of people he ought to warn: Maurice and his wife; Eric Burke; Eric's friend Horace; Robert Hall, the radio personality. Their lives were in danger.

She closed her eyes to rest, and at 3:30 A.M. hospital personnel draped her in a sterile robe and cleaned her belly with Betadine. They wheeled her into operating room number 5, where Dr. Gurbachan Soni, the on-call surgeon, sliced her belly vertically, from the sternum to the umbilicus. Exploring the abdominal cavity, the surgeon found gunshot holes in the left and right lobes of Millie's liver. A bullet of unknown caliber was flattened against her chest, so close to the spinal column the surgeon couldn't touch it. He controlled the bleeding and cleaned the liver wounds, closing the holes with catgut sutures. With silk stitches, he repaired two stomach perforations, sewed a deep, two-and-a-half-inch cut on her forehead, and went to work on the neck wound. The machete had missed her jugular vein by less than an inch. It had cut a major artery to the brain, and after identifying the bleeding vessels, Dr. Soni stitched the artery.

As the surgery proceeded, Detective Roadruck tried to figure out what kind of killers he was dealing with. At 6 A.M., he telephoned Detective John King's house, waking him up from a deep sleep.

"You're not gonna believe this," Roadruck said, "but you know your witnesses that you just debriefed about the Yahweh religion?"

"What about them?" King asked. "Why are you waking me up at six in the morning?"

"They were ambushed," Roadruck said. "Hooded gunmen were waiting for them. Carlton Carey's dead."

"Knock it off," King said. "That's not funny."

"I'm not kidding," Roadruck said. "His wife's extremely critical. They don't think she's gonna make it."

Detective King hung up the telephone in shock. Carlton Carey had spent his last hours cooperating with the police, and his willingness to help might have led to his murder. King called his sergeant at homicide, then jumped into the shower. By 7:15 A.M. he was on the road with Roadruck, prowling streets gripped by growing terror.

Even before the sun rose, the telephone rang at WMBM radio. "We just killed Robert Hall," an anonymous caller said. "We just cut off his head."

6

On Monday, November 16, as the police tried to break through a thickening barricade of fear, the *Miami Herald* headline screamed, HOODED GUNMEN ATTACK DROPOUTS OF SECT.

Anxious relatives called the police to check on the safety of loved ones, but no one showed up at the morgue to identify Carlton Carey's body.

Citizens became intimidated into silence, and others vanished into a shadow world of changing identities and untraceable locations. Eric Burke, the brash mechanic who started it all, bolted from his Liberty City apartment with nothing but his big-barreled pistol. When he reached a safe house, he called a friend.

"I think I might be next," he said.

Only Millie Banks fought back against the faceless killers. By Tuesday afternoon, November 17, she was breathing easier. Her arms and legs showed no signs of neurological damage, and her memory was improving. She now recalled a hooded assassin uttering the words "Catch Mishael!" or "Get Mishael!"

Mildred gave Detective Steve Roadruck the names of suspects: an ex-boyfriend, an auto-parts distributor, a utility worker, a former cop, all Hebrew Israelites from Liberty City's Temple of Love. She talked about her dead husband's gradual disillusionment with the religion he helped form—how his deepening involvement led to growing doubts, fear, and finally to his death. As his suspicions grew, Carlton had begun keeping notes on the enigmatic teacher who led the religion. He called himself Moses Israel and shrouded his past in mystery. But after a little digging, Carlton and his buddy Eric Burke had discovered Moses' real name.

As Millie went on with her story, the strain was visible in her eyes. Shotgun-wielding guards patrolled the hospital corridors, providing round-the-clock protection for the lone witness. Nurses walked into the room to change the bandages on her cut neck. Steve Roadruck cringed at the wound.

"One tough girl," he told himself.

She didn't seem to have a bit of hatred in her heart, and Roadruck couldn't understand how such a kind and gentle woman ended up with a bullet lodged near her spine. In time, Roadruck would grow so fond of the witness that his wife would accuse him of having an affair with her. One day, he asked Mildred if she planned to have plastic surgery on her neck.

"I'll never get rid of the scar," she said. "It's my badge of courage."

After a partial recovery, Millie Banks left Miami for a new life in a secret place, known only to the police. She would never stop helping them. A decade would pass before she returned. By then, Miami had been held hostage by even more brutal acts of terror, as the man called Moses elevated himself to new heights.

Part II

Divine Calling

7

A torrent punched through Kingfisher in the fourth week of October 1935. It was an almost biblical storm, the kind that shredded the cottonwood trees, and ripped down the power lines and sent them hissing along Main Street like so many serpents. In a small house near a wheat field, Pearl Olive Mitchell, eighteen years old, was just days away from giving birth to the first of her fifteen children to be.

It seemed as if it hadn't rained in Kingfisher, an Oklahoma prairie town of three thousand, for years. So much sand blew off the ruined topsoil that the townspeople had forgotten what the sun looked like. Migrants literally lost their way to the Jalopy Trail. Pearl, a bright and bubbly woman, knew that God would overpower the drought and dust. Pearl was poor like just about everybody else in Kingfisher, but she seemed unusually rich and happy. She never accepted handouts, no WPA welfare, no free turkeys at Thanksgiving. Relief was degrading, an act of desperation. Ever since Pearl gave herself to Jesus, she talked directly to the Savior. Her family had always walked with Jesus. The Holy Ghost healed them, pulled them out of poverty, delivered them from the wilderness of racial prejudice, and even cooled the fever of family squabbles.

Pearl Olive Mitchell was born into a world where visions were needed. She was the ambitious only child of George Leatherman of Texas and Ollie Razor of South Carolina. Her parents had moved to Kingfisher in the early nineteen hundreds to escape poverty and race hatred in the South. The ground in Oklahoma was as red and fertile as any place in southern Tennessee or northern Mississippi, producing some of the best corn, cotton, and wheat in the country. The town, named for a cattleman, King Fisher, who also operated a stage line, earned the designation "buckle of the wheat belt." But, for the exodus Negroes, Kingfisher was hardly the Promised Land.

As they started their own school, farms, and businesses, the KKK tried to chase them out of town. Mob lynchings and fiery cross burnings served as warnings to Negro entrepreneurs who stepped out of line.

In August 1910 George and Ollie were married in the traditional African Methodist Episcopal Church, but the services there were halfhearted, like going to a funeral. The coming kingdom never seemed to materialize. George and Ollie found more comfort in the Church Of God In Christ (Colored), a Holiness sect organized in the late eighteen nineties by militant preachers. Pearl went with her parents to the prayer meetings. She discovered she could reach God through her rich, clear voice. She sang her way through high school, playing basketball and making 90s in cooking, sewing, and reading, and in 1933 her mother deeded her a quarter-acre lot on the edge of town. They built a little four-room house with Sheetrock walls, pine floors, and wood heating.

One day Pearl met a tall, hulking deacon with a deep voice. His name was Hulon Mitchell. He was the man of her dreams. Like Pearl, Hulon was strictly Holiness Pentecostal, though his parents, William and Callie, had been married in the Baptist church. Hulon was raised in nearby Purcell, a town of three thousand shaded by mistletoe-hung maples and elms. His father hailed from Grayson County, Texas, and his mother was born in Oklahoma Indian Territory. From dawn to dusk, the family picked cotton, earning one dollar for every one hundred pounds. Hulon later sold fish and ice blocks. Then, as sand buried houses, as farmers sold pigs for $3.50, and as people stood in breadlines outside Kingfisher city hall, Hulon and Pearl tied the knot. Together, they dreamed of raising a Holiness family.

On October 27, 1935, a Sunday, their prayers began to be answered. Sun leaked through the roof of rain clouds that had covered Kingfisher for days. Pearl had her number-one child at home as twenty-one-year-old Hulon sat beside her, holding her hand. They called the boy Hulon Junior. He had light skin like his mother, a few freckles, and radiant eyes that seemed to change color, like a flame, from blue to gray to hazel.

There was something otherworldly about him, and instinctively Pearl knew something special had happened. "You are my Jesus," she later told her son. Right after the birth, Senior and Pearl rushed Junior to church and dedicated him to God. The Holiness preacher placed his hands on the infant's head and prayed for a divine blessing. People came from around town and brought gifts for him.

Eight months later, Pearl was pregnant again. She would have fourteen more babies, nine boys and five girls, in the next twenty-one years. The kids would call her Mama Pearl. Some of them believed they'd been sanctified in her "blessed womb."

From Junior's earliest days, his mother was his support and inspiration. She gave piano and voice lessons and worked as a domestic and a nurse even during her pregnancies. She took him to church often, and rocked him to sleep with songs like "Steal away . . . steal away to Jesus."

"Strive for perfection," she told the boy.

He listened attentively as his eloquent father spun uplifting tales from the Old and New Testaments. Senior preached to two congregations to make worldly ends meet. He played a number of musical instruments by ear. To church, he sometimes wore a big rhinestone lapel pin with the word *Jesus.*

"Sometimes people want to make themselves something," he once exhorted. "They get a title and want to pin it on themselves. For instance, I could tell you all that I am Christ!"

The small congregation, many of them Mitchells, giggled. Whenever a sinner showed signs of accepting Jesus, they all started hollering, crying, and jumping up and down. Almost every eye in the church would be filled with tears. "I must warn you of people saying all over the world: 'I am the messiah,' " the Reverend Hulon Mitchell would cry. "Don't you go follow them!"

Junior was an inquisitive boy with mood swings, crying one minute and belly laughing the next. But it didn't take him long to learn to shut up and do exactly what he was told without whining. If he refused, he knew his daddy would punish him. Senior demanded rigid obedience, or else.

At age three, Junior realized he was divine. Radiating pride, he ran to his mother one day and acted out the Exodus story. From then on, he performed the deliverance every Sunday, showing the way Moses led the children of Israel across the Red Sea. "I'm the burning bush," he'd say.

By Christmas 1941 Junior was holding sway over two sisters and a brother. The multiplying clan put small-town life behind them and moved north to Enid, population twenty-eight thousand. The parents borrowed $1,585 for a small house in the city's Southern Heights section, where most of the colored population was huddled.

Compared with Kingfisher, Enid was a bustling metropolis with lakes and rivers of oil and cathedral-like wheat silos. There were six hotels in town, a big white marble post office, a city swimming pool, free tennis courts, and fifty-four churches. Six were for Negro worshipers. Enid had five motion picture houses, with the balcony of one theater open to colored people. Downtown, there was a rest room for Negro use, and COLORED and NO COLORED signs to ticket lines, train waiting rooms, and public schools.

Senior and Pearl Olive didn't question Jim Crow. They got all the power they needed from the Lord omnipotent. Junior learned to do the same without complaint. In Southern Heights, he joined the colored Boy Scout unit. He explored the salt plains and camped in the woodlands. He cuddled greyhounds. He made slingshots from scrap rubber and fashioned a fishing pole from tree branches; he angled for catfish in Boggy Creek. Once a year, on Independence Day, he was allowed to fish in Government Springs Park, near a garden of roses and anemones. For that special day, the white people opened a small section of the park to Negroes.

At age seven, Junior had a revelation of his special calling. Knowing he had a "distinct job," he observed his elders and constantly sought new answers. He decided there was nothing he loved more than filling himself up with the Holy Ghost. He adored the passion of the worship.

Junior was a bright, but not especially diligent, pupil at Booker T. Washington, the only Negro school in Enid. He had a high opinion of himself. No one, he later boasted, had a mind like his. He was so intelligent his IQ couldn't be measured. "Mother," he used to say, "I'm a genius."

Not everyone thought Junior was special. He was picked on constantly by the mostly Baptist children and teachers, both for his light complexion and his religion. Holiness kids, the Baptists thought, were strange, ensconced in old-fashioned customs. They didn't go to dances. They didn't smoke or drink. They didn't fight or steal. They didn't even go swimming with girls. Sometimes Junior broke the rules. In third grade, he swiped a pencil from a classmate. His teacher decided to send a message to all the Holiness kids by pinning a sign on Junior's back. "I'm a thief," the sign said. The teacher forced Junior to parade up and down the school halls with the sign on his back.

The humiliation stayed with Junior forever. "I have been persecuted all my life," he said years later, "for being Holiness."

Neighborhood kids used to sneak up to the Mitchells' church, standing on wooden crates and peeking through the window at the wooden pews. "Look at 'em dance!" the kids shouted, chuckling, as Junior and some two dozen congregants praised God in jerking motions induced by the Holy Ghost. Things could get so boisterous at Mitchell revivals that the noise not only stirred the devil but scared the neighbors. One August night, long after Junior was gone, Helen Childers would complain about it. Senior was charged with creating a public disturbance.

"Such screaming and hollering you never heard," the neighbor told Judge Robert Gregory.

"We are men of the gospel," the Reverend Hulon Mitchell replied. "We were praying for the sick. . . . We're Pentecostal. We don't pray quietly. We cut down the noise. We cut down the speakers. We closed the windows."

The judge wasn't impressed. "You don't have to be loud to praise the name of Jesus Christ," he said. "Just because it is a religious service doesn't give you the right to violate the rights of others.

"I've been a member of a church for forty-five years," Judge

Gregory went on. "I have never been in church after nine P.M. I'm a believer in religious freedom as long as it doesn't violate someone's rights."

Since the noise had ceased, the judge ruled the Reverend Hulon Mitchell innocent. His congregants in the courtroom waved their arms in the air. "Praise Jesus!" they chanted. "Thank you, Jesus!" The judge told them to shut up or face contempt charges. They left the courtroom whispering. One woman continued to wave her arms, gazing heavenward, whispering "Thank you."

By the end of World War II, Pearl Olive was working on what the family called "the second section" of kids. Junior had authority over four sisters and two brothers. They rarely challenged him. By Thanksgiving 1947 there were nine Mitchell children, and Junior had a new revelation. The neighborhood kids had new ways to poke fun. They joked about the prolific Mitchells sleeping in tents, wearing hand-me-down clothing, and causing traffic accidents getting to the dinner table. The Mitchell kids sloughed off the slights as jealousy and envy.

Junior woke up at five o'clock to care for his sisters and brothers. He helped to feed and clothe them, turning to his mama for reassurance. His dad was usually busy converting souls or wearing himself down so the family could eat. Eventually, Senior got a job as a porter at Union Equity Cooperative Exchange, a big grain firm. He didn't have much time to do fatherly things with the older kids. Junior's grandma and his great-aunt got to be two more parents to them.

Two other things held the Mitchell family together: singing and swinging. Sometimes at night, Senior administered group whippings to the children for sins ranging from roughhousing to sneaking out of church. The kids thought of it as tough love/discipline, but Senior had a fierce way that could scare the daylights out of some of the neighbor kids.

The family was also tied together by gospel hymns that told from the bottom of their hearts how they felt about their fellow man. As the "Musical Mitchells," they sang in just about every auditorium and sanctuary Negroes could enter in Oklahoma. Their spine-tingling renditions of old spirituals such as "Them Bones" shook the prayer houses on sharp winter nights. Senior was the manager and Junior the baritone in the traveling gospel show. The family performances prepared child number ten, soprano Leona, for stardom. The fifth and last girl, she would one day learn an aria from *Aida* by rote, since she couldn't read music. She would become a diva with the Metropolitan Opera Company.

To the Mitchells, music was a religion of its own. They believed it was their anointing, a blessing from God that set them apart from other families. Still, by the time Junior entered high school, he needed more encouragement than his family could provide.

Sometimes, he'd watch Green Hornet movies with his fishing buddy, Eugene Pitts. The movie house had special performances and seating arrangements for colored people. Eugene and Junior whooped it up and sang along with Gene Autry and Roy Rogers.

Junior searched for other activities that could bring him recognition. Fast, strong, and coordinated, he channeled his energies into sports. He also played cornet in the high school band.

And he reached out for new concepts of divinity. After his father's services, Junior walked along Southern Heights' unpaved, muddy streets to listen to the styles of other colored ministers in town. He read about exotic religious groups that glutted Oklahoma in the forties—the Mennonites, who wore unclipped beards and black caps; the Peace Mission of Father Divine, who rose to black messiah from obscurity; the Cheyenne Indians, who practiced the sun dance, an elaborate ritual of self-torture.

As a teenager, Junior discovered another area in which he felt completely adequate: sex. Sex was a forbidden subject in Holiness households. In the eyes of the church, sex outside of marriage was sinful and contrary to the purpose of God. Junior picked up tidbits from his friends. He had plenty of girls wherever he went. There was even speculation that once he had a white girlfriend. No one ever heard of a colored person in Enid dating a white girl.

Skin color had never really been a big issue for Junior. His parents always taught him that the human race descended from a single pair, Adam and Eve. The color line was washed away in the blood of Christ, and all of mankind shared the same human nature, the same original sin, and the same provisions for salvation. But as Junior discovered he was legally a Negro, he wanted to be white. His friends said he seemed proud of his light skin, and once he put together a family tree, tracing an Indian and European lineage. "I have never been black," he said years later. "I can't change my color."

The more he got out of Southern Heights, the more Junior saw that the world was populated not only by mean Baptist Negroes, it was populated by white people with guns. They had a saying in Enid: "If you're black and caught after dark, you're dead."

Traveling around was a big headache. "Hey, nigger!" white people would holler as Junior and his pals tooled around in a black Ford. They carried lunches and water bottles wherever they went. They stood up in the back of streetcars and ate in dirty restaurants. One day, when Junior and Eugene tried to take a shortcut to school through the "No colored" park, the prejudiced parks director fired his gun. The teenagers ran like hell.

In the early 1950s, as the NAACP launched a frontal attack on Jim Crow, the KKK recruited on the front steps of Enid's all-white high school. Everyone knew the Klan was bigger in Oklahoma than just about any place in the country. At Booker T. Washington, the teenagers heard a story almost daily about someone who had been clubbed or insulted on public transportation. One boy supposedly got kicked out of a drugstore for trying to drink a Coke. "Niggers can't sit here," the store owner snapped, snatching the drink from the boy and tossing it in a wastepaper basket. The kids tried to figure out which of Enid's sitting judges were Klansmen in good standing. They started complaining about their parents, who seemed frightened of white people, and about their preachers, who refused to challenge Jim Crow.

Junior had always been taught never to show indignation toward any person, colored or white, for any reason. Assertiveness was something to be relished privately, something to be kept in the family. But he was growing more frustrated, and the anger had to come out somewhere. Flashes of Junior's volatile nature showed up on the basketball court. One day, his Holiness brother, Phil Porter, was refereeing a game, and he called a foul on Junior. Junior threw the ball at Phil. "Don't you call no foul on me," Junior said.

Testing, Phil called another foul on Junior, who marched up to his church brother after the game. "I want to talk to you," Junior said.

The teenagers left the gym and walked to the bottom of the stairwell. Junior stared at Phil, then slugged him. "Don't you ever call a foul on me," Junior said. "We're brothers. We belong to the same church. You can't call fouls on me."

By 1953 the old verity—family loyalty—had started breaking down. Junior had fire in his belly. He began hunting for scholarships and told his friends he was going to make something of himself. Nothing would hold him back. After he graduated from high school, several things took him over the Oklahoma line: his childhood memories, his ambition for personal power, and the Jim Crow rules against attending a local college. Struggling to reconcile his experiences with religion and discrimination, Junior left for Texas College in Tyler. Tyler was a town of rose-coated neighborhoods ninety-nine miles east of Dallas—far enough away from his strict family, but near enough to go home when he needed them. At Texas, Junior studied math and music, branching beyond the gospel hymns of his childhood, and hoping to make his stamp as jazz bebop gave way to a new, avant-garde sound. To compensate for shortcomings in his high school education, he took general survey courses, earning mostly Bs. Then, after less than a year away from home, the draft board put a monkey wrench in Junior's game plan. He got what he called "a welcome from my Uncle Sam." He returned to Enid, and a few weeks before Thanksgiving 1954, he enlisted in the air force. Enid had a big air force base, and it was common knowledge among Negroes that that was a better service for them. Besides, the air force was a lot cleaner than the army. Junior wouldn't have to be an infantry grunt in Korea or some other quagmire ground war. "I did not want to die," he explained.

While waiting for his assignment, Junior got a little rebellious. He partied, played guitar, joined social organizations, and tried to prove he was a leader. He dated women. One of his girlfriends was eighteen-year-old Nodie Mae Chiles, who was tender, kind, and liked whatever he liked.

On October 15, 1954, Junior married her at his father's altar. "Keep the solemn vows you are about to make," he told them, as they joined right hands and kneeled before the Lord. "Live with tender consideration for each other. Conduct your lives in honesty and in truth, and your marriage will last."

The Reverend Hulon Mitchell blessed the union in perpetuity. Carrying on the family tradition, Nodie Mae would have four babies in four years. But Junior's marriage wouldn't last. By the time it ended, he had shed his Mitchell skin and turned into someone else.

8

The first transformation of Junior came under the guiding hand of Uncle Sam. Bound up in brass buttons, bursting with pride, Junior created himself anew as Airman Mitchell, AF 18206878, ready to test his courage in war, if necessary. With Nodie Mae, his pregnant bride, the green cadet from the Oklahoma frontier moved to Parks (California) Air Force Base (AFB). Parks was an old Navy Seabee training camp converted into an air force basic training installation during the Korean War.

The military, Airman Mitchell discovered, was a religion of its own. It turned malleable young men into disciples of the United States of America. From grizzled vets to post-adolescent enlistees, they attended a school of sanctioned violence that converted them from thinking like civilians into thinking like killers.

Junior, age nineteen, had grown up following orders, and in the air force, he went straight by the book. He shined his shoes, did pushups in the mud, and marched in perfect step, chanting about how great the military was. As his indoctrination proceeded, he devalued family ties and promoted the righteous goals of the United States before all other loyalties. Junior never had to hurt a soul. He enjoyed the training so much he wanted to teach it to others. In the summer of 1955, he completed the air force's general instructor's course and began teaching math to recruits. He proved to be so gung-ho that his superiors made him a tactical instructor, giving him rights and privileges of an officer. Airman Mitchell's new mission: to turn raw troops into productive service members. He taught them how to operate light weapons and how to respond on command, instilling in them the classic military virtues of unquestioning duty, loyalty, and physical courage.

He observed leadership techniques of U.S. officers of all types, watching how they handled their men psychologically. If psychology failed, there was always harassment and brutality. Ninety-five percent of his trainees were white, and some were the most serious discipline problems on the base. Junior later bragged about transforming them into "the best soldiers in the U.S.A." "That includes becoming the best barracks on the base, having the least amount of demerits, troops with the best decorum that would win honors, not only in drill but in overall decorum, ready to take their position throughout the military," he said.

Airman Mitchell coveted honors, promotions, and raises. He earned stripes but never made sergeant. Nodie Mae sensed he felt let down, upset at not making rank more quickly or getting the chance to develop his talents to the fullest.

By the summer of 1956, he was almost twenty-one and had two daughters. A third girl was on the way. The Mitchells were transferred to Amarillo (Texas) AFB. While Junior was trying to decide his life path, two transforming national events could not have eluded him. The first: the brutal murder of Emmett Till, a Negro teenager from Chicago, who was kidnapped and lynched in Money, Mississippi, for purportedly whistling at, or speaking disrespectfully to, a white woman. The second: the work of a young Baptist minister named Martin Luther King, Jr. In Montgomery, Alabama, the old capital of the Confederacy, King was leading a city bus boycott, trying to change the seating accommodations. He preached that segregation was an evil, contrary to God's will. He believed the church had to be awakened to its moral responsibility to fight Jim Crow.

In Enid, the Bible thumpers never were very interested in God's kingdom here and now. They seemed to care more about collecting dues for Sunday school, getting to heaven, and waiting for the ground to shake. The preachers perpetuated their congregants' inferior positions. All Junior's life his family promised he would be special, if he just left his fate to Jesus. Slowly, he realized it wasn't true. "You knew your life wasn't different," he reflected later. "You faked and pretended to be different and tried to live the life they expected you to live."

Eventually, Junior became irreparably bitter toward Christian preachers who tolerated racial violence at home, though he never directly attacked his father by name. "I feel bad 'cause they took advantage of me," he said. "They tricked me and it makes me mad now.

"They all believed that one day the whole physical ground was gonna open up and they wanted to die a saint. And they thought a saint was someone who didn't go to night clubs, didn't drink no wine, didn't go to movies and ballgames. . . . And they say the Lord saved them . . . and they tried to put that off onto us. . . .

"In your nature you know there's a God . . . it's in your blood to want to be close to God. It's in your blood; it's in your genes and chromosomes. . . . And bein' a child, you didn't know the preacher was a crook. You didn't know he was a dumb dog. You didn't know he was blind as a bat in a snowstorm."

Airman Mitchell questioned why Negro soldiers had to kill for a country that refused to serve them, and looking for other paths to power, he made his first foray into a nonblack religion. He entered the occult world of the Rosicrucians, who believed they possessed exclusive wisdom about nature. Novices studied monographs that told of Egyptian ritual ceremonies, a person's latent magical powers, and the doctrine of reincarnation. Trying to attain harmony with the cosmic forces around them, Rosicrucians started each day with a prayer, inhaled seven deep breaths, focused their mind on each body part, awakened their psychic center, then showered and drank a glass of cold water before eating. With discipline, study, and prayer, they believed they would one day realize their divine nature and reach their highest potential.

It was too cosmic for Nodie Mae, who was concerned about economic security for her growing family. "I wasn't into any of that stuff." She wasn't interested in starting a fight against segregation either. "When you're used to it," she said, "it doesn't bother you."

Nodie always figured Junior would become a lawyer. He preferred being a housekeeper—taking care of the kids, teaching them to read and to count, molding them.

But he couldn't mold Nodie Mae. Though she tried to be a good military wife, Junior wasn't satisfied with her. After receiving an honorable discharge, they returned to Enid, which was still smothering in holy-roller folkways. He filed for a divorce. He moved in with his folks, who had purchased a house on East Oklahoma Street in Southern Heights. In the years he was away, Pearl Olive had completed the third section of children. Sister Leona was ten, a tomboy starting to sing solos in the church choir. Some of the boys showed signs of rebelling, against family, church, and music. Junior wanted to take them places—to movies, to restaurants—but their movements were still restricted. He had long discussions with high school buddies about the immorality of segregation. The 101st Airborne had recently landed at Little Rock, Arkansas, to escort nine black students to Central High School.

"You know," Junior told his boyhood pal Phil Porter, "the world doesn't love us."

Junior still hadn't quite let go of his dream of a career in music. By taking advantage of the GI Bill and a changing racial climate, he began to study American government and social problems at Enid's Phillips University. The fifty-year-old Disciples of Christ school had started to accept Negro students in response to the landmark *Brown v. Board of Education* case. Phil Porter was the first to break the university's color line. Junior followed his Holiness brother in January 1958. It didn't take long for them to realize that Negroes in Oklahoma didn't have the rights of full citizens, including the right to the best education the state offered. As he got older, Junior complained bitterly about white-run schools, hinting strongly at his personal experience of blocked ambition. "They gave you only enough knowledge," he said, "to be like a bird trying to fly with one wing."

Still trying to overcome his second-class education, Junior got a job as a college library assistant. He earned thirty-five cents an hour and read everything he could get his hands on: books about history and war, books about leaders—why some disappeared, how others sustained a following.

Then Junior relished his first taste of student rebellion. With two high school friends who felt as he did about the treatment of Oklahoma Negroes, he attended rallies and integration strategy sessions sponsored by the Oklahoma NAACP Youth Council.

"What do we want? Freedom!" they chanted.

"When do we want it? Now!"

The activists sang "Go Down, Moses" and "Joshua Fought the Battle of Jericho," gospel hymns that had warmed Junior's soul as a child and brought new meanings to him as a man. He sometimes wept when he heard those old sad songs that he grew up singing in church.

The NAACP council was full of gallant boys and girls who felt betrayed by their elders. Sometimes, Junior took his brothers of elementary school age to the meetings. They began a letter-writing campaign to the churches in a drive to break down segregation in public accommodations. The leader of the movement was a dynamic teacher from Oklahoma City named Clara Luper. Luper had always wanted to do something about a system that paralyzed her movements and "made me an outsider in my own country." Junior felt much the same way. She described him as an obedient follower welling with ambition and idealism.

At one Youth Council meeting, someone asked, "What are we going to do?"

"I move that we go down to Katz drugstore and sit down and drink a Coke," another person said.

There was no way for him to know it at the time, but Junior was about to be caught up in a movement that would change America.

For months, the young activists studied Luper's rules of nonviolent combat: "First, our objective was to eliminate segregation in public accommodations," Luper wrote in her memoir. "Second, we had to be honest. Nonviolence is not an approach to be used by hypocrites—honesty pays. Third, you must love your enemy . . . you aren't up against a deep-eyed monster, you are up against a man who has been handed an overdose of segregation and who knows

51

that segregation is wrong, yet he practices it. You are not to ridicule, nor vilify him at any time or any way. . . . Fourth, give the white man a way out. Nonviolence demonstrates a kind of strength that shows up the weakness of injustices. . . . Find a way to let him participate in victory when it comes."

In August 1958 Clara Luper launched the first sit-in in Oklahoma City. Junior followed in Enid, leading about fifty Negroes to two downtown lunch counters. Wearing coats and ties, the activists camped quietly in booths and stools at the soda fountains. They read magazines and books. Police officers hovered quietly in the back. At Downs pharmacy, Junior and a friend strolled down the aisle. As soon as white customers got up and left, the activists directed followers to occupy booths. By 11 A.M., the protesters had filled most of the seats and were politely demanding service. The owner said no. Competition among the various downtown lunch counters, he explained, prevented him from serving Negroes.

Junior chatted briefly with Garfield County Sheriff Mason "Bud" Hart who explained there was nothing he could do. Junior handed a reporter a prepared statement: "This country has emerged as a national power and how was this accomplished? Through preaching freedom and justice for all. If we expect to continue as world leaders, we cannot expect to continue to throw bricks in a crowd and hide our hand. There are many of us who are veterans, who fought that this country could exist as it is today."

The Jim Crow walls tumbled one by one in Enid. Sit-ins spread quickly throughout Oklahoma and the country. Junior briefly savored success, but his private struggle with his family and himself showed no sign of easing. On January 7, 1959, he appeared in Garfield County Superior Court for his divorce trial. Junior asked the judge for custody of Nodie Mae's four children: Terry Lynn, three; Venita Della, two; Levia Pearl, one; Hulon III, four months. Junior saw himself as a fitter parent than Nodie. She didn't show up to fight him. Judge George Howard Wilson granted him custody.

While educating and keeping house for the kids, and putting whatever hurt too much out of his mind, Junior resumed his college studies. He took a couple of classes in religion, but his main passion was psychology. He searched for answers. How does personality develop? What are the symptoms of mental disorders? What motivates people? Why do they show emotion? What issues face children with developmental disabilities? What forms of influence and conditioning make people conform?

Junior didn't fit in at the college rush parties or frats, and on Saturdays he drifted over to the house of Edward R. Jorden, his psychology professor and adviser. A small group of psych majors would gather there and discuss the confusing world. Junior was struggling to find a role for himself in a society where blacks were not fully accepted. He told Dr. Jorden he wanted to be accepted without regard to color. Jorden found the young man bright and ambitious. "There just weren't a lot of opportunities for blacks in leadership roles," the professor said.

On June 1, 1960, Junior received his B.A. from Phillips with less than a B average. He thought about a career in clinical psychology, then questioned whether any psychologist earning a hundred dollars an hour really understood how to treat mental disorder and human suffering. "After you get up [from the couch], you're still crazy and confused, and left in misery, anxiety, hell, and poverty," he later explained. "If they have power, they ought to be able to look inside your head and tell you what is wrong. Why can't they tell you the problem and offer the solution?"

Why can't they "analyze the mind and change it from immorality to morality?" Why can't they "go inside the minds of poverty-stricken people and cause them to rise up and be rich?"

Junior rejected psychology. In the fall of 1960, he showed up at the University of Oklahoma Law School, looking like a model of conservatism: spectacles, jacket, tie. The civil rights movement was not yet in full gear at Oklahoma—just a couple of "squat-in" protests at Campus Corner. Junior, the only black person in his class, was quiet and uncontroversial, plunging into contracts, legal accounting, and torts. With financial support from family and friends, he moved into a cluster of prefab homes called Sooner City, used mainly by married couples and GIs. There Junior met a doctoral candidate in education named Chloe Hight. Daughter of a Georgia brick mason, she was attractive, warm, and bright. Junior was interested in her research on the learning rates of Negro and white children. Chloe had concluded that the Stanford Binet Intelligence Test, used widely in the public schools, didn't measure the true abilities of Negro children. She wanted to find out if they would fare better on an intelligence test freer of cultural bias. She administered the Good-enough Draw-a-Man Test to fifty-five second- and third-graders in an Oklahoma school system. Their task was to draw a man. Chloe arrived at scores depending on the number of details attempted (such as arms, legs, clothing, and so on), or on the correctness of relative proportions. On the Draw-a-Man Test, her study showed, the Negro children got higher test scores than the white children.

Chloe, three years older than Junior, shared certain qualities with his mother. She set high standards and moral codes. She valued hard work and independence. In time, she became Junior's new total spiritual and financial supporter—"as good medical doctors' wives do," he said. Even if he treated her badly, she tolerated it. She idolized him and found him supportive. "Hulon," Chloe once said, "is one of the most brilliant men I ever met." She became the second Mrs. Hulon Mitchell, Jr., but there would be no children. Junior never talked about the reasons, but after his failed marriage, according to three family members, he got a vasectomy.

He stayed in law school less than a year. He moved to Georgia with Chloe, who got a teaching job at Albany State. Albany was a segregated, backwater city of 57,000, 40 percent black. The shock troops of the civil rights movement had begun to gather there, to make it a test ground for sit-ins, protests, and economic boycotts. If Albany could integrate peacefully, then any place in the South could. It turned into a long struggle. Albany Police Chief Laurie Pritchett tried to crush the activists' demonstrations through mass arrests.

Curiously, Junior sat out the protests, watching from the side-lines. On occasion, when people in the so-called Albany movement saw him, he seemed mad at the world, angry with white people who kept him and his Negro brothers down, and angry with black people who didn't stand up to white people. Chloe, once full of vitality, seemed to change. She became withdrawn. The nonviolent combatants kept a distance from Junior. A "very heavy revolutionary, no, not revolutionary, revelatory period," he called it. He'd already prayed at the courthouse steps and sung "We Shall Overcome." It didn't seem worth it to go to more sit-ins when their only options were to become track stars or "comedians on stage."

"The civil rights movement," he later said, "was not about becoming free from the oppressor. The civil rights movement was about fighting and dying to get inside of oppression, to be better oppressed. The civil rights movement was about being able to go and stay in a hotel that you couldn't afford to pay one night's rent in. The civil rights movement was about being able to stop giving your money to your black brother and give it all to your oppressor. That's what the civil rights movement was all about. You wanted to sleep in the white hotel and eat in the white restaurant, so you wouldn't have to eat in the black restaurant no more. The civil rights movement was not about owning a hotel."

His sense of fair play weakened, Junior looked for quicker means of personal liberation, another path to success stressing economic clout. He incinerated another old self. About 1961, he began to study the teachings of the Honorable Elijah Muhammad, "Messenger of Allah" and spiritual leader of the Lost-Found Nation of Islam (the Black Muslims). In a mosque on Edgewood Avenue in Atlanta, he listened raptly as Jeremiah X, one of Mr. Muhammad's qualified ministers, revealed secrets concealed by the white race for six thousand years. The Muslims combined black American rage with a few odds and ends of Islam, a protective attitude toward women, a nontraditional theology about the origin of the races, and a strict disciplinary code not unlike that of Junior's father: self-help, no smoking, no drinking, no swearing, no gambling, no sparing the rod on children.

Suddenly, a new world opened up for Junior. "Muhammad

taught that the black men of America was God across the planet Earth," he said. "That was the first time I heard we were God." The Muslims were proud to be black, even more than proud. They gloried in it, treating one another with respect. They believed they were the original man, Allah's choice to survive the final conflict. Though his family had tried to exalt him, Junior always seemed to view blackness as a stigma, a curse he was born with. Now he was sick of acting like someone he didn't want to be. "Talk like them, act like them, dress like them, think like them," he later lamented. He wanted to set his own standards of beauty, conduct, and accomplishment, not the white man's standards. He had enough of black people who "fry and dye" their hair, cooking it, baking it, oiling it, and chemicalizing it, and black women who put on "war paint" to imitate white people. He had no use for the elders who infused him with white values and programmed him to mimic the white man. "You don't care if the whole world rejects you," Junior would say, "as long as white people accept you.

"I don't want to be white anymore."

In Albany, about thirty to forty Muslims met in a small house. They ran a grocery store, but people in Albany didn't take kindly to a group with a reputation for violence. The business failed.

By 1964 Junior and Chloe had moved to Atlanta, cradle of the civil rights movement. He joined the Muslims canvassing the streets and fishing for converts, telling their black brothers and sisters how the white man had brainwashed them. They needed to come into Elijah Muhammad's movement. He hawked copies of the movement's newspaper, *Muhammad Speaks*, and traveled to Chicago for audiences with Mr. Muhammad. He said he wanted to discard his evil ways and cut the umbilical cord tying him to his family's Christianity. He wanted an X.

9

Elijah Muhammad welcomed him into the knowledge. Hulon Mitchell, Jr., became Hulon X, a man unknown, robbed of his identity, stripped of his homeland, his language, his culture, and his family name. Hulon ex-Christian. Hulon ex-veteran. Hulon ex–girl chaser. Hulon ex-Mitchell.

According to Mr. Muhammad, Mitchell was a "slave name." Slave masters took away his real name, forced him into the wilderness of North America, and gave him this phony name. "I truly did not know the name of my forefathers" he said. "Our names and land were taken from us, and the ones who gave us their names . . . were owners of the plantations, so if Mr. Smith owned the plantation, we became slaves of Mr. Smith, and if we were on Johnson's plantation, we became the slaves of Mr. Johnson."

Hulon would keep his X until Allah gave him a holy name. Seeking to rise in the Nation of Islam as quickly as he could, Hulon X became a proselytizer without peer. He poured his energy into interpreting the Holy Qur'an to explain current events. He tempered his inner self to survive in the wilderness. He cropped his hair, which the Muslims said carried germs. He exercised, fasted, ate lightly. Usually, Muslims ate only one meal a day of bean soup, a fish salad, a choice of broccoli, spinach, carrots, or white cabbage. Pork destroyed an individual's mental powers and beauty, and the only seafood they were allowed to eat was fish with scales and fins weighing less than fifty pounds. The Muslims considered bigger fish scavengers. They insisted on buying from Negro merchants whenever possible.

Chloe stayed in the background. People remember her wearing long skirts, covering her head, never complaining. According to Muhammad, a man had to control a woman if he was to gain her respect. While continuing to teach, Chloe kept house and helped educate

Nodie's kids. Public schools, the Muslims thought, were breeding grounds for sadists, drug addicts, radicals, and perverts.

In a later identity, Hulon X would wax indignant about integrated public schools and their harm to black children. "When he comes home to the ghetto, he sees black people standing under trees talking loud, drunk, cursing, disrespecting our beautiful, sweet, lovely black women, speaking nasty words to our women as they pass publicly in the street. . . . He goes to an integrated school in a white suburban neighborhood where all the lawns are manicured. They live in big, fine, spacious $200,000 homes, and he comes home to a ghetto house where there's no grass on the front lawn, no air-conditioning in the home, hot, hell conditions. He sees the opposite kind of life on white television, white magazines, and white newspapers. Your child learns white supremacy in the white schools."

Hulon X observed and learned to articulate Mr. Muhammad's teachings to a T. He befriended Malcolm X, the Nation's most media-savvy member. At the University of Islam in Atlanta, he listened to the fiery Jeremiah X, who once labeled a confidant of Martin Luther King "one of the most low-down creatures I've ever met . . . a tool of the white man . . . an educated Uncle Tom." Jeremiah taught not to hate the white man, but not to love him either. The black man's problem was economic. He had been held down and stomped on by the white man.

The Nation of Islam was essentially a conservative organization, more interested in building an independent economic empire than in making a frontal attack on racist institutions. For legal advice, they sometimes turned to James Venable, an imperial wizard of a KKK faction. ("I'd represent Martin Luther King if he paid me enough," Venable once said.)

To learn more about economic institutions, Hulon X enrolled at Atlanta University under his slave name. The university, a complex of schools housing Martin Luther King's alma mater, was setting the pace in the civil rights movement, but progress was still slow and restless students were vowing to take the fight into the streets. Others were becoming receptive to the Muslims' ideology of racial separation. Hulon took courses in banking and monetary policy. His

58

seventy-page thesis, submitted in August 1964, explored the "exploitation of the masses" and the demise of capitalism. He singled out the crushing plight of the "laboring Negro masses, the truly forgotten men of American life."

"They have no security in their employment," he wrote. "There are few that cannot be fired on a day's notice. They do not have union protection for reasonably fair wages even in hazardous occupations. Their pay, even in times when there is a strong demand for their services, is far from adequate." Elijah Muhammad's servant concluded that world socialism was the wave of the future. "Until all men can enjoy an economic freedom, justice and equality, the world will experience chaos."

On May 31, 1965, less than three months before President Johnson signed the Voting Rights Act, Hulon X left the university with his master's degree in economics and a renewed sense of mission. "Society is a product of will and action," he proclaimed. "Only human beings are able to will and act."

Mr. Muhammad showered him with praise, naming him minister of Muhammad's mosque number fifteen. Hulon X received the holy name Shah, meaning the ruler. People around town started calling him the Shah or Mr. Minister. His ministry took place amid a rising tide of urban warfare gripping the country. In 1965, a Muslim hit team gunned down Malcolm at the Audubon Ballroom in New York City. The civil rights movement was in volatile flux. Many of Atlanta's older preachers wanted to continue the struggle within the framework of Dr. King and existing organizations. They viewed the Muslims as anti-Christian extremists going straight to hell. But few of the older leaders knew how to go into a hot ghetto and be listened to. The man who could speak to the young people was Minister Shah. Muslim membership swelled. After they outgrew their cramped quarters, they paid $110,000 for what had been a white Baptist church in the city's northwest section. They transformed it into a mosque with stained-glass windows. Hulon and Chloe lived in a brick house next to the sanctuary on Bankhead Highway.

Racial unrest in Atlanta's Summerhill section spurred attendance at the mosque and added to Minister Shah's prestige. He gained a reputation as one of the coolest, smartest militants in town. Just hearing his name on the street was enough to bring a taste of respect, or fear, to a non-Muslim's mouth. "A brilliant man schooled in the art of discourse," Sam Wright called him. Wright was a high school English teacher and supporter of Dr. King. He remembered peppering Shah with questions over coffee at Paschal's, a famous black-owned motor hotel and restaurant just a few blocks from Atlanta University Center. "How can we get the white man off our neck?" Wright used to ask him.

The only way they could get the white man off their neck, the minister replied, was to love each other instead of the enemy. Wright sat riveted to Shah's words. He was charming and polite, never raising his voice in public. He had a serene exterior and so much rapport with whomever he was speaking that he probably could talk a person into giving him his socks if he wanted them. If he had any rage, he kept it stewing inside him. "You had to like him," Wright said. "He loved a challenge and liked to be sparred with."

At Paschal's, Minister Shah debated strategy with movement activists of all stripes, from Martin Luther King to Stokely ("Black Power") Carmichael, from H. Rap ("Burn, baby, burn") Brown to Louis Farrakhan. Everyone who knew Shah recalled his radical eloquence when he explained how the so-called Negro was in a state of mental and spiritual captivity, brainwashed to think that "white man's ice is colder, his flour is whiter, and white folks' sugar is sweeter." Integration, he came to believe, was "the worst thing that ever happened to us," a "trick" leading to a few window-dressing blacks who were selling out. "The white man was in control in slavery, he was in control in segregation, and after integration he's still in control," he once explained. "They used to only let a black policeman arrest a black person, then they came up with the trick called integration. Now black police forget that we marched for them to get on the job. Now they get on the job and turn white. If they try to stay on the job and be black, whitey persecutes them."

At the mosque, Minister Shah presided over meetings that could turn into boiling kettles of emotion. The Muslims were secretive, verging on being paranoid, and every man, woman, and child who entered was searched for weapons, cigarettes, alcohol, and drugs. The showman in him blossomed as he exhorted his hearers not to fear the white man. He quoted Elijah Muhammad: Be peaceful, courteous, respect the white man's law, and never be the aggressor. But if anyone puts a hand on you, may Allah bless you.

Hulon Shah had finally found respect, walking in his path, not in the path of his father. He went around Atlanta with bodyguards from the ranks of the Fruit of Islam, the Nation's paramilitary security force. Trained in karate and judo, they knew how to handle weapons and ward off police dog attacks.

The minister put his wife in charge of the Muslim school, where boys and girls attended classes separately. They had special classes about the nature of the sexes—lessons for men learning to be husbands and fathers, and for women learning to keep house and care for their children. He helped men find jobs and counseled ex-prisoners in need of spiritual comfort. Muslim ministers also recommended punishment for backsliders and acted as a sort of courtship czar between male and female followers. Away from the mosque, Shah managed the Muslims' businesses—a bakery, a clothing store, and restaurants featuring whiting.

As his powers grew, his self-esteem rose. He coolly showed off his bodyguards in front of his family. "I wasn't so impressed with the Muslims," said brother Jefferson, ten years younger than Junior. Jefferson and a few of his brothers lived in Atlanta for a time and got to meet stars like Muhammad Ali. "Growing up in the church, it was too fast a jump for me," Jefferson said. "They were pretty violent."

Junior's blood brothers said he never preached violence, but Atlanta police were less certain about Minister Shah's followers. The cops considered the Muslims a sinewy semicult of bow-tied soldiers, contemptuous of civil liberties. Secret tape recordings of Muslim meetings, an Atlanta police officer said, suggested that at least a few militants wanted to do away with the white man. Citizens traded insults and punches with them on Broad Street when Muslim newspaper peddlers came at members of their own race too hard. Whether Minister Shah's thundering words incited followers into acts of violence was an open question. Without a doubt, though, he showed extreme loyalty when a follower operated outside the law.

One Saturday night in March 1967, Hulon Shah received a phone call at Paschal's. Five of his men had been in a fight with a citizen who refused to buy the Muslim weekly tabloid. Angry street people ran to the aid of the injured man, pinning the Muslims against a building. When the police arrived, the crowd swelled to hundreds and the Muslims, broken broomsticks in hand, were shouting, "We're not going anywhere until the minister gets here."

By the time the minister arrived with his entourage, the cops had already hauled the Muslims to jail. Shah hurried to the station house, where his belligerent followers were refusing to give up their slave names. He ordered them to cooperate, and then left to see a bondsman named Alley Pat. While Shah was gone, the Muslims got into another fight. This one was with the cops.

The police said the Muslims attacked them with crowbars and drill bits, but at two separate trials Shah's men insisted the cops attacked first, without provocation. Fearing for their lives, the Muslims responded to violence with violence. The minister took the stand for his men amid tight security in Fulton Superior Court. The second-floor courtroom was packed with Muslims and members of the Student Nonviolent Coordinating Committee (SNCC). Plainclothes deputies, investigators, and detectives ringed the courtroom.

The minister matter-of-factly recounted events on the night of the assault, describing the way the brothers had been "mutilated."

"They were disheveled, limping," he testified. "I saw bruises, half-closed eyes, things like that."

Atlanta's Solicitor General Lewis R. Slaton, Jr., cross-examined him. "Are you referred to as mister or reverend or minister?" the prosecutor asked.

"Minister Shah," he answered in a soft voice. "I don't use the counsel of anyone other than Elijah Muhammad and some legal attorney."

When Shah referred to the injured policemen as "so-called Negroes," the prosecutor stopped him. "Does 'so-called' have any particular significance?"

"Well, Elijah Muhammad teaches us that we are . . . really descendants from the Asiatic people, not from Africa," Shah explained.

Slaton had tried a lot of militants in his life, but Shah was one of the calmest, most articulate he had ever seen.

Slaton's assistant, Roger Thompson, was curious about the minister's educational background. "You say you received your training for the ministry at the University of Islam?"

"Yes, sir."

"And what courses did you take, what major and minor field?"

"There is no major and minor field in the study of Islam."

"Do you agree with me a university is a group of colleges?" Thompson asked.

"I think according to Webster's dictionary, a university can be a high school or even a grade school," the minister replied.

"What strata of academic attainment was required at the University of Islam?"

"The attainment was being able to teach Islam as taught by the Honorable Elijah Muhammad."

On the witness stand, Hulon Shah proved to be an exceptional verbal sparrer, a portrait of a righteous, straitlaced man, with complete regard for human life and total respect for authority. Though his followers were convicted of assault with intent to commit murder, prosecutor Slaton never believed Shah had sanctioned their violent acts. "He seemed like the type who tried to shepherd them along a nonviolent path."

Minister Shah could attract both devotion and danger. The more authority he amassed, the more he had to protect. And the more he had to lose. After the trial, the shadows of police riots fell over the country. Rumors of FBI-sanctioned plots against black leaders were widespread. The Muslims were fighting a series of harsh internal battles, and reports hit the desks of Elijah Muhammad's right-hand men at national headquarters in Chicago: the Shah was abusing his ministry, wielding power for private gain and personal satisfaction. Unnamed informants accused him of skimming $50,000 in legal fees that Elijah Muhammad had wired down for some of Shah's incarcerated men. According to Taalib Ahmad, a close aide to Mr. Muhammad, Chicago also received unsubstantiated allegations of sexual improprieties—possible battery of minors and "homosexual tendencies"—a grave violation in the Muslims' manly world.

"He was weak," Taalib said. "The reports we got was that he was taking the teachings and using them as a shield for his own purposes . . . to secure power and wealth for himself and hide his immoral side."

Elijah Muhammad ordered a no-holds-barred investigation, dispatching Taalib to Atlanta to look into charges. "Brother," the messenger told him, "don't be surprised at anything you hear." Taalib directed the minister's lieutenants to keep a sharp eye and report any possible misconduct to Chicago.

A Muslim's most chilling fear was to be put out from the brotherhood and family of the Nation of Islam. He looked upon a suspension as a "return to the grave." Rather than be cut off from the Nation, Hulon Shah quit, before the investigators substantiated any of the charges. "It was obvious to him we were going to get rid of him," Taalib said. "He saved us the trouble."

The Muslims said they did not seek vengeance. "Allah will punish him for it in his own good time," they quoted Elijah Muhammad.

Shah never talked publicly about his reasons for leaving, but he told his family the Muslims had set him up as he tried to break away. He feared assassination and knew any death talk had to be sanctioned by—if not actually arranged by—one man: Elijah Muhammad.

The ex-minister dropped from sight and tried to bury the past. Thirty-two and unemployed, he had to start over. The Holiness airman, who had gone to a Disciples of Christ school and somehow found himself in the Nation of Islam, vowed never again to take orders from a religious hierarchy. But he wasn't going to languish in obscurity or let Elijah Muhammad intimidate him into silence. Never again would he be an apostate in any faith in which he was a mere follower.

His respite from turbulence was brief. Only a short time after he disappeared, ex–Hulon X resurfaced in Atlanta with a fancy house, a new name, and a new crowd to run with.

10

Billy Steven Jones, sometimes known as B.S., made his living selling clothes in Atlanta. He was a friendly, decent man who loved silk suits, pointy shoes, pistols, and the Word of God.

B.S., age twenty-six, always wanted to do God's work, and in June 1968, Elijah Muhammad's onetime servant gave him the chance. The two men hooked up and found a way to make the love of God pay their bills. They exalted themselves with French-sounding names. Hulon Mitchell called himself Michel (pronounced Mee shel). Jones took the name Jone (pronounced Jo nay). They also bestowed upon themselves the very honorable title "Father." And they set out to prove their worth.

Father Jone and Father Michel took to Atlanta's gospel airwaves, quickly becoming successful radio evangelists. Their total-blessing plan was destined to save "needy, and oppressed" listeners, as well as any other casualty of America's system, from ruin. They could bless and heal thousands by the power of God. They held the key to solving any kind of problem, be it personal, social, or financial. With their spiritual powers, they could even see into the future and predict the winning numbers. The numbers game in Atlanta was like a Wall Street brokerage firm. Winning hits paid off big, so big that people could buy big cars and houses.

Although the FCC frowned upon dispensing lucky numbers over the air, the prophets told interested listeners to set up an appointment. For a small contribution, Fathers Michel and Jone would reveal all. Listeners of WIGO and WAOK flocked to see them. The more people they recruited into their orbit, the more contributions Michel and Jone received and the more airtime they bought. Around Atlanta they became known as "the prophets."

In less than ten years, the former Hulon Mitchell, Jr., had revealed himself as a bona fide religious genius, embracing Christianity, renouncing it, going on to Islam, renouncing that, and then inventing a new creed, using discarded pieces of the old ones. The former psychology student had come to believe that only God could "change the mind from the left to the right, change the mind from bad to good, change . . . the mind from darkness to light."

His success as a reborn evangelist of the airwaves foreshadowed a burst of interest in exotic swamis, Zen masters, and gurus, as well as a boom in born-again churches. These were, after all, the strange days of hippies and Vietnam. Lots of people were looking for a new spiritual consciousness. Father Michel, in his many identities, always had a divinelike sense of timing.

To serve their financial needs, the prophets of Atlanta set up a nonprofit company called the Modern Christian Church. Father Michel's wife, Chloe, served as an officer with them. The church provided for their major expenses. Father Michel started tooling around town in a white limo, delivering tapes of his message to gospel radio stations. New bodyguards were in tow. He and Chloe settled in a spacious, pagoda-style house on a hilly street in northwest Atlanta. He called the brick house, lavishly furnished with gifts from his followers, his $75,000 "palace." It had a sophisticated alarm system and burglar bars on the windows. Two Eldorados were parked in the driveway. Father Michel exchanged his bow tie and fez for a long white robe. He cited scriptural authority ("He that overcometh, the same shall be clothed in white raiment") for his new wardrobe.

One day, Father Michel's ex-Muslim friends spotted him on the street. "Brother's really flipped out," one groused. "He's running around Atlanta in a dress." The Muslims tailed Father Michel to his new house, then reported to national headquarters in Chicago: They knew where Mr. Muhammad's $50,000 went. Father Michel was living off it in skirts.

As a religious man, Father Jone had a lifestyle conversion too. He put on satin robes and adorned his apartment with all the accouterments of a prophet. He set up a prayer room where candles cast a flickering glow. Father Jone would sit on a velvet throne, reading the Bible. The prayer room had an altar replete with incense and packets of herbs and spices. The throne itself was covered with a tasseled white canopy and was propped up on a foot-high platform. Underneath the cushion was a loaded six-shot revolver.

The gun didn't do him any good. On Friday, May 23, 1969, at 10:30 P.M., Father Jone was in the dining room, studying the Bible. The doorbell rang, and the prophet's wife answered. Three men wanted in. Mrs. Jone figured they had an appointment and told them to have a seat in the meditation room. Suddenly, they pulled pistols and opened fire. Father Jone bled to death on the floor, shot three times in the back. After the shootout, the police announced that B.S. Jones had managed to kill two of the gunmen. One killer collapsed in the parking lot. A second was found dying after he wrecked his car.

Although witnesses heard no demands for money, the cops thought robbery was the motive; the killers probably knew Father Jone had made a little money in the religious racket. But the prophet's friends speculated that there was more to the story. According to the police version, the two dead killers came from Jacksonville, Florida. So did a third suspect, later captured in Chicago but never prosecuted. Why would robbers come from out of town to kill Father Jone? How much money did he have anyway? According to documents filed in probate court, he left his widow and daughter only $1,994.30—of which he owed creditors $1,588.80 (including $733 for clothes). Robbery didn't make much sense. Not a shred of proof existed that Father Jone had his hands in the offering plate. And even if he did dip into it from time to time, so too, probably, did quite a few other religious men in Atlanta. Nobody really cared. It wasn't something a man got killed over. Besides, it wasn't as if Father Jone was living in super-opulence. Father Jone's homicide looked as much like a murder-for-hire job as a robbery.

The homicide wasn't something his partner, Father Michel, ever discussed. The police never pressed him. If the surviving prophet of Atlanta was frightened, he didn't show it. After the homicide, his congregation got bigger and Father Michel got better at working a crowd. His Modern Christian Church spread to Detroit, where the prophet could be heard five days a week on WJLB radio. With his encouragement, his followers started calling him the King. Only a month after Jone's untimely passing, Michel appeared at the first anniversary of his ministry in Atlanta's City Auditorium. The program for the event pictured him carrying a scepter and wearing a white satin tunic and a robe with a zebra lining. He also had a gold crown with red jewels. He preached prosperity and a you-are-somebody message. Quoting the Twenty-third Psalm, he urged his congregants to make a difference in God's heaven on earth. "God wants you to be rich," he wrote. "The Bible says, 'Riches and wealth is the gift of God.'"

Father Michel did miracle cures with his "blessed prayer cloth." His supporters were housewives craving spiritual power, young people tired of the drug culture, and small businesspeople who wanted to strike it rich. His blessing plan, they testified, put money in their pockets and brought happiness to their homes. He restored peace of mind and removed unnatural conditions, ranging from cancer to frayed nerves. Supposedly, Father Michel could even replace lost teeth.

"The Lame Walk!" Father Michel's brochure proclaimed. "The Blind See! The Deaf Hear! Disorders Disappear! Operations Are Cancelled!" The brochure cited many happy customers. Mrs. Helen Straughter said that thanks to the Father, she was blessed with a Cadillac. A man named Mr. Chaz, photographed in his beauty shop, was quoted as saying his profits had skyrocketed because of a "mighty miracle through Father Michel."

"His prayers," another disciple said, "mean everything."

The former Hulon Mitchell, Jr., airman, psychology major, and law student, had applied his organizational skills to conquer the God business. Atlantans remembered the church as unorthodox, but as deejay Harrison Smith put it, "not so belligerent that you could classify him as a racist."

The more Michel's followers showered him with adulation and gifts, the more he dreamed of awakening their fantasies of eternal life. He wanted them to feel as much pride and satisfaction about themselves as he felt about himself. He wanted them to believe, as he believed about himself, that they possessed divine gifts.

"I love hearing about me," he bellowed almost two decades later. "I'm the supreme narcissist. I'm the one who gets off on myself supremely. I look in the mirror and say, 'You're lookin' good, lookin' good . . . the best lookin' man in the universe. I know I'm most beautiful. No one is as beautiful as I am 'cause I created beauty. . . . The beauty of my mind is incomprehensible."

In his quiet suburban neighborhood of professional people and retirees, the King was less flashy. He kept a low, almost invisible, profile, leaving small, neighborly things—domestic chores, shopping, and so on—to Chloe. She attended homeowners' meetings and taught at Morris Brown College. She also helped him run a nursery school for the church children. They called it The King's Day Care Center.

As time went on, the Modern Christian Church became like one big happy family, a paradise free from suffering and pain, where everyone was completely committed to their glorified teacher and father. The depth of loyalty became apparent on a spring night in 1970. About two hundred of Father Michel's followers had gathered for a Sunday meeting at their church on Edgewood. Michel was being guarded by his recently hired bodyguard, Lucious Boyce. As the service drew to a close, the Father turned to the bodyguard. "Lucious Boyce is a hired killer and a cold-blooded murderer," he allegedly declared.

Lucious, age thirty-one, was an ex-cop and air force veteran trained in the use of M-16s and Thompson submachine guns. But Father Michel had a bigger weapon: words.

The King told the congregation he had proof that Lucious was a hitman. An assassin had deposited five thousand dollars in Lucious's bank account and five thousand more was coming after Father Michel was dead.

Lucious tried to defend himself against the King's verbal onslaught, but nobody was listening. A large crowd suddenly surrounded the bodyguard. The attack, he said later, was sudden, violent, and came from all sides. They beat him and ripped his clothes. One woman struck him on the head with her high heels. "I was shocked and terrified," Lucious said.

Five weeks after the attack, he filed a slander lawsuit against Father Michel. The preacher's remarks, Lucious said in court papers, were calculated "to incite a crowd of people to physically attack and seriously injure or kill me.

"The undeniable effect of the language, utterances, and implications falsely made against me to the crowd of people present at the time complained of, did cause persons to react with hatred, contempt, ridicule, and lack of confidence in me which they expressed by their words and deeds to me and to each other."

Father Michel denied Lucious's charges while cloaking himself in religion. If he made the statements at all, his lawyer said, the preacher made them "in performance of a morally obligatory private duty," to protect himself and his family. "This question and all matters complained of transpired in an ecclesiastic court and tribunal," attorney J. L. Jordan wrote in court papers. The First Amendment, the lawyer contended, protected not only a church's doctrines but also its discipline.

Eventually, Lucious's lawsuit was tossed out of court. The assault at the Modern Christian Church never caught the attention of Atlanta's lawmen. Prosecutor Slaton had kept files on the church because he suspected it was a scam. But it wasn't a big enough scam to warrant attention. What's more, proving it was a scam was something else entirely.

Back in Enid, Oklahoma, legends about Hulon Mitchell's life were growing. The talk among family and friends was that Muslim hitmen had invaded his home, held his kids hostage, and threatened to cut out his tongue. "They put bullet holes in his windows," said brother Marvin, child number thirteen. Everyone in Enid was worried about him.

In 1971 Phil Porter went to a convention in Atlanta and decided to check on Junior. Father Michel sent a limo to his friend's hotel.

Sydney P. Freedberg

It was an emotional reunion. The men hugged and reminisced. The tumultuous sixties had left even Enid reeling. Shortly after the assassination of Martin Luther King, Jr., houses in Southern Heights had gone up in smoke. The police suspected three of Junior's brothers in a firebomb attack after two Molotov cocktails were found in a Mitchell car. The charges provoked an angry denial from the Reverend Hulon Mitchell, who appeared before a grand jury to clear his boys. He testified they were in Tulsa with him, singing in a church choir, the day the fires were set. Civil rights leaders used the incident to illustrate the mistreatment of black people by the Enid judicial system, which they called the worst in Oklahoma. The charges against the Mitchells were dropped.

The sixties had seen an ungluing of some of the Mitchells' tight ties. The family singing performances weren't as much fun. The Church Of God In Christ itself had gone through a dark period. Many spiritual friendships had been broken. Attitudes had gotten so radical and lifestyles so promiscuous that the churchmen complained they could no longer distinguish between "holy and unholy" and "clean and unclean."

Despite the upheaval, Phil Porter had stayed in the church. Now he was a respected minister. Junior seemed surprised and a little awed by his friend's commitment. Junior had always been persecuted for being Holiness. He started to weep, and so did Phil. Junior's memories ate away inside him. He would have liked to have stayed in his father's church, but every time he went back, he saw the same thing—gutless preachers giving otherworldly sermons that perverted human hopes and dreams. Father Michel, at least, accepted that humans had a right to be happy on earth.

Phil asked him to give the church another try.

"Do you think these people will accept me?" Junior asked.

Of course, Phil replied. He introduced Junior to a Holiness bishop in Atlanta. Junior agreed to go back to the Christian church of his childhood, and for a short time he called himself the Reverend Hugh Mitchell. But before long he was back in the pulpit of his tailor-made Modern Christian Church, with an even more ambitious

72

program of social uplift. In 1974 he amended the church's corporate charter to make himself almost omnipotent. His new Modern Christian Church was an all-encompassing social, economic, and spiritual center with self-perpetuating machinery. Father Michel would be the final arbiter in all matters—president and national minister for life. "No other person shall be eligible nor shall any other person qualify for such office," the incorporation papers stated. His church would help needy people. It could borrow money and other personal property and make loans to the poor. It could provide transportation services, housing, clothing, and food for children. It could sell religious sermons and musical recordings. It could receive gifts and contributions "made by will or otherwise." Finally, it could offer a burial service.

It was a ministry built on a foundation of sand, and as the Bible says, it was destined to crumble. The church disbanded over disagreements about splitting communal property. In February 1978 congregants sued Father Michel for fraud. By then, he was already gone, and another metamorphosis was under way.

11

···

Father Michel left almost everything in Atlanta, including Chloe and his crown. He popped up in Orlando, Florida, to perform his magic. It is a town built on magic, and it called out to the mystical Brother Love.

Before Disney World, Orlando was just another sleepy central Florida town of untouched palmetto brush, flatlands, and long lines of orange trees vanishing toward the horizon. Then Mickey Mouse came along and awakened the place. Hotels, fancy restaurants, and superfantasy attractions mushroomed almost overnight, turning Orlando and its suburbs into Florida's most famous tourist spot.

Brother Love, like the earlier Father Michel, had murky origins. By most accounts, he surfaced about 1976 in a storefront pulpit not far from Church Street Station. The area was blossoming with Dixieland bands, can-can dancers, discos, country-western music, and a hot-air balloon museum.

He strolled among the masses on Church Street. "Just call me Brother Love," he'd say. He had always been lucky in love. For twenty years, women supported him, and in Orlando, Brother Love commanded fifteen to twenty disciples, among them a coterie of women who took care of his every need. They pooled their resources, giving themselves up to him spiritually, financially, and, prosecutors hinted years later, sexually. The women worked for him and paid the rent, leaving him with enough blessing money to survive. He read Scripture to them and gambled at the dog track. As their prophet, Brother Love didn't feel he had to work. He hadn't held a secular job since his days as a college librarian.

Nodie Mae and Chloe, the wives of his past, faded from his memory. In time, he would even forget their maiden names. They tried to erase him from their minds. "I don't want to talk about that man," Chloe told a friend in Georgia. A decade later, she would try

74

to explain Junior in a rare interview with the *Miami Herald*. "You don't have to look at his background," she said. "Look at society. Society creates people like Hulon."

As his ex-wives struggled to start over, Brother Love found a new woman, Linda Merthie Gaines. She was an attractive, twenty-nine-year-old clerk at Florida Power & Light. If there was anyone Brother Love could relate to emotionally, it was Linda. A pretty, expressive woman with a radiant smile and a big dimple, she seemed to have her feet planted firmly on the ground. She was smart and trusting, a self-starter. "She is the most peaceful person I ever met," he once said. "A wonderful person." Like other important women in his life, she was light-skinned.

Linda grew up in a large, closely knit Baptist family in Sanford, Florida, a railroad town north of Orlando. Her parents, Lillie and Oscar Merthie, ran a day-care center. Linda's mother always supported the children through right and wrong. Oscar Merthie was loving but stern. He taught his kids the necessary skills and applied the strap when they didn't obey him.

Eager to succeed, Linda rarely needed discipline. She attended Florida A & M, a historically black school in Tallahassee, during the tumult of the civil rights movement. She majored in business administration and belonged to the thespian society, the chorus, and the band. She was a cheerleader and secretary of the student council. In 1968 she married Freddie Gaines, who turned out, according to Linda, to be a no-good son of a bitch. He made one hundred and ten dollars a week as a construction worker, if he was lucky. The couple argued constantly, and she had to fight him for child support—one hundred and thirty dollars a month.

Enter Brother Love. On the rebound from her divorce, Linda was raising three kids alone: Freddie, Jr., ten; Kelly, eight, and Lydia, six. She met Love at a social event in Orlando, and he seemed to be exactly what she was looking for. Eleven years older, he was tough and strong and stood up for what he believed in. He didn't need to get drunk or high to have a good time. Linda was impressed by his intellect, his charm, his spirituality, his good looks, and the way he could give her almost anything she wanted. Her initial attraction deepened into a complex relationship. They'd always deny they had sex, but like Chloe, Linda began to support him. He spent so much time at her house that the children thought they had a new, out-of-work father.

From what little the Gaines children could remember, Brother Love tried to ingratiate himself. He hugged them and called them "son" or "baby." They knew him as Love and Shah. He could be a warm, loving man, but he also could turn into an angry grand inquisitor. Being little kids, they tried to make him feel good and obeyed his commands with a "Yes, sir!" As they got older, though, the Gaines children would grow to distrust him. "If I told him the truth he would get heated up," Linda's son Kelly told the authorities. "We all knew not to say anything against him in his face." Added Freddie, Jr., "It wasn't any great love there."

In time, the Gaines children also would question how their mother, or any person, could be so devoted to someone else. "I don't know how she feels deep down," Kelly said. "She's a very strong-willed woman. . . . She can hide feelings . . . I don't know how she does it."

In whatever way, Linda found inner peace with Brother Love, who was busy reading about religion, meditating, and talking to God. He dabbled in Hebrew and studied Buddhism, Hinduism, Krishna, Brahma, Vishnu, Siva, Sikhism, and any other "ism" he could find. He started seeing the Bible as a cryptogram written in nine ways: figuratively, literally, prophetically, metaphorically, allegorically, in prose, poetry, similes, and parables. He tried to decipher the book's whole, perfect, secret truth. Along the way, he came to believe in karma, that the totality of his actions would determine his next fate.

Then he had another revelation, prompting him to pack his bags for Miami, Babel by the sea. In 1978 Miami was full of people claiming to be God and others who thought they were Jesus Christ. He later said that Miami's established prophets tried to warn him away. "This is not the place you want to come," they told him. "This is the most ignorant group, the most downtrodden, the most divided, the most impossible to do anything with."

The naysayers made Brother Love more determined. "To take them and do something with them," he thought, "proves that I am the divine."

Blacks were a forgotten minority under Miami's old, tight-fisted Cracker leadership, and they were still a forgotten minority under the new Cuban one. The man who made the new Miami what it is lives in Havana. In 1960, a year after Fidel came to power, only five percent of Miami was Hispanic. By 1978 the percentage was six times that. The Cuban influx created potent exile politics and profound economic inequities. As the Cubans overcame barriers of exile to reap financial success, much of black Miami stagnated in poverty. Many blacks believed the Cubans had pushed them to even lower levels in the social pecking order. Blacks felt cheated, locked out of the system. They thought the police were free to harass them, break into their homes without warrants, brutalize and even kill them. Prosecutors were just as likely not to prosecute the police, and no politician did very much about the problems. The elected officials, for the most part, took their cues from a clique of bankers, developers, and media moguls who tried to run Miami in private. The city's power elite became a sort of shadow government known as the Non-Group.

Throughout the nineteen seventies only a few idealistic leaders emerged to challenge the system. Some so-called leaders were secret establishment allies. Others were out to take advantage of the very people they promised to help. Although the civil rights movement had promised steady work, a better education, and a just society, the war on poverty in Miami had been virtually called off. Middle-class blacks left town or integrated themselves into the careerism and apathy of the majority society. Discipline snapped in poorer neighborhoods, and a string of police and prosecutor abuses led to small riots. By the time the stage was set for Brother Love, some young black men thought the only way to grab their piece of Miami's bounty was to take it at gunpoint.

With Linda Gaines and the kids, Brother Love would settle in an all-white apartment building in Hollywood, Florida, south of Fort Lauderdale. Hollywood had a spiffy dog track. Love kept a low profile, receiving mail at a Hollywood post office box. The apartment was in Linda's name. The signature on the rent checks was hers.

The whole Atlanta-to-Orlando-to-Miami journey was shrouded in mystery. When investigators asked about it later, he couldn't recall the simplest dates and places. He said he was evolving, forming a new religion rooted in Judaism. As a boy, he had always loved Old Testament stories. He recited the tales of Gideon, Joshua, and all of God's warrior kings and acted out the Jews' search for the Promised Land.

At some point, he received a message from within: God's true name was designated by the four Hebrew letters Yod Heh Vav Heh, or YHWH, sometimes pronounced Yahweh in English. Millions of Masons and Jews consider the name Yahweh too sacred to be spoken. According to Jewish custom, the word Lord or God is substituted each of the more than five thousand times that YHWH appears in the Old Testament.

Black Hebrew movements had flourished quietly in America since the 1800s. An early supporter was a chef on the Santa Fe railroad, who founded a sect in Kansas. Shortly thereafter, a prophet named F. S. Cherry preached that black people were the Jews mentioned in the Bible. White Jews, he believed, were interlopers and frauds. Cherry used to pull out a picture of a white Jesus Christ and howl, "Who in the hell is this? Nobody knows! They say it is Jesus. That's a damned lie!"

Another group, Commandment Keepers Congregation of the Living God, identified with the Falashas. They were the lost Ethiopian Jews who traced their roots to the union of King Solomon and the Queen of Sheba.

Miami had a black Jewish church dating back to the turn of the century. A thriving sect, its members met in a storefront in Overtown, the city's oldest black neighborhood. The congregation liked the feeling of camaraderie, a sense of belonging they never felt in the big, more established religions.

In the 1970s the media had taken to calling some black Hebrew movements "cults." One of these, the Original Hebrew Israelite Nation, took hold on Chicago's South Side. It ran into controversy when some of its followers went to Israel to reclaim their homeland. Israeli and American authorities accused members of the group of trafficking in stolen credit cards and airline tickets. The Anti-Defamation League of B'nai B'rith compared the Hebrew Israelites to right-wing Aryans who teach that people of northern European stock are the "chosen people."

Now Brother Love was about to put a new face on the Black Hebrew tradition. When he checked his Bible interpreter's dictionary, he learned that Yahweh was the only name of God. Why, he wondered, was Yahweh's name kept secret from him? Why did they hide the name with titles like God, Lord, the Most High, Elohim, Adonai, Emmanuel, Jehovah? The more he read, the more he understood the answers—what he described as "the shocking truth," later to be revealed in a ninety-six-page yellow paperback entitled *You Are Not a Nigger! Our True History, the World's Best-Kept Secret: Yahweh God of Gods.*

But before he could reveal the secret to the world, he had to share it with his family. The prodigal son, the one who rose from the dust bowl in 1935, went home to Oklahoma.

12

He was the messenger. But it wasn't Junior, Airman Mitchell, X, Shah, Father Michel, or Brother Love who delivered it. It was someone evolving into Och Moshe Israel, Hebrew for Brother Moses Israel. "Our people need deliverance," he concluded. "Our people need to be saved."

The biblical Moses rescued the Jews from the brutality of Egyptian slavery. "This time," said the modern-day Moses, "it is a spiritual deliverance."

With his new disciple, Linda Gaines, he returned to his boyhood town to begin the task of gathering his lost sheep so he could shepherd them from spiritual bondage. "I am here to save you," he'd tell potential converts, with gentleness and rapport. "I am here to take you out of hell."

Physically, very little had changed in Enid. The streets in Southern Heights were still muddy and unpaved. The people still munched on ribs at Elmer's BBQ and prayed at a dozen Houses of the Lord. Enid's poor still lived, loved, worked, and died almost entirely within the bounds of Southern Heights, fenced in by the railroad tracks, a busy highway, a park, Boggy Creek, and their own history. But the Reverend and Mrs. Hulon Mitchell, Senior, had escaped the past and gained a new respectability in town. In the years since their number one son left home, Senior had laid a cornerstone for a new Holiness church, on a street to be renamed for daughter Leona, the soprano who had made it all the way to New York City. The fastest-rising diva in the country, she gave her parents a spacious house in the suburbs. Not many people make it big in Enid, and for sure Leona was the only one from this backwater place who performed *Aida* at the Metropolitan Opera House.

The ecstatic hymns of praise for the opera star drowned the din of sorrow in the Mitchell household. Over the years, Hulon and Pearl probably had enjoyed more happiness than any parents in town. But they also had plenty of heartache. Leona's "unexpected Cinderella story," as the hometown press called it, had its downside. Her husband, Robert House, survived two tours in Vietnam and a near-fatal crash in June 1971. Less than two years later, he was killed when his car barreled into a Frisco freight train. Senior had high blood pressure and a tumor on his cheek that kept growing back after operations. His health and age seemed to have mellowed him. He toned down the foot-stomping revivals and took the younger kids to ball games and movies. He seemed more concerned with loving them than saving them from sin.

There was sin in the Mitchell household, but everyone kept quiet about it. Some of the preacher's fifteen children were pregnant out of wedlock or in trouble with the law. Religion had been hammered into them all their lives, but the nails didn't always hold. The Mitchells, despite all their faith, were still only human. Only Pearl Olive seemed above it all, the rock, unaffected by time. She still pounded away at the piano, and people said Sister Pearl's voice got fresher and richer with age.

They welcomed Junior back, even though he had spent a big part of his life rebelling against having been born one of them. He had sought to blot them out by casting off his old name and adopting new ones. Still, he was the bone of their bone and the flesh of their flesh.

Junior would always love them, but he had come to believe all unconverted black people were "dry bones," asleep in mental graves of ignorance. He had died in his thirties, he explained, but now, at age forty-three, he was rising from the dead with a divine mission. He had been called to breathe life into their bones, to wake them up and heal them, breathe spirit into them, and to rescue them from their blind, deaf, dumb, mental, and spiritual condition. Anyone who walked around with "a dumb cross" around his neck proved he was a dead man, spiritually lost.

"Cross represents death, the death of a fool," he once said. "You show me a black man that wears a cross on the planet Earth and I'll show you a man that loves the white enemy to your exclusion. He loves white people, but he hates black people. He lies and says he loves everybody but he's a damnable liar, going straight to hell. He doesn't love everybody. He loves the white enemy. He doesn't love his own black brothers and sisters, except to use them and to steal your money . . . steal your crumbs."

Never singling out his father by name, Junior vilified the false prophets of his childhood—the "lying, blind, greedy, dumb-dog preachers" alluded to in the Book of Isaiah. "His watchmen are blind," according to the Bible. "They are all ignorant, they are all dumb dogs, they cannot bark; sleeping, lying down, loving to slumber. Yea, they are greedy dogs which can never have enough, and they are shepherds that cannot understand. . . ."

But Enid's prodigal son understood the plight of his people. "I know all of your feelings and heartaches and sufferings and pain," he told them. "Because I have endured them for your sake."

On his trip home for a family reunion, Junior assembled interested listeners in an Enid classroom. He held daily lessons to share the mysteries of Scripture and the secrets behind verses holding the key to family prosperity. The Christian preachers, he said, deliberately withheld the whole truth.

The messenger wanted to teach them the truth. "Have you heard people say that God is black?" he'd ask. "Have you heard people say that the prophets are black? . . . Well, let us stop dealing with hearsay."

"Reach up and feel your own head or look at the nappy head of our people, the so-called Negroes." Their hair was like pure wool—proof, "absolutely clear, beyond a shadow of a doubt" that the Scripture, Daniel 7:9 ("I beheld till the thrones were cast down, and the Ancient of days did sit, whose garment was white as snow, and the hair of his head like the pure wool") meant a black God.

He shot out more evidence, more Scripture "proof" that the son of God was black (Revelation 1:13–15), the prophet Job was black (Job 30:30), Jeremiah was black (Jeremiah 8:21), Solomon was black (Song of Solomon 1:5), and David was black (Proverbs 1:1).

Psalm 119:83: "For I am become like a bottle in the smoke;

yet do I not forget thy statutes." What color is a bottle of smoke? he asked. Black.

Jeremiah 14:2: "Judah mourneth, and the gates thereof languish; they are black unto the ground; and the cry of Jerusalem is gone up." The tribe of Israel, known as the tribe of Judah, is black unto the ground. What tribe did Jesus belong to? Hebrews 7:14: "For it is evident that our Lord sprang out of Judah."

So if the tribe of Judah sprang from a region where people had color and Jesus sprang from Judah, what color was Jesus? Black.

Lamentations 4:8: "Their visage is blacker than a coal. . . ."

Now, he explained, if the Chinese come from China, the Spanish from Spain, the French from France, and the Germans from Germany, where does the so-called black man of America whose ancestors were slaves come from? "Where is a land called Nigger land or Colored land or Negro land or Black land?" He'd chuckle. His listeners would laugh.

"How many of us speak Negroese or Blackese or Coloredese or Americanese? Or how about Coonese? How about Niggerese?"

He'd pause, then come alive. "Have you been wondering why white people spend billions of dollars . . . laying on the beaches, burning for hours, trying to turn black?"

And if the Christian God is so great, then why does he inflict black people with evil? He told them to turn to Acts 7:6 of their King James Bible. "Read!"

"And God spake on this wise, That his seed should sojourn in a strange land, and that they should bring them into bondage, and entreat them evil for 400 years."

Genesis 15:13: "And he said unto Abram, Know of a surety that thy seed shall be a stranger in a land that is not theirs, and shall serve them; and they shall afflict them for four hundred years."

The messenger interpreted: the afflicters are white people and false Christian prophets. The afflicted are so-called Negroes, brought to America on slave ships in the year 1555, serving in a strange land in bondage for more than four hundred years. "We have served our time, according to the Bible," he'd say.

This was the "world's best-kept secret." The afflicters, white people and false prophets, were deliberately covering up God's real name, Yahweh, to conceal that so-called black people are the chosen people of the Bible. By lying about the exalted status of the black race, the white race could dominate, oppress, control, and murder the black race.

"All white people who say they are Jews are liars and impostors," he concluded, "and Yahweh has made them the Synagogue of Satan (Revelation 3:9)." One day, he vowed, Yahweh will make white Jews "come and worship at our black feet."

His family gave his new religion mixed reviews. In their eyes, Junior had always been an enigma, not really crazy but special and gifted. "They always said genius was right next to it," said his brother Jefferson. He loved Junior, but Jefferson carried too much middle-class baggage simply to take off to Florida for good. "I wasn't much interested in living in a hole and not owning anything of my own," he explained. Sister Leona would never say a word in public about her brother, preferring to protect the family image. And Senior confided to friends his boy was a little lost.

Other Mitchells were more sympathetic. Brother Marvin felt like a Hebrew Israelite and believed everything Junior said. Sister Palmor Jean, child number six, listened hard. Like most of the Mitchells, Jean had good instincts, a warm personality, and a heavenly voice. From the time she was small, she had a complicated relationship with Junior, who was eight years older. Years later, she'd wonder in a conversation with a prosecutor if Junior's failed love affair with a white girl might have turned him against white people and women. Or maybe, as the family lore had it, his eccentric life path had something to do with the time he was changing a flat tire and a car fell on his head. He had never acted quite the same after that. Jean buried other, more disturbing memories of her brother. She loved him as much as any Mitchell and thought he was so brilliant that his words sometimes went right over her head.

Junior told Jean of his great expectations for her. A housewife, she had married a former cop in her father's church in Watonga, a small town where members of the Cheyenne and Arapaho nations still wore long, black braids interwoven with colorful ribbons. Now she was raising three kids, including a younger brother's daughter. Junior took a special interest in Jean's only son, Anthony. During the recruiting trip, Anthony was just finishing the fifth grade. When he brought home a report card of Cs and Ds, his Uncle Junior marched into the teacher's office and accused her of being prejudiced. Anthony had never really experienced discrimination before, but Junior raised his consciousness.

Never expressly pressuring her, Junior persuaded Jean to be his ambassadress in Enid. She agreed to distribute his literature and try to coax as many people as she could into believing his teachings. After her brother and Linda left town, Jean hosted history classes at her house in Enid's Heritage Hills section. A few friends read the Bible, talked about neighborhood issues, and tried to take control of their lives. They discussed articles tracing the black man's journey from Jerusalem to Africa to the West Indies to America—and "four hundred years of hell and white brainwashing."

"Be on the lookout for someone who will be different from your false preachers," the pamphlets said. "If you're tired of being ruled over, kicked about, if you're tired of being mistreated, misused, and abused, come to Yahweh and I'll show you how to rule the world forever!"

Twelve-year-old Patricia Lynette Albert, daughter of Jean's girlfriend Charlzetta, read the leaflets and attended classes at Jean's house. She loved both. They made her feel special, unique, maybe even a little better than anyone else. "We believed in a black heaven and earth," Pat reflected years later. She tried to persuade her stepfather, Jeffrey Glover, that the Book of Job says white people are lower than dogs. Jeffrey, a former air force policeman from Columbus, Texas, was skeptical. He had just recently married Charlzetta and was busy working in a propane refinery. He had better things to do with his time than to attend Jean's meetings. But finally, after a special appeal by Junior, he agreed to sit in.

Throughout 1979 Jean Solomon and her small corps of missionaries spread Yahweh's message. It caught on slowly in the pockets of poverty dotting Oklahoma's oil and wheat fields, and in small towns where black people were still openly called "the coloreds." When an Enid high school senior was found hanged one fall morning in 1979, it produced trigger-harsh memories of Oklahoma Klan lynchings—and a surge of interest in the fledgling Black Hebrew faith. The victim, Mitchell Lee Sanford, had been dating a white girl. He was found dangling from a tan cowboy belt nailed to a tree. The police ruled the death a suicide, though Mitchell Lee's denim pants didn't have loops for a belt. The Oklahoma Hebrews used the incident as evidence of a nationwide plot to kill the black race. "Wake Up Blacks, Whites Daily Plan Our Death," their leader, Moses Israel, wrote in a pamphlet.

A contingent of fifteen to twenty Oklahomans, eager to escape the oppression of small-town life, prepared to join Ock Moshe Israel in Florida. Jean Solomon longed to be near her brother and his teachings. Her husband, Leo, had always dreamed of living in a bigger city, and he wanted the chance to start a business. He thought south Florida offered greater financial promise than Enid. Anthony, almost twelve years old, was full of ambition, eager to check out his Uncle Junior's school of divine learning. Eighteen-year-old Vonzell, Jean's oldest daughter, persuaded her college fiancé, Lawrence Lee, that going to Florida would be an adventure. They could get married in paradise.

In 1980 the Oklahomans quit school and jobs, sold houses, and packed U-Hauls for Miami, just a rest stop en route to the Promised Land. It wouldn't turn out to be anything like what most of them expected. It would turn out to be so disappointing that a decade later Jean said: "Something that horrible that happened . . . I tried to put that in the sea of forgetfulness and at some point it comes back in pieces."

Like Enid, Miami would be a place of fallen idols and only temporary dreams.

Part III

Heaven on Earth

13

Linda Gaines printed the fliers about Ock Moshe Israel's new religion and distributed them by mail. He never signed his Christian name to his writings. Suspecting the post office was spying on him, he simply typed the name Moses Israel at the bottom of each document. But he also used the personal touch. He drove around Miami in Linda's Lincoln Continental, sometimes stopping to preach in front of movie theaters. At Lums restaurant, he shared his beliefs with anyone who attempted to make eye contact. His light eyes were penetrating, yet understanding. He was mild-mannered. His long, carefully manicured nails were coated with clear polish. He wore a suit, but no tie, and his hair was in a medium-length Afro. His full beard, specked with gray, gave him the look of a scholar. He introduced himself as a Bible teacher, spending hours with the curious, always encouraging conversation. "You got a lot of questions," he said with a warm smile. "I am just answering them with the Bible."

Some people saw him as a man with more-than-usual amounts of soul, heart, and caring about people. He made them feel as if they were making a connection. His message satisfied their yearning for information about the history of the black man and the failure of traditional religions to acknowledge that at least some biblical characters are black. Other people, though, thought he was a con man, just another self-proclaimed prophet out to rip off the poor. They took his literature because it was free, but then they set it on fire.

If a skeptic asked about his biological name, Brother Moses simply smiled and quoted John 16:13: "How be it when he, the Spirit of Truth, is come, he will guide you into all truth: for he shall not speak of himself; but whatsoever he shall hear, that shall he speak: and he will show you things to come."

Or he hinted he wasn't earthly at all: "My father's name is Yahweh!" he'd say.

"Where do you come from?"

"Heaven!"

"How old are you?"

"Four hundred twenty-five years old!" He pegged his age to the arrival of slaves in America.

"Where are you from?"

"Jerusalem."

His earliest disciples, mostly middle class, went house to house, holding prayer meetings. They hugged and greeted one another warmly with the Hebrew word for peace, *shalom*. They joined for a variety of reasons. Jessie Hill, Moses' sister-in-law, had followed him since his days in Atlanta. Herman Sands, a government social service administrator, was looking for financial success and a leadership role. Carter Cornelius, Moses' heavyset, thirty-something cousin, hoped for a music comeback. In the seventies, Carter's group, Cornelius Brothers and Sister Rose, had recorded two giant hits, "Treat Her Like a Lady" and "Too Late to Turn Back Now." More recently, he suffered from poor health and the excesses of success. Moses pulled him from his "dark world," and the singer denounced modern music, saying it "set black people back thousands of years."

All of them recruited friends and loved ones: Jessie brought along her young daughter, and Herman, his wife. Recruitment proceeded very slowly. Carlton Carey, the accountant, began studying with them, hoping to make a difference in Miami's black community. Eric Burke, the handyman, started searching for his roots.

Everyone—even kids—brought a King James Bible to the meetings. Sitting in a circle on the floor, they studied the Word and looked for clues of their Hebrew heritage. Moses expounded on the powers of their "Great, Good, and Terrible Black God." A God who controlled everything from natural disasters to economic recessions. A God who punished sin. A God who showed compassion for the chosen people. The God of Deuteronomy 10:17: "For the Lord your God (Yahweh) is God of gods and Lord of lords, a great God, a mighty, and a terrible . . ."

At the meetings, Ock Moshe encouraged them to jot down Scriptures. Study, he said. Do research. Read the white man's dictionary. Look behind the meaning of words and dig out the truth. He asked them to pledge ten percent of their wages to help the black community, but no one was forced to give any money. No one had to renounce the outside world. Linda collected the tithes and offerings and, taking up where Chloe left off, she organized a school and became the primary teacher. Located in a two-bedroom house in Miami's Haitian quarter, the school wasn't licensed, but in Florida no school had to be. Linda's kids and about two dozen others came in car pools, and at first they were lumped together in a single class. They memorized Bible verses and facts about the planet Earth, learned a little Hebrew and math, and did some cooking. Moses' sister Jean would teach them to sing.

Moses taught lofty subjects, too, but he never spoke in stuffy, pious phrases. He whipped out news clippings to make his point. In February 1979 the cops in Dade County pistol-whipped a black man in a wrong-house drug raid. Prosecutors didn't indict the officers. In September 1979 an off-duty cop fatally shot a black man who had stopped to urinate. The policeman got a merit pay increase with the notation that he needed to improve in the "area of tactfulness." Moses used current events to prove a conspiracy existed against the so-called Negroes of America.

Then came the Arthur McDuffie beating case. As civic cheerleaders prepared for the annual Orange Bowl parade, no fewer than six and possibly up to twelve police officers beat the insurance agent to death with heavy flashlights. The police had been chasing him for a traffic violation. They tried to cover up the killing by pretending he died in a motorcycle accident. Although Dade County's criminal justice system rarely took steps to stop police intimidation, the McDuffie case was so outrageous that most people figured brutal cops were finally going to get jail time. The legal issues weren't of great public interest, only the bottom line: Would the four white McDuffie officers get off? Not guilty = riot. Guilty = no riot.

Moses let his disciples in on secret government plans that would become operative after a riot. One was called King Alfred. Its purpose was to destroy the Negro threat. He said he had copies of classified documents proving the FBI's overt policy "to expose, disrupt, or otherwise neutralize" black leaders and organizations. The U.S. government, he warned, was on the lookout for a messiah who would be harassed to deprive the masses of effective organizers. During a riot, United States foot troops would storm the ghettos, make wholesale arrests, institute nationwide search and seizure, issue census cards to citizens, place Negroes in concentration camps, and appoint Uncle Toms to do the white man's bidding.

As the McDuffie officers inched toward trial in Tampa, another cataclysmic event heightened racial tensions. About 120,000 Cubans fled to Key West in a flotilla of small boats. The new immigrants got kid-glove treatment, sharpening the grievances of those already there. Miami was hot and angry, fine kindling for a riot.

Moses' message, wedding racial rhetoric with religion, was sealed with his gift of oratory. It caught on. With their numbers growing, the Hebrews moved classes to the Joseph Caleb Center in Liberty City. It housed a thousand-seat auditorium, a library, a black archives history room, food-stamp offices, and classrooms rented by assorted counterculture prophets, fundamentalist revivalists, and faith healers. There, the new prophet in town exposed the "World's Best-Kept Secret" every Wednesday night and Saturday morning.

When they weren't in class, his fresh-faced disciples, always smiling, recruited in steamy neighborhoods sick from drugs, joblessness, crime, broken homes, and domestic violence. They attracted down-and-out people, disenchanted radicals, and middle-class college kids who just wanted to be accepted for who they were. Lloyd Clark, an outgoing dancer who loved to dazzle an audience, was rolling up good grades in college when he picked up Moses' literature at the house of his frat brother Tatahead. One quarter Cherokee, Lloyd came from an air force family where race talk wasn't permitted. In college, he'd gotten a dose of racial consciousness by meeting black Muslims and joining a black fraternity. He attended his first Hebrew meeting in April 1980 and enjoyed the feeling of black unity. Lloyd started to pass the Word. "Hey, brother, check it out! It's about Yahweh, the black God!" Lloyd shouted, as he knocked on doors in Overtown, the old "Harlem of the South" in the shadows of Miami's skyscrapers. Lloyd tried to hide his fear as he handed Moses' leaflets to dopers pressing needles into their arms and drunk men cursing pregnant women in the doorways of leaky tenements.

"We don't want your God!" a woman yelled, throwing a beer bottle at him. "Get lost!"

As the all-white jury listened to testimony in the McDuffie case, about fifty regulars filed into Moses' classroom carrying their Bibles. It was May 1980. A few women were dressed in colorful, ankle-length skirts. Men wore loose-fitting dashikis, coming just below the waist, and skull caps slightly larger than a traditional Jewish yarmulke. Most people had on regular street clothes. Lloyd Clark was wearing his blue and gold frat jacket. Carlton Carey had a tape recorder in his hand and a Star of David around his neck. They called the star a hexagram. Moses taught that it was a sign of resurrection from their mental graves of ignorance. Its two entwined triangles contained spiritual secrets and represented the "highest knowledge of the universe."

The minute the hand struck eight o'clock, a voice came over the loudspeaker.

"Shalom!"

"Shalom!" the people in the audience responded.

Moses stood at the podium. The people recited a prayer from the Book of Jeremiah. "Oh, Yahweh, God of our salvation, save us and deliver us from evil, that we may give thanks to thy holy name, and glory in thy praise. Oh, Yahweh, let them be confounded that persecute us, but let not us be confounded. Let them be dismayed, but let not us be dismayed. Bring upon our enemies the day of evil and destroy them with double destruction."

"Praise Yahweh!" Moses Israel declared.

"Praise Yahweh!" the people replied in unison.

Two sentries, looking more like scholars than bodyguards, took positions near the podium. "How do we love our brothers and sisters?" Moses Israel asked.

"With all our minds, with all our hearts, with all our souls, with all our might," the audience answered in perfect unity.

"What is our motto?"

"Our motto is one God, one mind, one love, and one action!"

"We're all for one!"

"And one for all!"

"What color is Israel?"

"Black unto the ground!"

"What's the name of the fourth tribe?"

"Judah!"

"What did Yahweh choose Judah to do?"

"To be a ruler!"

"The color of all his prophets?"

"Black!"

"Who is Judah?"

"We are!"

"What did Yahweh choose you to do?"

"To be a ruler!"

"How long?"

"Forever!"

"How long is forever?"

"Eternity!"

"Yahweh chose who?"

"He chose me!"

"Who is Judah?"

"We are!"

"How long?"

"Forever!"

"How long is forever?"

"Eternity!"

"Praise Yahweh!" Moses boomed.

"Praise Yahweh!" the people said.

Moses asked his listeners to turn to Zechariah 11:5 in their Bibles.

"Read!" he said, and they read.

"Whose possessors slay them and hold themselves not guilty . . ."

The McDuffie cops, Moses prophesied, would go free. Miami's "criminal injustice system" had one law for blacks, one for whites. White people who killed blacks always held themselves not guilty. So-called Negroes would seek justice by rioting, by tearing down their neighborhoods. But rioting, Moses said, wasn't the answer.

The Great, Good, and Terrible Black God Yahweh gave the so-called black man of America his law of justice. Moses said the only way they could get righteous judgment, the only way black people could get real power, was to come to Yahweh.

The prophet preached until his voice dropped. He knew how to ride an audience like a wave. Their hearts pumped with desire, and his voice rose and fell, depending on the response he got. His appeal lay not only in the energy of his words but in the ringing tones of his voice and in the beaming expressions on his face.

After his lectures, Lloyd Clark and his frat brothers always left feeling ten feet tall, invincible against the white man. On Saturday, May 17, 1980, at 2:45 P.M., they were washing cars on the corner of a busy, six-lane thoroughfare in Opa-locka, north of Miami. Opa-locka's downtown looked like something out of the *Arabian Nights*—ironic commentary since the place had little luck and little money. Ice Man, the afternoon deejay on WEDR (FM 99.1) radio, came over the airwaves. The Ice Man sounded like he was weeping. The all-white jury in Tampa had acquitted the McDuffie cops. Not guilty of anything. Set free. All their misgivings, all their doubts about the system, all turned out to be true. The Ice Man told his listeners to keep things cool, but Lloyd turned to his friends. "Here it goes," he said. "Ock Moshe was right to the letter. Town's gonna burn."

Within minutes, the Ice Man's radio show was flooded with angry callers. At 5 P.M., the first rocks and bottles were lofted in Liberty City. At 6:20 P.M., a mob attacked its first victim, a white vagrant, name unknown. By 8 P.M., fires raged out of control, darting through store roofs in front of the eyes of the Hebrew Israelite neophytes. Black youths surged from behind parked cars and charged white motorists with rocks, beer cans, bottles, and rotten eggs, anything they got their hands on. As darkness descended, flames silhouetted the scurrying shapes of looters ferrying liquor, meat, window fans, and cosmetics 'from stores. Cops with rifles rolled into the lawless, fiery streets, but it was too little force, too late. Miami was out of control.

The next day, Lloyd hopped into his beat-up Chevette to check on his fiancée, Karen. She lived in Opa-locka. Overnight, Opa-locka and other black districts had turned into a carnival of burning and looting. Lloyd parked the car outside a smoldering grocery store, took a whiff of tear gas, and for reasons he never fully understood, joined the ranks of brazen looters. He sorted through the remains, out of sight of helmeted police. He gave the stolen food to Karen's mom. He knew Moses Israel wouldn't approve, but Lloyd, like many others caught in the riot, told himself, "It's black justice! It's God's justice."

Exodus 21: "And if any mischief follow, then thou shalt give life for life, eye for eye, tooth for tooth, hand for hand, burning for burning, wound for wound, stripe for stripe."

Violence—cruelly sweeping up blacks, whites, and Hispanics alike—pulsed through Miami for three days. Eighteen people died, 417 were injured, 1,110 were arrested, and 71 businesses were destroyed. The bare statistics didn't tell the story. The McDuffie riot would cast a spell over Miami for decades. Civic leaders promised jobs. But a chance to scrub floors or flip hamburgers for $3.35 an hour was not what blacks in Miami needed or wanted.

With the smell of acrid smoke still in the air, newcomers streamed to Brother Moses Israel's sermons. They wanted a chance to spew out their opinions, to testify about everything they felt and the brutality they had seen with their own eyes. Moses listened, and his eyes filled with tears. He said later he could sense the buildup of hate in their minds. He forbade guns at his classes, but a few men packed them secretly, the way some kids hide squirt guns.

The riot, Moses preached, was a sign that the world was building to the last days of unrighteous rulership. He told them to think beyond their cares, to press on unafraid and, through willful prayer, to bring down the persecutors. "Oh," he'd bellow, "there's an End Day comin'! There's a Judgment Day comin'! There's a great gettin'-up morning comin'!"

His voice quivered as he promised to love them, feed them, clothe them, protect them, deliver them from their enemies, and restore them to the Promised Land.

The Righteous People, he said, wouldn't have to endure this country for long. They'd sell their clothing and gather for the trip from the hells of North America to New Jerusalem. They would go by ship or maybe by eagles' wings. "We're gonna need our running shoes!" he declared. After leaving Miami, they'd wait out cosmic nuclear battles in a safe place. Then, when God defeated the persecuting powers, the Hebrew saints would march into their homeland, bury the dead, and set up the kingdom of Yahweh. They alone would rule the world. "Get ready to be on the run!"

14

As they waited for the climactic battle with the evil forces, Ock Moshe insisted they stand as a "solid wall"—pooling their energy and their resources, their time and their minds. Interpreting verses from the Book of Acts, he proclaimed: "We move like one! We look like one. We dress like one! We act like one! We talk like one! We eat like one! We love like one! We are one! We get rich as one! We rise up as one! We are high above all nations as one! We rule the world as one!"

Disunity, he cautioned prophetically, would destroy their cause. So long as they faithfully observed Yahweh's laws, statutes, judgments, and commandments, they would learn to love themselves. They would forever remain safe and distinct from their common "modern Pharaoh," the white nations trying to crush them. "God is concerned about us, the so-called Negroes *only*," he wrote.

Step by step, they discovered their new culture. Pooling cash and salable possessions, they rented houses together and learned to separate themselves from the "evil ways" of white people. Men stopped shaving. Women stopped straightening their hair. They spent most of their waking hours discussing Scripture and trying to master Yahweh's statutes without competition or jealousy. As he weaned them from their pasts, they began to call him "Abba," Hebrew for father. Gradually, their allegiances changed, along with their lifestyles. Ock Moshe taught that the Righteous People wore holy robes down to their feet, the same as God. He called the robes their culture. He openly rejected luxuries: tobacco, alcohol, drugs, gambling, movies, and "devil vision." Yahweh, he said, didn't bless people who lived above their means or worshiped worldly trappings. Blessings for keeping God's covenant, and curses for violating it, were detailed in Leviticus 26 and Deuteronomy 28. Yahweh threatened to bring drought, famine, disease, poverty, and total ruin on people who disobeyed the rules.

The diet was modified kosher. Moses wrote a divine dietary law book with recipes for Hebrew dishes such as heavenly grainburgers and blessed bean soup. He considered pork, oysters, and shrimp "filthy and abominable." He forbade foods with additives and preservatives. Eating cookies was bad; eating pork was worse. He likened it to sucking on a woman's menstrual pad. "Have you any idea what unclean is?" he once asked. He paused for a second, as though inviting comment. "Unclean is like sitting down every month and taking all of the women's issue and lick and suck her pads. That is unclean. Do I have any disagree-ers? How many agree with me? . . . If you saw someone sucking a woman's issue pad, would you call them a fool? Would you call him stupid? . . . And you want people to respect you, look up to you, honor you, with an issue pad in your mouth?"

Moses' loose and trashy talk made his followers roar with laughter. His earthy commentaries jumped from family economics to warnings of nuclear-war attacks to the black man's law in one spellbinding brew. "If white people pluck out our eyes, we should try and pluck out theirs," he once wrote, trying to shock them into reality. "It is better for us to just go and commit suicide than to allow the enemy to come in our homes and drag us down, drag our mothers and daughters out, beat, lynch, and rape them while we stand by looking."

No topics grabbed him like power and death and sex. His mandate on sex: There would be none except for procreation. There would be no sex with non-Hebrews. Children, at puberty, should have babies. "The younger will make your blood boil, brother!" he advised.

"Get it, brothers! . . . Sisters, give it up!"

"Some brothers waitin' around on the perfect love to come," he said in another class. "You shouldn't do that, brothers, you should be tryin' to get it. . . . If the sister can have a baby, you should be tryin' to help her get what Yahweh wants her to have. We have all these brothers tryin' to be a bachelor instead of tryin' to get it. . . . It's not about fallin' in love, it's about multiplyin'."

His four biological children would have twenty-six babies. He

99

wanted his nonbiological family to multiply like his flesh and blood, into a tribe, into many tribes, into what he called his "human family."

Birth control, abortion, vasectomies, hysterectomies, and tubal ligations were strictly taboo. Moses condemned them as genocidal tricks of the white man. "If you got your tubes tied, go untie them," he said. "If you got them cut, go get them sewed back together, and have all the black babies you can have. Have them as fast as Yahweh lets you have them. . . . Have babies and let's subdue and control the earth."

To increase the tribe, Moses took on the role of impulsive match-maker. He blessed couples and performed marriages, sometimes in mass ceremonies. When a man and a woman had sex, they were considered married by Yahweh law, not by Florida law. People who didn't feel a romantic commitment were urged to do it for God. Moses also became the tribe doctor, sometimes wearing a lab coat, handing out health opinions, and prescribing back-to-Eden herb treatments with authority.

Besides the twice-weekly Bible classes, he presided at special lectures. On Fridays, he conducted midwife classes, attended by a dozen specially selected prepubescent girls and women. Like the other students, Karen Clark, Lloyd's pregnant wife, stayed tight-lipped about what she was learning. Ostensibly, the midwives read how-to books on baby delivery. They learned first aid and relaxation techniques and did gynecological examinations on preg-nant members.

The midwife classes weren't the only secret study groups. Moses also introduced sisters' and brothers' classes on Tuesday nights. The sisters weren't supposed to tell the brothers what they learned, and the brothers weren't supposed to tell the sisters. But the topics, at least as far as the men were concerned, didn't stay quiet for long.

The main male laws focused on cleanliness and circumcision, a ceremony commemorating God's bond with the people of Israel. Moses taught them not to be "box boys" or "CHUMPs." "Box" was his word for a vagina and "CHUMP" was the acronym for men "completely hung up on mama's pussies." If they were to be righteous world leaders, he explained, they had to stop "running behind women's skirts." Lloyd Clark never forgot one of Moses' more racy talks to the men: "I know a man that if his pussy went to China, he'd take a slow boat to get there. You gotta stop fuckin' the pussy so much. Say no sometimes! Some of you are just old 'come freaks,' gotta come. . . . How many of you have masturbated? . . . Well, stop it because Yahweh once killed a man for spilling his seed on the ground. . . . There are some of you that like men, too. At least one of you in here that I know. Yeah, I'm talkin' to you. Yahweh hates faggots!'"

Among the Hebrews, man was expected to be boss. Woman's role was more complex. "What is the duty of a Hebrew woman?" he'd ask.

"To follow in righteousness!" they'd reply.

On one level, Hebrew women kept their place, but on another, Ock Moshe promised to make them strong and powerful, equal to the brothers in every way. Whenever a new woman or girl came to class, he left the impression that he was solely responsible for spiritual instruction. Female novices, he explained, were weak-minded, giddy, foolish, lustful, greedy, and promiscuous. "Tree sisters," he called them. "Tree" was his word for a penis. Like the biblical Eve, a new woman member was a "mother of bestiality" who had eaten from the forbidden tree and taken on the mindset of Lucifer. His mission was to reshape them into morally perfect, female Adams.

A popular theme in his lectures was "The White Woman as She-Devil." Once Lloyd attended an X-rated movie of a white woman having sex with animals. Unlike white women, black women had "that big wide nose. . . . those big old thick, juicy lips . . . big behind . . . big black cheeks," and Moses loved them with a vengeance. "My Adam female, she is grateful to Yahweh and she accepts the power of Yahweh," he said.

Women went wild when he preached, finding him sexy, brilliant, and funny. During class, they'd smack their lips and stare at him with open mouths and eyes popping with adoration and ecstasy. He had a baby-me quality to him, and he encouraged his flock to baby him. At the same time, he thought of them as his children. Moses molded them accordingly.

In classes on the "law concerning parents and children," he discouraged parents from sending kids to public school. There, he said, they were daily in the company of selfish, disrespectful, immoral, evil, wicked, drug-using liars, thieves, homosexuals, and haters of God's law. "If you want your children to be righteous," he asked his followers one day, "must you integrate them or separate them?"

"Separate them!"

"Let white people teach them or teach them yourselves?"

"Teach them yourselves!"

Moses' divine university struck a chord in Miami, where the inner-city public schools were in turmoil. Yahweh University, as it became known, would grow rapidly. As Hebrew doctrine became codified, parents would impart it to the children through a system that Ock Moshe called "reciting knowledge." For example, the children would recite, rapid-fire, all the chemical elements and their symbols in numerical progression. Teenagers called it "Scripture rapping." Flubbed lines, embarrassed giggles, or hints of negativity weren't allowed.

"Yahweh is teaching us to take little apple seeds and turn them into big trees!" the children chanted, punctuating their lines with swings of fists. "Yahweh is causing us to be!"

In time, people who didn't approve of rote education or who were unwilling to accept the laws Moses set down dropped out. He called non-Hebrews "dead Jacobs" and "dead Eves."

"The people you thought were your friends turn their back on you," he explained. "They start calling you crazy. They'll say, 'You are part of a cult, you are part of somebody brainwashing you.' "

As old-timers left, new people came, and by October 1980 his following was about 150 strong. He led them into more change, or really a series of changes. First, he renamed them, wiping away their slave names. "We are white people's property as long as we keep

102

their names," Ock Moshe declared. "Don't ever forget that." He handed out a sheet of biblical first names from which to choose. Their common last name would be Israel. Moses' companion, Linda Gaines, took the name Judith Yakira Israel. Judith was the feminine form of Judah, meaning praised one. Children tore through the Bible, looking for uplifting ancient characters to emulate. Judith's son Freddie was excited about living up to his biblical namesake. He picked Solomon Israel.

Hebrew newborns would never know a slave name. Before dawn on Friday, November 28, 1980, the first baby in Yahweh's human family was about to be born. Marlcah Hadassah Israel, the former Karen Clark, went into labor at home. Her husband, Yehudah, the former Lloyd, summoned a midwife, who summoned the other midwives and Brother Moses. As Marlcah Hadassah sat on a birthing stool, Moses encouraged her, calmly reporting progress to the dozen people gathered for the event. He pulled the heavenly girl from the uterus and cut the umbilical cord with finesse. He didn't spank her; that practice, he explained, was cruel and inhumane. "Yehudah, you're a father!" Moses announced, as Dad stood off in a corner, terrified. "The devil is never going to see this baby! The devil is never going to know about this baby!" They called the little girl Keturah. Moses was determined to protect her from the white medical establishment, which, he said, murdered black babies. Keturah would never receive the standard childhood inoculations against polio, measles, or tetanus. She never got a birth certificate. As far as the state of Florida was concerned, she didn't exist.

Ock Moshe would keep his own records. He listed his lost sheep, by Hebrew and slave names, in the *Lamb's Book of Life*, a black three-ring binder. When Judgment Day came, they all had to be accounted for.

15

Moses beamed with pride as he broke the news of their first "kosher baby." A few weeks later, he had even better news: his followers had collected enough tithes to buy a new home: a gutted, fifteen-thousand-square-foot warehouse at 2766 Northwest Sixty-second Street, Liberty City, in the heart of the riot zone. The building, spanning a city block, would serve as their temporary headquarters, a "nation within a nation," until they left for New Jerusalem.

It had holes in the roof and loose wires hanging from the ceiling. Moses encouraged them to pitch in to fix it up. What's more, he'd selflessly give them everything—good health, food, an education, a job, whatever they needed, if they moved in and worked for Yahweh full time. Most Hebrews resisted. "Going full time," as they called it, was a bridge-burning decision they weren't ready to make. But Moses, a master at getting people to do what they didn't want to do, spoke of the Book of Matthew and its instruction to love Yahweh more than their biological families: "He that loveth father or mother more than me is not worthy of me."

"Who you gonna serve?" he asked. "Yahweh? Or your mother, or father, sister, brother, husband, wife, or children? What's it gonna be?"

"Yahweh!" everyone screamed.

"Praise Yahweh!" he'd prompt, and the audience would repeat "Yahweh! Yahweh! Yahweh!" until the words ran together in a hypnotic chant.

About thirty followers responded to the call. They chucked cars and homes, dropped out of jobs and college, and cast off material lives for their struggling new religion in the ghetto.

Assisted by some part-timers, they chipped in for supplies and began the remodeling job on Christmas Day 1980. They plastered walls, installed wiring, repaired the roof, and fixed the plumbing.

They painted the building white, the color of sainthood. They scrawled a big hexagram on it. They called it the Yahweh temple or the Temple of Love.

Inside, they hung pictures of an all-black Last Supper, a black Noah, a black Madonna, and paintings of futuristic cities populated by black people and of flying saucers representing salvation. Under one portrait was a caption: "The black Christ is risen among us today to deliver us from white people." Small signs exhorted "Life is better with Yahweh" and "Come on up to Yahweh."

The Hebrews set up a large worship auditorium with folding chairs, television monitors, and loudspeakers. They had a cafeteria, a laundry room, an infirmary, an ice-cream parlor, a grocery store, an art room, a sewing room, and a print shop. In the print shop, equipped with presses, collators, and binders, Sister Judith's three children went to work on Moses' literature. They churned out the *Original Bible*, a standard King James edition with pictures of black deities—"the way it was before the white man changed it." They helped manufacture the little yellow book *You Are Not a Nigger!*

Because the building was zoned commercial, nobody was supposed to live there. To keep fire marshals and zoning inspectors at bay, Moses' disciples hung OFFICE signs on the doors of sleeping quarters. Each family got a cubicle, about ten-feet-by-fifteen-feet, with a small closet and a dresser. Some people brought beds and other home furnishings. Job Israel, a master barber, tossed a prayer rug on the floor. He once went by the name Richard Ingraham and did soft fingerwaves for stars like Nat King Cole and Duke Ellington. Now he combed Moses' hair.

Yehudah's room was bare. With his wife and baby, he slept on a blanket. He kept a few mementos from his frat days and pictures of his high school prom night. Nobody needed worldly possessions anymore. They had Yahweh.

Sheetrock partitions, about eight feet high, separated one room from the next. There were no ceilings, just the roof of the warehouse itself. It didn't take them long to discover they could hear everything. And by climbing to the top of the Sheetrock—to the space between it and the roof—they could see exactly what was going on below.

The temple quickly became a kind of all-purpose, land-based cruise ship: a clubhouse, an amusement park, a theater, a place to romance and learn. The full-time disciples formed a band, a dance troupe, and a singing ensemble. They hosted fashion shows, raffle contests, and karate classes for kids. They kept up a front of serenity, but the temple life was rimmed and edged in tension.

Moses' disciples adhered to a rigid schedule, waking up to a loud knock on their cubicles at 5 A.M. From sunup to sundown, they touched and prayed. They cleaned bathrooms, cooked, proofed literature, and did whatever was required of them. Thirteen-year-old Sister Sherah, the former Patricia Albert of Enid, believed if she didn't work for Yahweh full time, she would be kicked out of heaven, or worse, go straight to hell. After only a few months in Miami, Ock Moshe already had made an imprint on her young mind. "He became a father figure," she wrote in a diary.

Much of the temple's family dynamic revolved around meals. They placed orders for beef, fish, and vegetables at a local market, and at mealtime they'd sit together. Someone would gulp down spectacular ice cream prepared by Deborah Vashti, the former Jean Solomon, Moses' sister. Someone else would plead for seconds of her corn bread. Parents scolded children caught munching on peanut butter. The kids learned to stash their nonkosher delights in secret temple cubbyholes. As a family, everybody tended to do the same things, in the same way, every day, and in just a short time, Moses' disciples were bickering over everything from food to washing machines to domestic chores to responsibilities to God. Brother Job, a onetime army sharpshooter, barked like a drill sergeant whenever somebody showed signs of selfishness. "Brother," Job said to people who uttered profanity, "let your conversation be holy!"

To keep the household in line and to protect them from untoward outside influences, Moses' muscular followers set up a security force. Known as the Circle of Ten, it was based on a verse from the Book of Exodus: "And Moses chose able men out of all Israel, and made them heads over the people, rulers of thousands, rulers of hundreds, rulers of fifties, and rulers of tens." Members of the circle paced the temple property with knobby, wooden shepherd's sticks, about five feet long, the width of a baseball bat. They called them "staffs of life." The white man, Moses said, thought of the staff as a phallic symbol. "And in the hands of a black man that's a terrible weapon to him. So therefore it shows you in authority."

Eventually, the Hebrew men became vigilantes in a neighborhood the police didn't want to mess with. They warned away dope peddlers, scared off purse snatchers, and ran down smash-and-grab robbers from a food-stamp office across the street. The word went out: Don't rob people while you're around the Yahweh temple.

Even more than providing for his followers' security, the Circle of Ten protected Brother Moses. Sensing that old enemies were out to hurt him, he asked the circle to guard him. They followed him everywhere and attended to his personal needs, setting up his speaking podium and carrying his Bible. As time passed and they showed their willingness to be corralled, they took on added responsibilities, such as pouring him water from a silver pitcher or polishing his Bally loafers. Zedekiah, the former Hulon Mitchell III, served as a bodyguard for his father. Other members of Moses' blood family got important assignments too. He taught his twelve-year-old nephew, Joshua Israel, the former Anthony Solomon, to do circumcisions. Joshua felt important, like a real doctor. But few people knew about Ock Moshe's biological relatives. He deliberately kept them—his children, his sister, his nieces, nephews, and cousins—at a distance.

His life, unlike his followers', was not open to anyone who wanted to peek inside. But it didn't stop them from snooping. When Abba wasn't looking, they sneaked into his off-limits temple suite next door to Sister Judith's room. Their quarters were separated by a bathroom. His room had a ceiling and was modestly furnished: a large bed, a table, a couple of chairs, and a refrigerator. He kept a small library of Bibles, concordances, interpreter's dictionaries, and a Holy Qur'an.

As they grew more curious, Ock Moshe told them a little more. He said he woke up at 5 A.M. to meditate and prepare his lessons.

They observed his huge bursts of energy—and how he could drop into a terrible angry state when something didn't go his way. Sometimes, he wrote so much he complained of a writing bump on his hand. He loved to read and sing, and he had music in his head. But he silently suffered from earthly tendencies: an occasional severe headache, a dust allergy, and some sort of sleep disorder.

Moses said he was working day and night to wake them up to Yahweh. At night he moved around the temple to check on his flock, occasionally tiptoeing from a sister's room at 2 in the morning. He said he was teaching the Bible, but a few people began to wonder how he could teach with the lights off. In the morning, he would resurface, sometimes with bloodshot eyes, bragging that if he could function on just a little sleep, so could his disciples.

One day a rumor swept through the temple after Sister Judith emerged with what looked like a passion mark on her honey-colored skin. People whispered that she must be Moses' wife. The couple insisted their relationship was strictly spiritual, one of mutual admiration. Yahweh required him to keep sex out of the picture, and he denied she even used his bathroom. She said she was like a nun, sworn to abstinence.

Either way, it was clear Moses trusted Judith completely. The Hebrews thought she would do anything for him. As temple treasurer and Moses' "executive secretary," she signed the checks, deposited money in the bank, and kept a cash box in her desk drawer. She purchased supplies: everything from deodorant for the disciples to ink for the print shop. She handed out daily job assignments, so his followers, hoping for a position near Moses, worked to stay on Sister Judith's good side. Whatever she said went. She didn't have to go to classes if she didn't want to. If Brother Zerubbabel, the former Ricky Woodside, got tired of working fourteen-hour days, Sister Judith would tell him, "Too bad! Better get in there and go to work for Yahweh!" But if Judith was tired, she didn't have to work. She slept. She tooled around in her Lincoln and shopped at fancy department stores.

Jealousies flared because some followers thought Judith's children got special privileges, like their mother. After her kids finished assembling Moses' literature, he rewarded them with a weekend trip to a nice hotel. Other disciples distributed his fliers throughout Dade County, by car and on foot, knocking on door after door. If a white person came to the door, they'd say, "Sorry, wrong door." But if it was the right door, they offered the yellow book for a suggested five-dollar contribution. The Bible went for an "introductory offer" of twenty-five dollars.

The door-to-door missionaries captured the attention, and the dollars, of Liberty City. By early spring of 1981, hundreds of people were hearkening to Moses' prophetic warnings. On Saturday mornings, for Shabbat or Sabbath class, as many as five hundred visitors would line up, waiting for a glimpse of Liberty City's radical prophet. As they filed inside, Hebrew guards with hand-held electronic devices scanned them for weapons. Women's purses were thoroughly searched.

Moses waited in the wings until the crowd was properly worked into a frenzy. Electric guitars struck up. Drums crashed. People shouted, whistled, clapped. And then, flanked by his circle, he swept into the room. He walked to the podium, grabbed the mike, and launched into his sputtering doomsday messages. "I'm not leavin' America until you turn Fort Knox over to me!" he'd rail. His voice exploded in the auditorium like a hand grenade.

"Praise Yahweh!" the people would holler, vying to scream louder than whoever was sitting next to them. Moses said the Word burned like a fire in his bones, and he liked to preach for hours and hours, until his voice gave out or until he was simply too sapped of energy to stand anymore. "I'm come to set a man at odds against his father," he'd say. "And I'm come to put the daughter against her mother!"

He began to talk about how the Federal Reserve had defaulted, and since the dollar was worthless, he wanted them to invest in Yahweh's silver company. Precious metals, he explained, were the only hedge against disaster. "You had better hurry up and buy."

Nobody ever saw the silver, but people rushed to Sister Judith's office to buy thousands of dollars' worth of Yahweh's "silver certificates." The certificates, they were told, could be redeemed for the actual silver sometime after Judgment Day.

Gradually, people attending the meetings encountered new demands. Temple dwellers put pressure on the part-timers to give more money, time, and possessions to Yahweh.

In case some people weren't sufficiently motivated to contribute, Moses cautioned that God would put them under a "double curse." He praised big contributors, who, in turn, made life uncomfortable for those who didn't give so much.

To handle donations, Sister Judith helped set up a nonprofit company called Temple of Love Inc. Moses' name was nowhere on the incorporation papers, but he became the chief fund-raiser. "How many would give up their house for Yahweh?" he'd ask. Most people in the audience would raise their hands. Enforcers would scan the room for doubters. "If you're not bringing it to me," Moses would say "you're taking it to white folks."

Instead of just tithing ten percent, people began forking over cars and property. They donated checks, record collections, home appliances, and in one instance, a cherished fluegelhorn. "You gave up all liberties," said Amariah Israel, the former Lawrence Lee. "Everything you had went to the temple."

To avoid any appearance of coercion, Ock Moshe was quick to point out that the donations were strictly voluntary—freedom of choice. Then he set before them the choice: life and prosperity versus death and disaster. There was no barbed wire around the temple that stopped them from leaving. But on the other hand, he saw retribution at work for every person who refused to accept Yahweh.

For those who went on with Yahweh, life grew more bizarre. To make sure the men were circumcised and clean, Moses asked them to pull down their pants for a "D.I.," or dick inspection. He presided over a mass circumcision for uninitiated grown men, who paid one hundred dollars apiece for the honor. After promising the procedure would be quick and painless, he picked up his clamps and removed penis foreskins on men in the auditorium. Some fainted and shrieked with pain. The midwives stood by with disinfectants.

Men fussed about the circumcision practices. Women began confiding to spouses and friends about goings-on in female-only classes. Moses, they whispered, went to extremes to ensure they were chaste and clean. He even made them disrobe so they could examine one another. Sister Sherah said he personally taught her to douche and clean her behind properly. One day, Brother Joshua, the temple's young doctor-in-training, peeked into a midwife class. "They were conducted in a lot of funny ways," Joshua told the authorities, "sometimes in the nude, sometimes you know in—they had like orgy-type setups." Evidently Moses had one woman lie on her back, nude, as another woman blew into her vagina. This, he explained, was the technique for CPR on an unborn baby.

Since very few births were being announced to the congregation, a few skeptics questioned whether there was some ulterior purpose behind the midwife sessions. Yehudah Israel, one of Moses' most loyal followers, stood outside the classroom and heard his wife laughing and screeching. Marlcah had begun to pay more attention to Ock Moshe than to her husband. "I love that man," she would tell him. "I just love him."

Yehudah, meantime, had begun pumping iron to cut down on sexual urges, hoping to remain celibate, as required. He tried to convince himself that Marlcah meant she admired Moses spiritually. Then, one Friday night after a midwife class, he lit into her. He had been studying in the cafeteria, minding his business, when Marlcah playfully quipped to a midwife-girlfriend that she liked men with cucumber-sized penises. Yehudah leaped up, his face burning. What does that mean? he challenged. He didn't have a cucumber-sized penis. He called her names, and Marlcah stormed off in tears.

Later that night, the full-time disciples were summoned to an emergency meeting in the cafeteria. Yehudah knew instinctively that somebody was in trouble for something. Whenever they called an emergency meeting, it was never good news. For fifteen minutes or so, Moses stood before about forty followers, mostly women, and talked about Yahweh's blessings. Then his tone shifted. "What do you think about a brother who worries about another man's penis?"

Everybody giggled. Everybody except Yehudah. He knew right away his wife had tattled on him. Evidently she had twisted the story to make him look bad. Moses went on with the verbal lashing.

"You ought to get your mind on Yahweh and off the sisters," Yehudah quoted Moses. "You're wicked for thinking these kinds of things." Moses scolded him for other violations of temple law: sleeping on guard duty, leaving his clothes in the dryer. "Yehudah, stand up!"

"Weren't you the one who gave me that paddle?" Moses was talking about a two-foot fraternity hazing paddle that Yehudah had sanded, painted white, and inscribed with the word Yahweh. He had given it to Ock Moshe as a present.

"Sister Judith," he said, "go get that paddle out of your office."

"I should let the brothers beat you, but you could take that because you were in a fraternity. So instead I'm going to let the sisters beat your behind."

Moses made Yehudah lean over a chair. The women formed a line. "You, too, sisters," Ock Moshe enjoined, pointing to two little girls.

He handed the paddle to Yehudah's wife, who swatted her husband twice. Then the women and girls took turns giving Yehudah two licks apiece. Moses watched from a chair.

Yehudah fell on the floor and cried, out of embarrassment more than pain. After everybody left and went to bed, he thought about the "ass-whippins" his staff sergeant father used to give him. He thought back to his college hazing and a ceremony called "crossing the burning sands," when the frats blindfolded him, then whomped him with paddle boards and wet towels. This was worse. To be whipped by women, he said later, was the most humiliating thing he could imagine. Yehudah wept for half an hour. Marlcah finally picked him up and took him to bed. She said she was sorry, but Yehudah knew the intimacy they had felt as high school sweethearts was gone.

Without trust or sex, some of Moses' followers struggled to save their marriages. Life became a battle of wits between men and women. Everything the men did was about pleasing Yahweh. Everything the women did was about pleasing Yahweh. And Moses called on both genders to show more loyalty.

"Think not that I come to bring peace, I come with a sword," Moses once warned them, quoting Scripture.

"Oh, bring that sword!" someone in the audience replied.

"You need a sword!" the prophet said.

"Yes, Yahweh!"

"You better go buy one and sharpen it up!"

"That's right!"

"You see you need a sword," he insisted. "You don't need a .357 Magnum. He say a sword."

"He sure did!"

"Do what he says!"

"Yes, sir!"

Moses said later his sword was the Bible, but a few literal-minded men didn't get it. They went out and bought machetes. Residents of Liberty City then began to notice the temple dwellers with long and shiny objects on their hips. They weren't Bibles. Worried relatives began dropping by the compound to check on loved ones they hadn't seen in months. At first, Moses' enforcers simply flashed angry looks at the outsiders, but then the hateful stares turned to brute force. When a University of Miami student came to inquire about his girlfriend one day, Yehudah Israel and the other guards took him to a back room, stripped him, and beat him with sticks.

16

Before long, the media shone a spotlight on the Temple of Love. Robert Hall, a popular broadcaster at WMBM-AM radio, peppered his afternoon shows with talk of the Hebrew Israelites. The thirty-one-year-old Hall, a trusted source of black news, had attracted a big audience by following up on rumors of police misconduct. The rumors about the Hebrews were different. Hall didn't know what to make of them. His listeners spoke about the group with a mixture of fear and admiration. He decided to go to the temple and see for himself.

After a few classes, Hall became disillusioned. He announced on the air that he considered himself a Hebrew Israelite, but he had serious doubts about Moses' teachings. "What they were doing in that temple," the radio man said, "was not the teaching of the real Hebrew Israelites."

His commentaries stirred up Liberty City and drew people from the temple. Under pressure from the community, the Metro-Dade Police Department, the county's largest police force, briefly sent in undercover agents. But the cops were skittish about going after the Hebrews for a lot of reasons. One: religion. From Catholics to voodoo priests, from Jews to *santeros*, religions old and new came armed with money, the First Amendment, and the ACLU. The Hebrew Israelites were no exception. Reason number two: race. Because the Hebrews were black, the police were afraid to act tough, lest they appear or be branded racist. Miami, so often stung by banner headlines and front-page photos that showed the city in flames, wanted its national image to stress RayBans, not racism. Reason number three: fear. One undercover officer backed off because he suspected Moses had picked him out as an "Uncle Tom" infiltrator.

Despite the police's unwillingness to act, the commotion inside the temple didn't go away. Ock Moshe announced to the congregation one day that Robert Hall had cursed Yahweh and could be subject to a divine chastisement. Yakim Israel, the former Eric Burke, didn't like what he was hearing. After class, he and a few fellow doubters asked Moses what he meant. "If you have to ask my meaning, then it is not clear," the prophet answered ambiguously. In Yakim's mind, Ock Moshe wanted the radio man dead.

The episode compounded Yakim's confusion. His first misgivings had surfaced several months before, when he was under pressure to donate his possessions and go full time. Yakim valued his privacy too much to move into the temple. He felt as if he had already contributed enough, tithing a big percentage of his salary. What's more, he had volunteered his highly valued labor, installing air-conditioning ducts in the kitchen. Yakim started to wonder where his money was going. He had questions about Moses' explicit sexual talk. He confided to friends that the Hebrew history classes seemed to be turning into a white-hate cult.

Some of Yakim's pals shared his concerns, but nobody wanted to say anything. "If you had any thoughts or if you were convinced that something was wrong or disagreed with anybody," Yakim later said, "it would be wise not to make your disagreement or whatever you found that was wrong known to any of the individuals for fear of repercussion. . . . It was a type of fear that you had to toe the line if you didn't want your head to be taken off."

Putting the fear out of his mind, Yakim finally took the lead in speaking out. He talked to Mishael Israel, the former Carlton Carey, about the promise that their donations would help black teenagers find jobs. Why wasn't that happening?

Mishael, one of Moses' most loyal lieutenants, had personally contributed more than five thousand dollars to the cause. He enjoyed a reputation as a Scripture scholar and did bookkeeping for the Hebrews. He knew the temple was accumulating hundreds of thousands of dollars, mostly in cash, at breakneck speed. But once the money flowed in, Mishael claimed he had no idea where it flowed next. He just assumed the funds were going where Moses said: to support good works in the black community.

With no place to turn, disenchanted Hebrews started taking their gripes to Joe Oglesby, a reporter/columnist for the *Miami Herald*. They described Moses Israel as a vicious hatemonger who condemned all whites as "evil, wicked, savage beasts" and all blacks who rejected his view as Uncle Toms. They said children in Moses' divine university were learning only his version of the three Rs: religion, racism, and reproduction. One mother told Oglesby she pulled out after her four-year-old son came home one day and announced, "I hate whitey. I hate whitey."

On a Wednesday night in May 1981, Oglesby infiltrated a Hebrew meeting with two *Herald* staffers. Frisked at the door, they took seats in the large auditorium. Brother Moses stepped onstage and held a picture of Jesus Christ high in the air.

"Who is this?" he cried.

"The great white lie," the congregation roared.

"This is a white man's fairy tale," he said, "an invention of the painter Michelangelo, a wicked white devil."

"Tear it up," demanded a voice from the assembly.

Nobody by the name Jesus ever walked the earth nineteen hundred years ago, he told his flock. No such name existed because there had never been a letter J until six hundred years ago. "Go to your dictionary! Go to your encyclopedia! Look up the letter J. There is no Jah, no J, no Jesus. So just shut up that stuff. Go to the dictionary. THERE IS NO J!"

So how could a man living almost two thousand years ago have the name Jehovah or Jesus? No, he said, it was the white man, the trickster of technology, who changed the color of the son of God into a lie. It was the white man who changed the name of Yahweh. The white man handed out pictures of a white savior so the black man wouldn't recognize the true messiah when he made his appearance.

The crowd was in a frenzy. Joe Oglesby was frightened. Moses asked, "How many would die for Yahweh?" All hands were raised.

"How many would kill for Yahweh?"

Oglesby noticed the darting eyes of fanatical sentries positioned around the auditorium. He raised his hand with everyone else. He felt they might kill him if he didn't.

Oglesby's article, published on Monday, July 13, 1981, caused a swirl of paranoia inside the temple. Hebrews labeled him an Uncle Tom. Outside, Liberty City brimmed with distrust, and anonymous citizens asked the police to investigate rumors of child neglect and fraud. Eleven days after Oglesby's article, Dade County's fire marshals descended on the temple. They uncovered an array of safety code and zoning violations and were especially concerned about the children. Fearing a Russian-roulette type of mentality among the parents, the marshals demanded immediate evacuation. But after Moses classified the white firemen as open enemies of God, their superiors decided to void the order.

With the media pumping the thing up, Mishael Israel could stay quiet no more. He knew various revenues, including fees from circumcisions and possibly from baby deliveries, were unaccounted for. Mishael's name appeared on the incorporation papers for the Temple of Love Inc. If the IRS ever audited, he could be hauled in for questioning.

Sensing a scandal in the works, Mishael gathered his strength and asked Moses for a full accounting. The prophet seemed unruffled by growing dissatisfaction with his leadership. The whereabouts of the money, Moses told Mishael, was none of his business. Not only did Moses refuse to provide an explanation, he became deeply insulted by the slightest suggestion of impropriety. How could they not trust him? His whole life, he always said, was for his followers. Nothing was for him.

Even loyalists were turning restless and rebellious. They needed a new sign, some concrete demonstration of his power, for them to keep the covenant with Yahweh. During a temple Q & A one Saturday, they got what they were looking for. A newcomer stepped to the microphone and started to expound the teachings of the late Honorable Elijah Muhammad and his defiant servant, the assassinated El-Hajj Malik El-Shabazz, once known as Malcolm X.

Moses always welcomed a good challenge. He listened politely to the Muslim sympathizer at the mike, sending an air of fairness and support. "I want to ask you some questions," Moses said. "Turn to Revelation 1:1."

"The revelation of Jesus Christ, which God gave unto him, to show unto his servants things which must surely come to pass . . ."

"Can you explain this Scripture?" Moses asked.

A hush fell over the auditorium. Moses' enforcers locked the temple doors. The newcomer at the microphone stuttered.

"Yes, this talks about the revelation that was revealed unto John while he was in exile on the island of Patmos, and Jesus is the lamb of God who will open the seals and reveal the revelation," the man said.

"Who is the lamb of God?" Moses asked.

"I am," the Muslim sympathizer replied.

People in the audience stared down the son of God impostor. A few minutes later, everyone flipped to Job 38. " 'Who is this that darkeneth counsel by words without knowledge?' " he thundered. " 'You stand to speak words without knowledge . . . Gird up now thy loins like a man. . . .' "

As if struck by a bolt of lightning, the Muslim fell flat on his face. Men and women clapped and wailed. "The guy's getting struck down by God," Brother Yehudah thought.

Moses jumped up and down at the podium, in ecstasy. His whole life he had believed he was special, even anointed. Now he had proved it.

"There you go!" a follower heard him say. "That's Yahweh knocking him out!"

The shaking visitor lifted himself from the floor.

"Abound that black devil!" Moses bellowed, and the man at the mike hit the floor again, bursting into spasms. He was knocked down several more times without anybody touching him. Then the guards grabbed him and tossed him out the door.

No one ever saw the son of God claimant again, no one ever knew where he came from or why he just happened into the temple that day to be knocked flat by the strong right hand of God. "The way I feel about this today, I think this guy might have been paid to do that," Abyah Israel, the former Jeffrey Glover, said almost a decade later.

Setup or supernatural, the episode made Abyah and the other disciples fear Ock Moshe as much as they feared the Great, Good, and Terrible God. Moses lorded it over them. One day, he suddenly removed Mishael from his job as an English teacher at the divine university. Mishael's wife, Danielle, speculated that Moses didn't want the kids to read, because if they knew how to read, they would understand they were being brainwashed. Danielle, the former Mildred Banks, divulged her fears to Mishael. In her six months as a Hebrew Israelite, she had gladly made personal and financial sacrifices. Without complaint, she tithed ten percent of her $21,000 postal worker's salary. She gave up high heels and tight pants. She found comfort in Moses' teachings about black prophets and white injustice, deriving satisfaction she never felt as a Baptist or a Methodist. But the threatening remarks aimed at Robert Hall had bothered her. She couldn't see herself going out to kill anyone, white or black.

Danielle and Mishael cast their lot with Brother Yakim and the dissidents. Meeting secretly at Mishael's house in Carol City, they discussed everything that was happening to them: Moses' silver scam; the midwife classes; the group circumcisions; mind control; homicidal urges; beatings; the disappearance of an unruly member.

No one had the total picture, but they thought they saw through the facade of Moses' Bible teachings. The Book, they agreed, said nothing about racial hatred. The dissidents were well-educated, goal-oriented people and among Moses' most financially secure supporters. One suggested they stop tithing. By ceasing the flow of thousands of dollars to the temple, they might be able to bankrupt Moses into obscurity. When a few people began withholding contributions, the war between the devil and the righteous was joined.

17

....

Moses smote his followers with Scriptures about spies, anti-Christs, and hypocrites in the ranks. He cited a passage in the Book of Proverbs: "Trust in the Lord with all thine heart; and lean not unto thine own understanding." Then, on a Saturday in early fall 1981, Moses spouted an example of Hebrew people "leaning to their own understanding." Singling out Mishael and Danielle, the prophet demanded they stand up and declare their love before the congregation. The couple, who had married without Moses' permission, refused. Danielle didn't think her private life was anybody's business.

Moses didn't let up. He had the congregation read from the Book of Timothy. "For men shall be lovers of their own selves, covetous, boasters, proud, blasphemers, disobedient to parents, unthankful, unholy. Without natural affection, trucebreakers, false accusers, incontinent, fierce, despisers of those that are good. Traitors, heady, high-minded, lovers of pleasure more than lovers of God. Having a form of godliness, but denying the power thereof; from such turn away. For of this sort are they which creep into houses, and lead captive silly women laden with sins. . . ."

Danielle perched quietly in her seat, as Moses called her a silly woman, a "tree sister" who had broken the Yahweh law on sex. She scanned the audience. "People were acting like zombies," she later said.

Everybody turned to the Book of Titus: "For there are many unruly and vain talkers and deceivers . . . whose mouths must be stopped, who subvert whole houses, teaching things which they ought not, for filthy lucre's sake."

No way would the Hebrews allow the Temple of Love to be mugged by one of their own people, a vain talker who went into households and led silly women captive, a deceiver who was "leaning to his own understanding" and espousing his own, phony interpretations of the Bible. Moses meant Mishael.

Mishael crossed his arms, slumped in his chair, and forced himself to smile. Moses' loyalists had never really liked him. Mishael was of Jamaican heritage, and they thought he had an attitude that made him act superior to American-born blacks. They were suspicious of other Caribbean-born people in Mishael's clique.

Moses "wanted our minds," Danielle would say, but "we weren't going to submit to him." The couple continued to maneuver with the other dissidents. Should they try to reform the temple from within? Or should they leave and start their own group? No matter what happened, the rebels vowed they would stay loyal to one another.

As they searched for the best way to make a break, Moses moved to a final showdown. In class one day, he tried to coax his opponents into believing he was the messiah. His real name had been disguised as Shiloh, the stem of Jesse, the root of David, the branch, the lion of the Tribe of Judah, the lamb, the counselor. He quoted Revelation 1:13–15 as textual proof of what he would look like: "I wrote about me before I came," he'd declare. "I told you my skin color before I came. I told you my feet would be like fire and brass, my skin color is like brass, fine brown brass . . . I told you my hair would be like wool . . .

"I told you what kind of eyes I would have when I came. I won't have eyes like everybody. . . ." He had eyes like a flame of fire, mysteriously changing color, from blue to yellow to orange. Ever since he started teaching, people had quietly scrutinized Moses' powerful eyes and light skin. They wondered who was dark and who was light in his family. Quoting a verse from the Book of Jeremiah, he suggested God chose him because his heritage was like "a speckled bird." Here he was "high yellow," the heavenly messenger of the powerless and the uprooted, a living example of the injustices of slavery. If he'd come to his people jet black, who would have accepted him? "He sent me to you because he knew I would understand your case."

Moses' self-promotion convinced the dissidents he was a fraud. "A cheap crook and a swindler," Mishael called him. With Brother Yakim, Mishael began digging into Moses' past. They found out his real name, and from Muslim sources they learned about his previous incarnations and his foiled effort to start a Bible school in Atlanta. Evidently, he had skipped town after Elijah Muhammad's henchmen accused him of being a pervert.

Unable to hush his mouth, Yakim whined out loud in the temple one day. "Hulon Mitchell is a faggot!" Then Yakim stormed out the door.

Moses heard about the name-calling. He knew from the Scriptures that if a man walks in the footsteps of Christ, people will call him evil things. But questioning his divinity was one thing; questioning his masculinity was something else entirely, especially given the premium he placed on sexual prowess. Calling a servant of God a faggot, Moses told his flock, was like calling God himself a faggot.

He wouldn't allow rebels to start their own following in his house. Only one throne existed in the Temple of Love. "I don't care how big the stage is," he'd explain. "When I come out on it, there's just one chair."

"When I came to Miami, I didn't need your money and I am here and I am successful and I don't need your money," Yehudah Israel quoted him. "And when all you silly niggers are gone, I won't need your money then."

Get out! Moses ordered the rebels. And don't come back!

But one of them did. Ben Zion, a tall, handsome man in his thirties, returned to the temple. He was known to be communing with the dissidents, especially Brother Yakim. Yehudah stood nearby as Ben Zion watched a movie. Moses walked up and switched off the tube. Not in the least intimidated, Ben Zion looked up at him. "You're just a man like me," Ben Zion said.

Moses, according to Yehudah, loomed closer and exploded. "Don't you know Yahweh can kill you? Don't you see where you're at?"

After the confrontation, the splinter group jockeyed to solidify its power base. Mishael, the unofficial leader, warned his roommate, Elijah, to stop attending Moses' meetings. But the fun-loving Elijah, once known as Aston Green, still had friends in the Temple of Love. He kept showing up, acting as a sort of peacemaker between the rival factions. Perhaps it was Elijah, perhaps someone else, who inadvertently leaked word that Mishael & Co. were conspiring to steal Moses' writings and set up competing Hebrew businesses. What's more, a rumor circulated that a traitor had written a letter to Moses' flock accusing him of sexual shenanigans.

Word leaked back to the rebels of open threats at Moses' meetings. An informant told them that Moses had ordered the taking of hypocrites' heads. The congregation had read the law on blasphemers: "And he that blasphemeth the name of Yahweh, he will surely be put to death!"

The ominous words might have scared off most people, but not Brother Yakim. He went out and bought a new pistol. He knew how to use it. One evening, he and a few friends pulled into the temple's parking lot, where a cluster of Hebrew guards were sitting on the patio, brooding about something or someone. Yakim jumped from the car, waving the gun. The temple guards stiffened.

"Where's Ock Moshe?" Yakim hollered. "Tell that faggot to come out!" As he sprayed bullets in the air, frightened Hebrews ducked for cover. Temple children heard the burst of gunfire and scrambled under their beds.

"Tell that sissy to come out!" Yakim shouted. The passengers in his car continued to taunt the followers. "Look at you now! Bunch of fuckin' faggots!"

Moses, furious that the rebels had endangered his children, gathered his sons for a warrior talk. Yehudah Israel recalled later that Ock Moshe recounted the parable of David and Goliath: David was a small man who went up against an eight-foot giant. The only way David could beat Goliath was if he had an equalizer. A slingshot. David matched weapons with his enemy and prevailed. The modern-day Moses led his enforcers to believe that God would allow them to match weapons with the enemy.

"In the Bible," Yehudah quoted the prophet, "we use swords to cut their heads off. With a gun, you may not kill them; they may get away. But if you cut their head off, you know they're dead."

That night, half a dozen Hebrew men made Molotov cocktails and scraped together a small arsenal of rocks, bricks, and tree limbs. One man had a gun. Despite Moses' opposition to guns, there had long been talk about a weapons cache hidden somewhere near the fortresslike compound. The men set up an ambush. If a hypocrite came within the perimeter, they would cut him off, smash his car windows with the gas-filled cocktails, drag him from the burning car, and kill him. The air was clear and warm that night, the kind of autumn night that draws the snow birds to Miami to line the beaches and pray for life everlasting. The Hebrews waited behind trees, on a rooftop, and inside a parked car. Across the street, someone hid behind a bush. But the hypocrites never came back.

Before dawn on Wednesday, November 11, 1981, Zerubbabel Israel and two other men armed themselves with knives from the temple cafeteria. They headed west on foot to Yakim's apartment building, just a couple of blocks away.

A handsome, twenty-year-old cellist in Yahweh for a year, Zerubbabel had once studied engineering and dreamed of singing at the Apollo in New York City. His college frat brothers called him the Cool One. Attracted to Moses' positive message of black unification, he had dropped out of college, joined Yahweh full time, and persuaded his whole tight-knit family to come to meetings: two brothers, a sister, and his mother, a well-known PR executive in town. Ricardo Woodside took the name Zerubbabel, a potential messianic king. Now he washed Moses' car, guarded Sister Judith, and looked for recognition in the eyes of Yahweh.

With his two brothers, the modern Zerubbabel climbed the darkened stairwell to Yakim's apartment, grabbing the knob to apartment number 1. The door was locked. Yakim was waiting in

124

the dark, armed and hidden. As they tried to break down the door, one or two shots rang out from inside.

Zerubbabel jumped the banister, and he and his brothers ran back to the temple in different directions. The incident seemed to be over even before it began.

18

At 5:52 A.M., two and a half hours after the botched attack on Yakim Israel, two Metro-Dade patrolmen responded to a report of "shots fired" at the temple. Brother Job Israel told the police Yakim and Mishael had brandished handguns, fired three rounds, and called someone a "faggot motherfucker." Job denied a role in any assassination plot, and the police left forty-three minutes later. Just a short time after that, two of Moses' loyalists reported to him that the rebel faction planned another secret meeting that night.

It was not the news Ock Moshe wanted to hear. He vented his anger in a two-page flyer titled "Yahweh's Hypocrites Are Warned." It mingled apocalyptic Scripture fragments and his own prophecy.

"Knowest thou not this of old," he wrote, quoting the Book of Job, "since man was placed upon earth, that the triumphing of the wicked is short, and the joy of the hypocrite but for a moment? Though his excellency mount up to the heavens, and his head reach unto the clouds; yet he shall perish forever like his own dung."

The next morning, Thursday, November 12, 1981, twenty of Moses' disciples gathered for daily prayer. They sang a hymn to Yahweh, and Moses blessed them. He told them it was their duty as Hebrew men and women to protect the nation they were working so hard to build. Then he left with Sister Judith to run some errands.

Whenever Moses pulled out of the parking lot, his firmament was abuzz with gossip. Where was Abba going? Was he having an affair with a white woman? Had he run off to the Bahamas with the money? Or was he teaching a young sister spiritual ecstasy? Then, to their everlasting relief, he always reappeared and scolded them for having doubted him.

He wasn't around when the extrovert Elijah drew up in a Datsun station wagon. Moses' stoic-faced enforcers were patrolling the grounds, begging for a fight. Enwrapped in sweet feelings of righ-

teousness, they had learned to bark Yahweh's general orders on command. They practiced marching and close-formation drills but, most
of all, they learned to obey. Their orders, written on a small lami-
nated card, came straight from the operating manual Moses had
used in the U.S. Air Force. His security force was composed of
organization men—onetime Boy Scouts and police officers, frat
members and soldiers—recruited at a point in their lives when the
summons to some larger collective purpose seemed just what they
needed. "We are warriors," Zerubbabel told himself. "We're supposed to stand up for our nation, and anybody that comes into our
nation . . . they are to be killed."

Elijah hopped from his car and began flirting with a woman.
He seemed to be in a good mood. Most Hebrews thought Elijah was
OK, maybe a little slow-witted but always happy-go-lucky as he sat
through classes. He sang the praises of the black savior louder than
just about anybody. His biblical namesake, the stormy prophet, tried
to stop disobedient Israelites from worshiping idols. Although the
Hebrews tolerated Elijah, some of them still distrusted him. They
thought he might be the stool pigeon feeding information about
temple activities to his roommate, Mishael. They remembered the
class when Moses criticized people for "straddling the fence." Everybody knew he was alluding to Elijah—everybody, that is, except
Elijah.

Yehudah Israel walked up to the Jamaican and snatched the
Bible from his hand. "What do you want?" Yehudah demanded,
patting him down.

"I want to see Ock Moshe," Elijah replied.

Yehudah told him that Moses wasn't around, and Elijah started
walking back to his car. A group of Hebrew men congregated to
watch him go.

According to the Book of Exodus, the "able Israelites" were to
bring the hard cases to Moses. The small matters they were allowed
to judge for themselves.

"Remember what Ock Moshe said about the hypocrite?" one
enforcer asked.

"If he keeps disturbing us, we're going to have to kill him."

"Hypocrites must be destroyed."

Elijah might have gotten away untouched, if he had just started his car and left. But he remembered the Bible that Yehudah had taken from him. Elijah went back to get it.

Hebrews formed a circle around him. Ock Moshe was there, they lied, and Elijah could meet with him now. They took him by the arms and led him inside the temple.

As they walked down the corridor, Elijah didn't seem afraid. He didn't resist. He thought he was going to see Moses, so he was just walking briskly alongside the Hebrews with a yeah-you-just-take-me-to-him attitude. But as they approached a small room in the back, Elijah realized something was wrong. He began to struggle. They'd taken him to a storage room where they kept paper and ink supplies. Elijah screamed.

Suddenly, a Hebrew punched him in the face, hard. Elijah dropped, his head bouncing off the concrete floor. As many as nine men swarmed over him, striking him with their fists. Elijah's screams turned to moans. They kicked him in the chest, the groin, and the head and bludgeoned him with blunt weapons—a tire iron, a hammer, a closet rod, a pipe. It was never clear which weapons were used, or who exactly was involved.

Yehudah Israel would admit years later that he stood watch, pacing the hall, as his buddies crushed Elijah's 165-pound frame. "The guy is so strong," Yehudah thought, later denying that he had ever laid a hand on Elijah. "Incredibly strong."

Zerubbabel Israel looked at Elijah's bloodied face and, for reasons he couldn't explain, kept pummeling him. "He looked horrible," Zerubbabel would confess. "Any available spot that was open on his body, he was being hit there."

Zerubbabel didn't know Elijah personally. It was much easier to hurt a man when you didn't know him well. They beat him for seven, ten, or twenty minutes or more. Elijah lay on the ground, gasping for air. He wasn't moving but he was semiconscious, moaning.

Brother Micah, a Circle of Ten member who just months before had quit his job as a Broward County sheriff's deputy, was recuperating from a temple circumcision when he heard Elijah's quiet screams. Micah ran over and saw Elijah on the floor, "in pain and maybe agony." Micah, the former Charles Saunders, later admitted he did nothing to stop the beating. He shooed away a curious child who sneaked away from school after hearing the thump, thump, thumping sound.

Yehudah and Zerubbabel later said that Enoch Israel, captain of the Circle of Ten, suddenly stopped the beating. Enoch was a big, friendly man with a long, full beard, reddish skin, and freckles. In his first life, he was John Foster, juvenile delinquent and gang leader, proving himself by "fighting all comers." In his second life, he was PFC John Foster, Vietnam paratrooper, recipient of a Purple Heart after being wounded in hand-to-hand combat. After Vietnam, John Foster turned to crime before turning to Yahweh. He became Enoch, a model of divine wisdom, Moses' primary instructor in Yahweh military matters.

Enoch—Yehudah and Zerubbabel said—supervised the beating that day. The Hebrews tied Elijah's hands, taped his mouth and nose with duct tape, and wrapped his bloody head in a carpet. They carried his limp body to a side door and loaded him in the trunk of Enoch's big red Ford.

They tossed a machete in the car and vied for the right to take Elijah for his last ride.

"I'll go, I'll go," one said. On the one hand, Yehudah Israel wanted to go. On the other, he said he was horrified because he knew what was going to happen: Elijah was going to die.

Yehudah's friend Zerubbabel won the honors. He later testified that Enoch ordered him to go. "Get in the car," Zerubbabel quoted him. Thinking that to hesitate would have been a sign of weakness, Zerubbabel jumped into the passenger's seat. Enoch drove off, Zerubbabel said, as Job Israel trailed them in Elijah's station wagon.

Inside the temple, Yehudah helped clean up the evidence. He and other men poured bleach and acid on the bloody floor, scrubbing it with a brush and some rags. They took the rags out back and burned them. A bloodstain, embedded in the concrete surface, required a repainting of the floor—red. While Zerubbabel and friends were making their way to Elijah's undisclosed killing ground, Moses returned to the temple. Yehudah said he and another Hebrew broke the news that a hypocrite had been beaten. "Praise Yahweh!" Moses said. "Yahweh is killing our enemies."

Zerubbabel was quiet as the cars pulled to a stop at a rock quarry in western Dade County, on the fringe of the Everglades. Someone grabbed the machete. They lifted Elijah from the trunk. Zerubbabel said Elijah was alive but dying, groaning for mercy in a barely audible rasp. The men carried him behind some bushes, knelt him on a red blanket, stretched his head over a coral rock, and the moans were soon ended.

Zerubbabel's mind was reeling. "In the beginning I heard ummmmmmm ummmmmmm," he confessed, "and then after about two, three minutes of that I didn't hear anything else." No noise except for the thud of a machete crushing flesh.

"Damn," one killer said, "this blade is dull."

It took fifteen, twenty, or thirty hacks to chop off Elijah's head, to administer the biblical sanction for those who blasphemed Yahweh. Zerubbabel wasn't counting exactly. He felt a sense of dissociation, as if in slow motion, physically and mentally removed from the situation. "My mind was running around," he'd say after years of reflection. "I don't know if pieces was going everywhere or exactly what was going on . . . I wasn't even paying attention."

As the men walked back to the cars, the pumped-up Zerubbabel tried to convince himself he had done Yahweh justice. He sought to absolve himself of blame, thinking God had fated the revenge. About two miles up the road, the killers stopped to get rid of Elijah's Datsun. When they got back to the temple, Zerubbabel Israel burned his blood-stained clothes. He said he sat down for supper with Brother Moses. "When we take the next head," Zerubbabel said, quoting Moses, "we're going to put the head in a basket on a post so the whole city can see it and fear Yahweh." According to the Bible,

130

victorious warriors were supposed to celebrate. "So go up there and get something to eat," Ock Moshe told him. "It's time to feast."

Zerubbabel stood in the chow line, but he wasn't hungry. His mind had been trained to do things he had no idea he was capable of. Years later, he would feel betrayed by his own judgments, like a person without a heart. "It's like being dead," Zerubbabel thought.

For days, he would walk around the temple in a panicky daze. Deborah Vashti told her brother Moses that Zerubbabel, usually outgoing, seemed out of it—like he was "losing his mind." He needed counseling, she said.

Zerubbabel admitted the killing to several Hebrews, but his version of what happened fluctuated from one day to the next. He told one person he only stood guard, listening, as Job and Enoch took turns wielding the machete. He told someone else he caught a glimpse of the dull blade striking Elijah's neck. Yet another heard him say he wielded the machete himself, because Enoch couldn't go through with it. "We had to finish it," Zerubbabel said.

A decade later, both Enoch and Job would vehemently deny a role in the murder. Job, who would earn a reputation as Moses' most loyal supporter, said he had no idea who might have been involved. Job could cite a Scripture to justify anything. "For God Yahweh knoweth the way of the righteous," he once declared, "but the way of the ungodly shall perish."

Enoch reacted stoically, proceeding to the next day's mission without a trace of guilt. Just hours after the homicide, he told Brother Amariah, a fellow Circle of Ten comrade, "Elijah won't be coming by anymore."

Even before the police identified the corpse, word reached Eric Burke (the former Yakim Israel) and Carlton Carey (the former Mishael Israel) that sweet Aston was dead. That Saturday night, the dissidents told homicide detectives that Moses Israel either ordered or sanctioned the murder. With no proof, they left the station house, nervous that they would be next. Carlton toyed with the idea of disappearing for a while, but he thought that could make Moses' henchmen even more suspicious. Carlton decided to go home instead.

Yahweh's avenging angels were waiting for him. This time, according to Brother Joshua, it was four men in dark clothes, trained in martial arts. They wore ski masks and carried guns and a machete. Two of them, Brothers Dan and Amri, had told Moses earlier about the secret meeting of the infidels.

About 3 A.M., after the ambush, Brother Dan, the former Robert Beasley, Jr., went home excited, waking up his wife, Sharon, from a deep sleep. He asked her to face the east and promise never to say a word about what he was about to tell her. He admitted he had paid a visit to the hypocrite Mishael. They waited in the darkness for him and his wife, Danielle, to come home.

For months, police in cruisers and unmarked Aries sedans had passed by the Temple of Love daily, staring at the turbaned sentries. Now, they put the temple under full surveillance, jotting down tag numbers. Homicide Detective Steve Roadruck began gathering intelligence on the enigmatic Moses, aka Hulon Mitchell, Jr. He was forty-six years old. Reportedly, he had done time in Detroit, but Roadruck could find no rap sheet or fingerprints on file. The FBI was no help. Just about the only information available came from Moses' Florida driver's license. The social security number was traced to a white woman living in Enid, Oklahoma.

As the detectives tried to overcome tricky legal, religious, and cultural obstacles posed by potential terrorists on American soil, the Hebrew Israelites gloried in the death of hypocrites.

Inside the Temple of Love, thirteen-year-old Joshua saw his uncle exulting when he read the newspaper. "Yahweh got them," Moses chortled. "Yahweh called these niggers."

Joshua was bringing his uncle a drink from the temple juice bar when Dan and Amri approached with the details. Joshua eavesdropped. Amri, a former Eagle Scout whose slave name was Walter Lightburn, said they couldn't get the woman's head to "come all the way off." Mishael had staggered to a neighbor's house after Dan shot him, so they didn't know if he was dead either.

"Well, I see right there you got him," Joshua quoted Ock Moshe, as the sect leader pointed to the newspaper article.

Later, Amri joked about the killing. Dan sat at his kitchen table, sawing apart a sixty-two-dollar H & R revolver. His wife watched. The gun belonged to her. Thirty-year-old Dan, a bespectacled man who sometimes wore a black kung-fu ghi, wrapped the pieces of the gun in a white handkerchief. Then, as the couple drove over a bridge on the way to the temple, Dan lobbed the bundle over a rail and into a canal. Sharon, scared of her husband and even more frightened of Moses, didn't utter a word about it. If the Hebrews could kill Mishael, she thought, they could kill her, too.

When the couple arrived for class that night, a pep rally commemorating the hypocrites' death was in session. Yahweh did it, Ock Moshe told them, as they clapped wildly and wept openly, rejoicing that Uncle Toms were dead. They looked around to make sure everyone was together in the spirit. There was a feeling of communal euphoria, a strong, close sentiment that they were all in something together. Yehudah Israel tried to blend in, cheering along with everybody else. But deep down, he confessed many years later, he felt something different, something terrible.

19

T he Hebrew publicity juggernaut went into full speed. Sister Judith, the chief PR spokesperson, met reporters at the door and read a brief statement denying media accounts that linked the temple to homicide. She seemed firm and sincere. Later, the Hebrews saw her in tears.

They flooded Liberty City with a leaflet, "A Plot to Kill the Innocent." "Our Great, Good, and Terrible Black God revealed to us a plot by the Miami-Dade Police Department to conduct a secret raid against the Hebrew Israelites," the flyer said. They "sent black Uncle Toms out into the street to see if they could get away with raiding us and killing us without a cause.

"They seek to destroy Hebrew Israelites today and you tomorrow. . . . How long are we going to sit down and allow white people to kill us one by one? How long are we going to stand around allowing white people to kill every model of black excellence? All black people must now stand up in unity against lies and falsehood."

In the days ahead, a chill settled over the word Yahweh as up to fourteen dissidents went into hiding. Some disappeared in the dead of night. Others simply stopped showing up for work. After the anonymous caller had reported him dead, the radio man Robert Hall gave up his talk show and took a desk job. He went underground with eight bodyguards.

A few community leaders condemned the Hebrew Israelites as a hate group, but most said nothing. Black leaders didn't want to violate the eleventh commandment: Thou shalt not criticize a member of thy own race. White leaders didn't give a damn or didn't want to upset the shaky peace that existed between the races.

None of Carlton Carey's neighbors heard or saw a thing. In Dade County people knew instinctively when to keep their heads down and close their eyes. They knew what not to see, especially when white lawmen were asking the questions.

On Wednesday, November 18, at 10:30 A.M., detectives Steve Roadruck and John King prowled the temple perimeter for clues. As they circled the back, King spotted something green.

"Steve, go back," he said. "That looks like the carpet on Aston's head." He pointed to a strip of green carpet, about six feet long, draped over a fence on the west end of the compound. "Do you think it's legal if we take a piece?"

"Sure," Roadruck said. King got out of the car and removed it.

Despite the physical evidence linking someone in the temple to Aston Green's murder, the homicide bureau ruled out asking a judge to sign a search warrant. They voted against a new undercover infiltration. "No way am I gonna put anyone in danger," said Sergeant Frank Wesolowski, a straight, by-the-book supervisor known as Weso.

A prearranged meeting, though, seemed slightly less intimidating. On the Thursday after the homicides, Moses Israel waited for a visit from the detectives. His followers hid their beds, replacing them with desks. At 1 P.M., Weso and the detectives pulled up to the temple as backup squad cars with heavily armed officers circled the complex. Roadruck and King kept looking around as they approached the door. "Three cops?" Weso thought. "No way. It would be crazy for them to try anything."

An Israelite escorted the officers to Moses' office. There, he sat serenely, flanked by two men, their arms crossed in a militant posture. Sister Judith occupied a couch beside him.

The detectives began hurling questions at him. Did he have any knowledge of murdered former members?

Only, he said, what he read in the newspapers. People come and go from the temple strictly voluntarily. When a Catholic is murdered, do the cops go to the pope and ask him if he did it?

Did he believe in killing?

Moses replied that he believed in the Holy Bible, every book from Genesis to Revelation.

Did he teach hate?

No, Moses said, he taught the black man's history, before, during, and after slavery. How could the police possibly accuse him of teaching hate? Black people are the victims of hate. It was white people, he said, who lynched "us."

"He has hung us on trees ever since we've been here," he once said. "He has cut off our ears, our nose and our fingers and our toes and our private parts. He has ripped our pregnant mothers' bellies open and took the baby out, and stomped on his head, raped our grandmothers, and turned us yellow, and you ask me about loving a dog like that? No, I don't love him. I hate everything he did to us."

Moses would always give unbelievers a history lesson—starting with white people killing the Indians and stealing their land, to the murder of ninety-six million Africans, to the Alamo, to the War of 1812, to Independence Day and Pearl Harbor, to World War I and World War II. The Jews teach their children about the Holocaust, he'd say. They even make movies of Hitler and the Germans killing Jews, but would the cops say they're teaching hatred? How about the KKK and the Nazis? You don't see Hebrews going around burning crosses on white folks' lawns. You never hear about black people hanging white people.

Moses held up a photocopied picture of several black men being lynched. The picture had a quotation from Langston Hughes at the top. "I've been a victim. The Belgians cut off my hands in the Congo. They lynched me in Texas."

He handed the picture to Detective King. "This is what your people have done to us for the last four hundred years," the prophet said.

"You don't seriously believe we came to the temple because we want to hang somebody, do you?" King replied.

The detectives tried to redirect the questions to the homicides. Did Moses have a son who attended the temple? He refused to acknowledge his son was there. He interpreted Scripture. Had they heard about the cobalt bomb? It kills people, Moses said, but leaves the buildings standing. The Bible says the battle of Armageddon will be fought in the Valley of Jehoshaphat in the Middle East. Iran, Saudi Arabia, Israel, Jordan, the West Bank will be no more. The Hebrews will walk in and claim the territory.

The Hebrew leader recited a litany of why he believed the police and the media had singled his people out for persecution. The very label "cult," he said, denied them legitimacy.

What did his followers call him? a detective wanted to know.

His name, he said, was Moses Israel. In time, he'd reveal his true identity. Who did they think he was?

There was a long pause. "I guess," one cop quipped, "you're whoever you say you are."

The conversation lasted about twenty minutes, and then Moses invited the detectives on a tour. To the cops, the complex seemed orderly and well furnished. Hebrews operated printers and prepared salad in the kitchen. Children recited the Hebrew alphabet. Moses commented on the way he was turning blind, dumb, and ignorant people into productive citizens. After the tour, Moses asked them to stay for lunch. "We'll pass," Sergeant Wesolowski said.

As the officers walked to their cars, Weso shook his head in utter amazement. "Unbelievable," he said. "The guy's just like Jim Jones."

A month passed, and Mildred Banks made a slow recovery under an assumed name. She tried to keep the pressure on the police and finally went public with her story. Her head and neck wrapped in bandages, she confessed to reporter Joe Oglesby that she had not liked white people or cops when she joined the Hebrew Israelites. But her experience had changed her. "It wasn't a white man that killed my husband," she explained. "It wasn't whites who did this to me. It was black people that did this to me."

Millie hoped that by speaking out she would encourage witnesses to come forward. No one did, and the Hebrew homicides slipped to the back burner.

20

With the hypocrites dead or silenced, the way was clear for Moses Israel to elevate himself. "Who am I?" he asked one day. "How many of you know who I am?" He looked at them with his holy and hypnotic blue-eyed gaze. "Ock Moshe is *not* my name. My name is Yahshua!"

Yahshua was the deliverer, the Lord of salvation, the real Jesus. "I'm here!" he proclaimed, to tears and foot stomping. "I told you when I was coming. I said after you served the enemy four hundred years, I'll come and judge!"

His words were the meaning their lives needed. His dreams were taller, bigger, grander than almost anyone else's. He unveiled a plan for a national expansion drive under the divine guidance of Yahweh. They would turn America upside down by setting up missionary units known as satellite temples. About seventy Hebrews volunteered for the first elders' training course. They learned to conduct services, to map and canvass a city, and, perhaps most important, to raise money. All donations would be strictly accounted for and returned to Miami weekly by money order. Not turning in their money or spending it on junk food was a crime worthy of death, the messiah warned. Among his other lessons: how to avoid out-of-town seduction. Deeming wives too much of a distraction, he wanted his elders to travel alone and remain celibate. To test them, he had a woman come to class one day. She hiked up her dress to her buttocks. Yehudah Israel couldn't stop gawking. The messiah, who could see through skirts and anything else, promptly concluded Yehudah had too many shortcomings to represent him as an elder.

While the elders learned to build an empire, Yahshua opened another educational facility called Hebrew Israelite University. Tuition: ten dollars a credit. Degree: B.A. in three years or less. Goal: to qualify students for rulership in New Jerusalem. Among the course offerings: "The History of False Religions."

Study and preparations for the national drive kept them busy throughout the winter of 1982. For a while after the homicides of the hypocrites, a few men had been frozen in fear, waiting for the police to arrest them. Aware that every brother or sister might become a snitch, they started a buddy system to monitor one another's movements. To root out "talebearers," the Hebrews began bringing rumors and infractions to the messiah's attention.

By early spring 1982, things were getting back to normal. His devotees opened the temple doors to the public and reconnected with non-Hebrew relatives during the Feast of the Unleavened Bread. It was one of three national holy feasts of the black man, celebrated three weeks before the traditional Jewish Passover. Yahshua preached about the divine executioner. "Yahweh might decide it's time for the Passover, the death angels to pass," he'd say. "We know now that an angel is a man. And the death angels were the Hebrew Israelites. And they killed the firstborn of Pharaoh and all Uncle Toms."

He inspired his followers to reach for the heavens while selectively remembering their past. During feasts, the Yahweh Universal Dance Troupe sometimes performed a stunning routine called "1555: Slave Ships Ahoy." In tattered rags, their hands chained, fifteen male and female dancers reenacted the slave journey from Africa to America. Yehudah Israel played the role of a rebellious captive, resisting his slave master mightily at first, then was whipped and beaten into submission. As the messiah watched one performance from his cushy white recliner on stage, he wept. He cried a lot, and his followers were never sure what triggered the tears.

But just as quickly, he'd turn buoyant, and on Easter Sunday, 1982, he must have been ecstatic as his flock gathered at Miami International Airport to say good-bye to Yahweh's twenty chosen elders. It was midmorning. The messiah could almost touch his dream of going national. He sent them off to spread Yahweh's word in new corners of the United States: New York City, Atlanta, Washington, Chicago, among others. They carried a few books, some Yahweh products, and a one-way ticket. He told them to solicit donations for food and lodging. When they had enough money, they were to set up satellite sanctuaries in a poor section of their city. "Blacktown," the messiah called it. Wives couldn't stop crying.

When the staff-wielding elders stepped off the airplanes, many had only the robes on their backs and the sandals on their feet. In Houston, Elder Abyah propped his feet on an airport chair and wondered where to go, what to do. Finally, he started hawking *You Are Not a Nigger!* and panhandled ten dollars, enough for a motel room. "I barely could feed myself," Abyah recalled later. A soft-hearted person, he had never wanted to join the Hebrews in the first place. Abyah wasn't a rising temple star or a social climber, and he thought it strange that the messiah entrusted him with an out-of-town assignment. He pined for a nine-to-five job, but like other Hebrews, Abyah kept going because his wife and children in Miami firmly believed that his sacrifice would one day be rewarded. With the grace of Yahweh, he was building a future for them. Almost a decade later, Abyah would learn the real reason he had been sent out of town. The revelation would make him so angry he could have killed the messiah.

For whatever reason they were chosen, elders discovered that being out of town was not only an education in survival but also a spiritual adventure. Sometimes they found themselves in loud battles of holy words, competing on crowded street corners with emissaries of other, even stranger religions. They learned to defend Yahweh against Jamaicans sermonizing about the Rosy Cross and the occult. Black Muslims would holler that Yahshua had purloined teachings of the late Honorable Elijah Muhammad. Hebrew Israelites from different lost tribes of Israel instructed the elders in the history of Black Judaism, in a way their own messiah never had.

In Miami, Yahshua trained more elders for new cities. Yehudah Israel, who was having severe marital problems and was anxious to go somewhere, anywhere, proved his loyalty after he and another Hebrew defaced with graffiti a bronze statue of Dr. Martin Luther King, Jr. Yehudah spray-painted the statue's face white, and across the chest scrawled the words "false prophet." He said another Hebrew tried to hacksaw the statue's head. In the second Yahweh expansion wave, Yehudah was dispatched to Newark, a mecca of Islam. Its downtown featured high-rise offices with glass skywalks. The people who worked there usually lived in the suburbs and never had to set foot in the city streets, which cultivated sects reminding Yehudah of black Nazis. They wore camouflage fatigues, conducted paramilitary drills at secret bootcamps, and wielded M-16s and Uzis.

Slowly, the new elders gained confidence, independence, and status in their kingdom extensions. Their Miami family, meantime, heeded the messiah's call to build an insular economy independent of the white man. He wanted them to become producers, masters of their own destiny. They established a fashion boutique, a clothing factory, and a kosher cafeteria. They set up a food-distribution firm (Genesis Food Co-op Inc.) and a housing company (Exodus Housing Co-op Inc.). A giant bottling department could produce one thousand bottles of Yahweh beer, Yahweh wine, and Yahweh soda a day. Some followers scrubbed old Heineken bottles, filled them with homemade brew, and slapped on the Yahweh label. Others put their creativity to work on a variety of new products. At Hangar 18, a $100,000 recording studio in Hollywood, Florida, Elder Gideon, Moses' cousin, worked on his soon-to-be-released *Love Train*, a divinely inspired album, his first in fourteen years. Hebrew women smiled and bobbed their heads as Gideon sat at the console, playing tunes like "Can I Get a Witness?" "I Want to Be Connected to the Mighty God," and "Going Back to Miami, Going Back to the City of God."

While Gideon strived for a platinum record, Brother Job Israel went for the gold. He crafted fourteen-karat religious medallions and bracelets, hammering them by hand. And when he wasn't making jewelry, Job kept busy in the temple's beauty shop. He mixed petroleum jellies to come up with a line of divine hair products. Among his creations: an all-kosher soft wave and a holy hair food. "This product," Job would boast, "actually grows your hair."

To market and retail the new products, the Hebrews set up toll-free WATS lines. They conducted telephone sales under the direction of a supervisor. The temple also enlarged its printing operation with

high-speed duplicators, power book binders, and expensive recording equipment. The messiah had such a vision of his place in history
that he had his disciples put hundreds of hours of chilling lectures
on audio and videotape. Workers in the temple's tape department
recorded the classes on fast-tape cassettes, which they turned over
to Sister Judith. The tapes were labeled, dated, indexed, and shelved
in a library, with a brief description of each class written for a catalog.
Then they were copied and distributed to satellite temples, along
with the other products. The tapes, generally selling for five dollars
apiece, ended with a promo from the satin-voiced messiah. He
pitched Yahweh soap ("which helps to get rid of rashes and other
skin problems and blemishes"), Yahweh books (including "a brand-
new book that is going to shake the entire planet Earth up"), and
Yahweh music (including "the world's best-selling underground al-
bum," *Let My People Go*). All were available by mail-order catalog.

In Miami, the rank and file—those with less marketing genius
and fewer management skills—elevated fund-raising to a religious
ritual. The troops fanned out in teams to solicit donations and peddle
their goods to the same "dead" world they condemned. "Shalom,"
they'd say, buttonholing beggermen and thieves, doctors and politicians. "I would like to testify to you that Yahweh is God and that
his son, Yahshua our messiah, is here to deliver us from the hells of
North America, that all so-called blacks in America are Hebrew
Israelites. Our nationality, history, culture, and language are Hebrew
and our homeland is Israel. Even if you don't believe as we believe,
we're still the same people and I love you. Would you care to give
a donation?"

The Hebrews hit up estranged relatives and learned to pull in
hundreds of dollars a week. Occasionally, they recruited a convert
on the sidewalk or in the park of a fractured neighborhood. Hoping
to win praise, a weekend junket to the Bahamas, or a lavish dinner
with the messiah, they pleaded for contributions in exchange for
Yahweh literature, key rings, pencils, and T-shirts. The shirts, emblazoned with a picture of a black man behind bars and bearing the
words "Let My People Go," went for seven dollars apiece. They

came in twelve color combinations. Yahweh drinks sold for one dollar a bottle of beer, seven dollars a bottle of wine. The Hebrews accepted cash, Yahweh credit cards, and food stamps. Somehow, they found a way to convert the stamps into cash.

At the end of an outing, solicitation crews turned over the money, stamps, and unsold products to a team leader, who turned them over to Sister Judith. She kept meticulous records, including charts of leading earners.

"The people love you!" the Hebrews would tell the messiah after a long day in the field. It wasn't exactly true. Some people laughed. Others sicced animals on the missionaries. No way, they said, would they buy shampoo from a group that cut off heads. They called the missionaries "Yahwehs."

"You go Yahway," the street people would say, "and I'll go my way."

Making only marginal membership gains in Miami, the messiah moved swiftly to find new revenue sources. Chief Elder David Solomon, the former Herman Sands, ran a government-funded crime prevention project and a program called "Aid to the Hebrews." More privileged followers instructed the less privileged in applying for food stamps and aid to families with dependent children. The messiah justified the program by explaining that because America was a modern-day Egypt, modern-day Hebrews were entitled to any aid the government offered. Women learned to wear normal street clothes, known as dead clothes, to welfare interviews. Government caseworkers suspected that some of the Hebrews lied on their applications, giving phony addresses outside the temple and claiming not to know the fathers of their children or where the fathers could be reached. Once they got the checks, the women were supposed to turn them over to Sister Judith to distribute as she deemed fit. In time, the state office administering welfare would estimate that up to three hundred Yahweh women received monthly checks of between two hundred and three hundred dollars.

By 1983, marketing and distribution of Yahweh products were turning into a sophisticated nationwide operation. New tractor trailers parceled goods to the satellite temples. Job's hair supplies were going coast to coast. Among the customers, Job later said, were celebrities such as Joe Jackson, Michael Jackson's father.

The egalitarian ideal of the Yahweh movement was giving way to status distinctions among the followers. The elders, who managed businesses such as car washes and sandwich shops, gained clout, as satellite kingdoms reported weekly earnings of from three hundred to seventeen hundred dollars.

The messiah insisted they were all stewards of the money they collected, not for themselves, but for Yahweh and their children's inheritance. In collective sessions on moral attributes and laziness, he urged them to work harder. Believing they would be leaving for New Jerusalem any day now, thinking every penny they collected belonged to God, his followers picked up the pace of their proselytizing and panhandling efforts.

At the same time, he began corporate belt-tightening, appealing to his full-time disciples to accept rationing. "I'm not a welfare department," he'd tell them. He threatened to withhold food until they showed more devotion. "You'll turn out to like Yahweh, pretty good, pretty quick."

He quoted Scripture—"He who does not work, does not eat," and then the temple cut back on food entirely. Followers were fed only one meal a day, a diet consisting primarily of rice, corn bread, water, and beans. Baked beans, black beans, stew beans—the temple chefs came up with dozens of creative ways to prepare beans. The messiah, holding catharsis sessions to correct counter-Yahweh attitudes, threatened punishment for anyone who wanted more than Yahweh had volunteered to provide. "If you maintain that gluttonous spirit," he once warned, "I'm going to hang you and I'm definitely going to stone you and I'm going to cut your crazy, stupid head off!" It was yet another test of their moral righteousness. If they were going to leave America, they had to condition their stomachs.

His followers made more and more sacrifices to aid the nation's growth. They gave up small weekly allowances and then agreed to a quota that would earn Yahweh a minimum amount each day. It didn't matter how they made the quota—products, food stamps, donations—so long as they made it.

Quota violators were sent to the temple prayer room. At first, they sat and prayed in steel folding chairs, sometimes for days. They fasted as enforcers watched over them. Then the chairs were taken away, and unproductive people—"cheaters," "cookie monsters," and "gluttons"—were asked to pray on their knees. If their arms dropped or they tried to stand up, a guard hit them with a switch or a rod. Knees sometimes turned numb, raw, bruised, or bloody. The messiah wanted them to "Praise Yahweh!" about it. Strict discipline, he insisted, was a special kind of love. "He that spareth the rod," he said, quoting from the Book of Proverbs, "hateth his son. . . . [Discipline] says, 'I care about you. I will not let you get into trouble.' "

The messiah would allow no trouble in the Temple of Love, no pain, no crying, no suffering at all. When a Hebrew Israelite died, there was no funeral, just a small announcement and private grieving. He wouldn't even let his followers die. One winter night the messiah walked into Sharon Israel's room and stared down at her frail, thin body. "Don't die here," he said, and walked out.

Sharon, age thirty, had been a pretty, vibrant woman, but now her friends hardly recognized her except for her gold tooth. She lay sick from malnourishment, down to ninety pounds. Her medical plan provided only for fasting and praying. Sharon believed her husband, Dan, helped kill Carlton Carey. Now an elder in Atlanta, Dan had taken several wives. Sharon was jealous, bitter, and frightened—frightened to stay, frightened to leave. Finally, on Saturday, April 16, 1983, she walked out of the temple with her eleven-year-old son. She didn't have money or a job, so she wrote a letter asking the temple to return the one hundred dollars she'd invested in Yahweh's silver certificates. "I'm not asking for the car," Sharon said of the vehicle she had donated to the temple. "I just want the little money that I put in for the silver." The temple sent her a check, though not for the full amount.

Sharon was one of the luckier ones. After she left, details about

temple deaths began to dribble out. A two-month-old child supposedly suffocated while being breast-fed by her sleeping mother. A
ten-week-old girl, born a month prematurely, died after experiencing
respiratory problems—and a warning from the messiah to the
mother not to take the child to a doctor. "You could hear her wheez-
ing during the night, and we didn't take her to a hospital or anything," the girl's father, Amariah, admitted years later. The
Yahwehs, the children of God, didn't need doctors. They quietly
wrapped the tiny fatalities in plastic bags, removed them from the
temple, and buried them in unmarked graves.

True believers said the dead babies made good fertilizer. It was
the living they cared about, and dozens of new "culture babies," as
the messiah called them, were now joining his human family. The
exact number would never be known. Yahweh's kingdom was multiplying, but the Bible, Yahshua the messiah said, forbade census
taking.

Right: Aston Green's body, discovered Friday, November 13, 1981, at the edge of the Everglades. *(Dade County Medical Examiner's Office) Below:* Carlton Carey was gunned down after coming home from the police station on November 15, 1981. Carey's wife, Mildred Banks, was cut in the neck and shot, but she survived the attack. *(Dade County Medical Examiner's Office)*

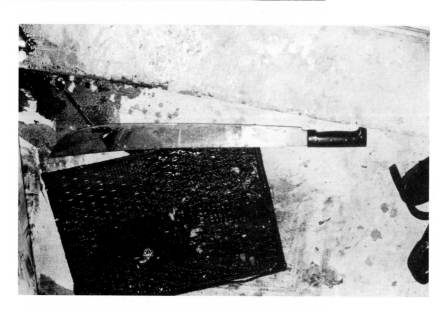

Crime-scene photo of a bloodstained machete and Mildred Banks's Star of David necklace. The police found the evidence at the entrance to the couple's house in Carol City. *(Dade County Medical Examiner's Office)*

Above: Pearl Olive Mitchell, the inspiration for her fifteen children, leaves the federal courthouse for a waiting limousine on November 20, 1990, after her oldest son's arraignment. *(Miami Herald/Candace Barbot)* *Right:* The Reverend Hulon Mitchell, Sr., the sect leader's father, taught his son discipline and the Bible. *(Miami Herald)*

EL'S $75,000.00 PALACE AND ELDORADO'S

FATHER MICHEL ANSWERS THOUSANDS OF LETTERS WEEKLY. PEOPLE ARE WRITING FROM EVERYWHERE AND ARE GETTING GREAT RESULTS!

ATHER MICHEL ADMIRES MANY OF THE WONDERFUL GIFTS RECEIVED FROM HIS FOLLOWERS.

THIS AUTOMOBILE HAS THOUSANDS OF MILEAGE AS A RESULT OF MEETING AND FULFILLING THE NEEDS OF THOUSANDS OF PEOPL

Above left: Father Michel prays for prosperity and abundance in 1969. *(Modern Christian Church brochure)* *Above:* From Michel's brochure: riches on earth, in Atlanta. *(Modern Christian Church brochure)*

Above: Former college frat brothers: Zerubbabel Israel, the former Ricky Woodside *(left)*, and Yehudah Israel, the former Lloyd Clark, eat beans and rice in the temple in October 1982, after giving up their slave lives. *(Miami Herald) Right:* Printers bind a book for nationwide distribution at the Hebrew publishing plant in Liberty City. *(Miami Herald/Carol Guzy)*

Aerial shot of the Temple of Love, with its fleet of white buses and cars, during the sect's heydey. *(Miami Herald/Jon Kral)*

Above left: Judith Israel, the former Linda Gaines, became the second most powerful person in the Yahweh hierarchy. She met the sect leader in central Florida during his days as Brother Love. *(Miami Herald/Chuck Fadely) Above right:* Leonard Dupree, a year before his disappearance. *(Miami Herald)*

Above left: Convicted Circle of Ten member Amri Israel, the former Walter Lightburn, was an Eagle Scout and member of the United Way before joining the Hebrew Israelites. "I am not colored, coon, jig, or any of those names," he testified in 1992, at a trial at which he was accused of having a role in four murders. "I am an individual." *(Miami Herald/Chuck Fadely) Above right:* Convicted Atlanta elder Dan Israel, the former Robert Beasley, Jr., said he was called to do God's will but denied a role in the ambush of Carlton Carey and Mildred Banks. *(Miami Herald) Left:* On television in 1981, Moses Israel denies media reports linking the temple to the murders of defectors. He is guarded by Yehudah Israel, who witnessed Aston Green's beating. *(Miami Herald)*

Above: A teacher at Yahweh Education Center asks questions about the Hebrew language. The students begin their answers with "Praise Yahweh, thank you ma'am." *(Miami Herald)*
Right: A mathematics class, where children learn that waste is not wise. "What is one apple seed plus one apple seed?" the child asks confidently. "The answer is two apple trees!" *(Miami Herald) Below:* A student sits in a sparsely furnished classroom and learns to read between the lines of the Bible. *(Miami Herald)*

In a bright white chapel with high ceilings, large windows, red carpet, and wooden pews, children chant their lessons in sing-song, sometimes clapping out a beat. *(Miami Herald)*

Above: Sentries with Staffs of Life guard a sect-owned building in Miami, in December 1985. *(Miami Herald/Carol Guzy)*

Above left and right: Ear case number three: Raymond Kelley, age sixty-one, a motor-pool mechanic for the city of South Miami. On September 6, 1986, his body was found in his car, parked at the Tepee Lounge in South Miami. Part of his left ear was missing; police found his severed right ear near the car. *(Dade County Medical Examiner's Office) Right:* Lyle Bellinger, who had recently converted to a new faith, relaxes at home, shortly before a fisherman discovered his body on September 5, 1986. The Hebrew suspect accused of Bellinger's murder was acquitted. *(Miami Herald)*

Above right: Ear case number one: Clair Walters, a Vietnam War veteran, after a Miami SWAT team, training in an abandoned motel on Biscayne Boulevard, found his body. His throat was cut and his left ear was missing from the crime scene. The Hebrew suspect accused of his murder was acquitted. *(Dade County Medical Examiner's Office) Above left:* The abandoned Aloha motel, where Walters's body was discovered on May 22, 1986. *(Dade County Medical Examiner's Office)*

The scene in Opa-locka,
Florida, on October 28, 1986,
after the Yahwehs took over
an apartment complex.
(Miami Herald)

Under a NO DRUGS warning
sign, sect members watch over
the just-purchased complex
on October 29, 1986.
(Miami Herald/David Walters)

Anthony Brown, holding daughter Tiquilla, in a photo taken from a Channel 4 WTVJ-TV interview October 29, 1986. Brown told reporters he would resist evictions ordered by the sect. About twelve hours later, he and his friend Rudy Broussard were shot dead. *(AP/Wide World Photos)*

Overcome by shock after learning of the shootings, the sister of a homicide victim is carried from the scene. *(Miami Herald/Michel duCille)*

Above left: Cecil Branch, a garbage man known as Big Man, before his confrontation with a Yahweh soliciting donations in Coconut Grove. Robert Rozier, Jr., pleaded guilty to the murder. A jury acquitted three alleged accomplices. *(Miami Herald) Left:* Before Yahweh. Robert Rozier, Jr., at Berkeley. *(University of California at Berkeley)*

Robert Rozier, Jr., number 96, rushes a quarterback during his days as a defensive lineman for Berkeley's Golden Bears. *(University of California at Berkeley)*

Above: After Yahweh. Murder suspect Neariah Israel, the former Robert Rozier, Jr., is escorted to jail after the shootings at the Opa-locka apartment complex on October 30, 1986. *(Miami Herald/Robin Cohen)* *Below:* Yahweh Ben Yahweh excommunicates Neariah Israel in June 1987, striking his name from the Lamb's Book of Life. *(Miami Herald/Carol Guzy)*

Above: A cameraman for YHWH-TV videotapes Mayor Xavier Suarez's state of the city address on March 1, 1988, as the sect gains civic respectability. *(Miami Herald/Marice Cohn Band) Left:* Miami mayor Xavier Suarez (standing) pays tribute to Yahweh Ben Yahweh in April 1990, at the opening of the sect's grocery store in the city's Overtown section. *(Miami Herald/Tim Chapman) Below:* Yahweh Ben Yahweh chats with his attorney and image man, Ellis Rubin, as they wait for guests to arrive at a wine-and-pasta luncheon sponsored by Miami's elite Manatee Bay Club. *(Miami Herald/Albert Coya)*

The real-estate portfolio. *Above left:* The Yahweh Motel at 7350 Biscayne Boulevard in Miami. *(Miami Herald/Albert Coya)* *Above right:* The sect's oceanfront motel in Sunny Isles, Florida. *(Miami Herald/Brian Smith)* *Right:* "The Fabulous Barclay Hotel" at 89 Luckie Street in Atlanta. *(Michael Cassell)*

Right: Yahweh Ben Yahweh leaves federal court after a grand-jury appearance on May 3, 1990. *(Miami Herald/Albert Coya)*

Above: Yahweh Ben Yahweh, in the firm grip of the law. FBI special agents Herb Cousins Jr. *(right)* and James Bernazzani escort the sect leader into the federal courthouse in New Orleans after his arrest on murder racketeering charges November 7, 1990. *(AP/Wide World Photos/Bill Haber)*

Left: Sect barber Job Israel, accused of bludgeoning Leonard Dupree with a car jack, is ushered to FBI headquarters after his capture at the Temple of Love. Simultaneously, on November 7, 1990, heavily armed agents fanned out in other southern cities, pulling in eleven followers. *(Miami Herald/Chuck Fadely)*

Above: Prosecutor Richard Scruggs, at his apartment overlooking downtown Miami. *(Miami Herald) Below:* The Prince of Peace returns to Miami. *(Bill Cooke)*

Above: Louretta Green leaves federal court in grief on May 14, 1992, after prosecutors showed the jury a photograph of her beheaded son. *(AP/Wide World Photos/Kathy Willens) Right:* Lloyd Clark, after leaving the faith. He informed on his old friends, bought a gun, and tried to put his life back together. "I know Yahweh is nothing but a mere man." *(Miami Herald)*

Despite Yahweh Ben Yahweh's conviction on a lone conspiracy count, his followers still believe in him. *(Miami Herald/Tim Chapman)*

21

Satellite kingdoms grew all over the country, branching out like fig trees, he beamed, with fruit ripening for harvest. As his elders widened their recruitment net, the messiah made room for people of every political persuasion, temperament, and skill. He even took in the police's Public Enemy Number Ones. "Come on down here!" he'd say, welcoming inmates into his heavenly court. "Who besides me will take a man straight out of prison—I didn't ask him what he did, I don't know what he did, I don't care what he did, the white man did it to him! The white man made him like he is! I'm here to remake him!"

Neariah Israel came to them from the white man's prison. He was six feet four inches, 235 pounds, mostly muscle. He was flamboyant, charming, and without a doubt one of the most aggressively masculine people in the temple. Most Hebrews didn't talk about their pasts, but Neariah bragged just enough about his slave life to let them know he had been something special, a pro football player named Bobby Rozier.

Athletics had always been the former Bobby's life. On the field, he was king, a brutal defensive lineman who felt glory when he took apart his opponents. But off the field, he was a washout. In high school, he graduated 594th out of 604 students. His D average wasn't good enough to get him a diploma, and certainly not into the University of California at Berkeley. But owing to his athletic prowess, Berkeley's affirmative-action program, and some skirting of the NCAA rules, he slipped in on a full scholarship. Number 96 promised to take the Golden Bears to the Rose Bowl. But roses weren't in the cards. Bobby became a college football thug.

In training camp, he posed for the team photo with a shiny gold nose ring, then promptly spent his scholarship money on dope. He bought a gun. He got busted for "contributing to the delinquency of a minor." The UC coaches pampered him and covered up his problems. Bobby called himself the Gorilla Pimp. His best friend was a sickly pit bull that he fed with an eyedropper. After nursing the puppy to health, Bobby named it Nig, short for nigger. "Don't ever say the end of the word," he would caution his teammates. They guessed the name was his way of making a statement against the world. Someone finally got fed up and made a statement against Bobby. Angry with him for stealing a stereo, a teammate put poison in Nig's food. When Bobby found the dead dog, he cuddled it, weeping for the first and only time anybody could remember.

By his senior year, Bobby's professors saw him as a major discipline problem, academically unfit, and a potential revolutionary. A few credits shy of graduation, he got tossed out of Berkeley, but he still believed football would carry him through life. The NFL's Saint Louis Cardinals, overlooking his problems, drafted him in the ninth round and signed him to a three-year $48,000-a-year contract. Bobby showed his gratitude by snorting coke and doing speed. He played in only two games, both losses, and was cut from the team. Turning on the charm, Bobby landed on his feet in Canada, where he signed with the Hamilton Tiger Cats and then the Saskatchewan Rough Riders. He didn't last long in Canada, either. While playing ball, he lived high and kept a rifle under his bed. People accused him of running up unpaid hotel bills, misusing team credit cards, writing phony checks, and falsifying loan applications. The Royal Canadian Mounted Police busted him for fraud, but before the Mounties could pick him up for trial, the Oakland Raiders, a team with a reputation for collecting misfits, took him on. Bobby's lifetime dream was to play for the Raiders, but he had no football left in him. In August 1981 the Raiders cut him.

Looking back, coaches at Bobby's high school in the suburbs of Sacramento, California, came to see him as a spoiled athlete, unbridled, with no self-control. He could manipulate the system because of his brawn, his charisma, and his race. "He wasn't the kind of guy," said Cordova High's athletic director, Guy Anderson, "you'd want to take home to meet your daughter."

But Bobby was just the kind of guy the messiah welcomed with love and kisses. Like other out-of-towners who joined during the expansion, Bobby Rozier stumbled upon the Hebrew Israelites in 1982 by accident. After coming to Florida to make a little money and do a little fishing, he landed in jail for driving a stolen car. Bobby told the cops he played for the Raiders, and prosecutors dropped the charges. Just a short time later, he burgled a house in Jacksonville, Florida, and popped some quaaludes he'd stolen. He put his bounty, including some money and a camera, in a car. Then he stole the car. When he wandered into a nice, all-white neighborhood after midnight, residents got suspicious of the big black guy on their quiet block. Again, Bobby found himself with inky fingers in the station house. This time, he cut a deal. A judge gave him six months in prison, but in deference to a celebrity athlete, he allowed Bobby a couple of weeks to get his life in order. That's when he found Yahweh.

He was walking past a grocery store on Pearl Street when he spotted a white building with a big Star of David on it. A bearded man milled about in a white robe and a turban, looking like some shepherd from a nativity scene. "He came straight out of the *Ten Commandments*," Bobby chuckled to himself. He had grown up a middle-class air force brat. His only real contact with religion had been in the movies. Bobby strolled up to the man. "What's this all about?" he asked. "I'm looking for the truth."

Micah Israel, the former sheriff's deputy, introduced himself and rapped about the Hebrews' black-God philosophy. Bobby liked Micah and found the religion "infatuating." Bobby always believed there was a conspiracy against nonwhite people, especially him. When Micah offered him food and lodging, Bobby agreed to stay. Anyway, he had no money, nowhere else to go, really. Bobby lived in the Jacksonville temple until he had to start his jail term. In prison, he read the Bible and *You Are Not a Nigger!* Micah visited. The Hebrews put money in Bobby's commissary fund.

Out of jail, he headed back to the Jacksonville temple. Brother Micah was gone; the new elder was Zerubbabel Israel, the young man who'd helped decapitate Aston Green. Bobby and Zerubbabel studied together. They watched videotaped sermons from the ultimate prophet and passed the Word in downtown Jacksonville. Then, in May 1983, Zerubbabel invited Bobby to Miami to attend the Feast of Weeks. It was a celebration giving thanks to Yahweh for a prosperous and bountiful harvest. By then, the Hebrews had learned to live without Christmas and Easter, birthdays and anniversaries. They kept track of time by the feasts. They greeted Bobby and the other newcomers warmly. He met military men trained in combat, ex-cons like himself, former entertainers, a boxer, and a deejay who had once gone by the name Bubbling Bobby Brown.

To make room for the growing flock, the Hebrews had renovated a big warehouse about ten blocks from the temple. They set up a wine-manufacturing plant and a mechanic's shop to service trucks and old school buses. They bought the buses from Dade County for about ten thousand dollars apiece, then painted them white and used them to recruit and transport new blood to Miami. The warehouse had dormitory-style, single-sex living quarters with bunk beds stacked three high. One side was for men and boys, the other side for women and girls. The warehouse was also equipped with dimly lit conjugal rooms and a sign-up sheet outside. Time limit: one hour. Purpose: procreation only. "They were full all the time," the messiah explained later. "It was kind of like going to a hotel every night."

But not a hotel tourists would find in an AAA guidebook. The messiah and his followers had begun to ensure that their secret world stayed secret. Stamps had to be authorized. Incoming and outgoing mail was censored. The temple pay phone had been ripped off the wall. The disciples had little access to newspapers or magazines. The messiah specifically outlawed *Jet* and *Ebony*, calling them materialistic "filth" and vowing to perform "a little exorcism" on anyone caught reading them.

As tough as life was, what he offered them was better than what awaited them on the unforgiving streets. For Bobby Rozier, the choice was particularly simple. With Canada's Mounties—as well as police in Maryland and California—hunting him for charges ranging from

150

bad checks to forgery, Bobby took the name Neariah Israel. He grew a beard and stopped reporting to his probation officer. On Yahweh's bottling line, he quickly established himself as a most-valuable player. He said later he could earn up to one thousand dollars a week, peddling Yahweh booze. He pocketed a quarter of what he made. To Neariah, that was justice for having to wash bottles. He wasn't in the temple to wash bottles. Neariah Israel was there for enlightenment, and to lash back at the system that had left him angry, bitter, drunk, and doped up. He became an enforcer in the temple prayer room, and then on a Wednesday night, July 27, 1983, he got his first chance to show off his raw power in public.

About three hundred Hebrews had gathered for class. They were singing and praising Yahweh when another self-proclaimed messiah walked to the microphone to express himself. His name was Melchizedek and he was a Rastafarian by culture and tradition. He dated a woman in the Opa-locka congregation, where Neariah had been assigned. Melchizedek believed Ethiopia was the cradle of the black race. He often carried a flag with a picture of Bob Marley, the dead reggae star and devoted Rastaman.

Melchizedek began preaching about his savior, Haile Selassie, as revealed in the Books of Ezekiel, Isaiah, and Revelation. He was King of Kings, Lord of Lords, Imperial Majesty, the Conquering Lion of the Tribe of Judah.

The messiah asked him to shut up, please. "That is not our philosophy," he said in a benevolent voice. "Yahweh is God."

Melchizedek kept interrupting, implying that he, Melchizedek, was the true son of God. Then he pulled off his head wrap and tossed it aside. "Why don't you come down and be a man and fight me yourself?" Melchizedek said, shaking his dreadlocks from side to side. Someone in the audience slapped him.

"Slap me, beat me! They beat Jesus!" Melchizedek thundered. "You might as well beat me, too!"

They needed no leader to tell them what to do. They were all leaders, of one mind, of one action. As in an instant reflex, about twenty Hebrews jumped Melchizedek. Fists flew. Another deity entered the fray. "I'm Jesus Christ!" he cried, but even so he was no match for Neariah Israel, the athlete who had always loved brute force, especially when it earned him applause from an audience.

As spectators cheered, Neariah and the rest of the pumped-up throng kicked and pummeled Melchizedek down the center aisle, to the front lobby. They dragged the heretic outside, dumped him on the grass, and grabbed a fistful of his dreadlocks. "It was like, if it was dust, it would have been a dust storm," Brother Joshua said.

Lip busted, cheeks bloody, eye knotted shut, Melchizedek stumbled to a pay phone at a Shell station on the corner. He dialed 911 and the police closed in. They went into the temple, where the dazed Melchizedek identified four of his attackers, including Neariah. "They did this to me," Melchizedek fumed. Neariah was sure he was going to jail again, but the skittish police left without making a single arrest. In the eighteen months since the homicides of the hypocrites, the lawmen had actually grown to appreciate the messiah. Miami's judges and prosecutors went easy on thugs. Doctors in the emergency room at Jackson Memorial Hospital were besieged with the kind of gunshot wounds normally seen only in war. With that kind of frightful crime picture, the police brass wouldn't say a word if the Temple of Love could keep a few troublemakers like Neariah in tow.

The lawmen wouldn't dare touch him, the messiah boasted to his followers. He said he had written to President Reagan, the Congress, the United Nations, the governors, the wardens, the FBI, and the CIA. "I told all of them, 'You are described by my God in the Bible as Satan, the devil, and you have orders, Don't you touch one Hebrew!' "

"Aren't you scared of the FBI and the CIA?" the faithful would ask him.

No, Moses rejoined. "They're just some devils with three-piece suits on. They're all redneck, Cracker, KKK devil dogs, all of them."

Neariah left class that night thinking this new messiah had a direct pipeline to the police department, if not to God. Neariah climbed into a car with Brother Amri, the Opa-locka elder. Like

Neariah, Amri had been an all-star football player in college. Unlike him, the thirty-three-year-old Amri, suspected of slicing the neck of the hypocrite Mildred Banks, played offense. Armed with a machete, he and Neariah drove off to hunt down Melchizedek. They waited in the darkness for him to come home. He never appeared. The Hebrews said they never heard from him again.

They had united to get rid of one common enemy, one man who believed differently, but Melchizedek's beating was just a prelude for increasing violence. As the messiah led his people deeper into a world of servitude, sticks, switches, ropes, paddles, and rulers were used to muzzle a growing number of nonconformists and people with lackluster attitudes. Anyone not smiling or praising the almighty God Yahweh could get punished at public meetings. "Yahweh, I've been a sinner!" they'd confess. "I think I need the rod of correction to drive the foolishness out of me!"

Yehudah Israel and dozens of congregants watched as an elderly man was tied to a pole because he couldn't stand the pain from one of Yahweh's punishments—kneeling for hours on the floor.

"I quit, I want to leave," the old man said. The messiah had bought the man's dentures. "Take those teeth out of your mouth 'cause they're mine," he told the backslider. The old man complied, but the enforcers continued to harass him.

In spite of the escalating violence, the temple's membership ranks grew faster than even the messiah's vision had dictated. In the fall of 1983, the morale of the original followers shot up with the arrival of hundreds of out-of-towners flocking to Miami for the Feast of Tabernacles. The pilgrims paid registration fees and purchased tickets on Yahweh's bus line, which offered stops in major cities across the country. Some neophytes were looking for an escape. Many others came thirsting for knowledge or salvation.

One thousand miles away, twenty-two-year-old Leonard Dupree was frantically trying to catch a ride to the feast. He had been attending Yahweh's classes for just a few months. His hair was growing, and he'd chosen the name Azariah Israel. It wasn't official yet, and one reason Leonard was so keen on getting to Miami was for the messiah to affirm the new name.

He jogged to the temple on Flood Street, in an area of old and decaying Victorian houses, a few blocks from New Orleans' French Quarter. He asked the Hebrews at the satellite temple if he could go with them. They didn't have room in their cars. Leonard pleaded with his parents to lend him money to make the trip, but Lartius and Mary Dupree viewed the Hebrew Israelites as a hate group. They tried to talk their son out of going.

"How are you gonna live?" his mom asked.

"The Yahwehs will help me," Leonard replied. His Hebrew name meant helped by God.

Leonard was a clean-cut, spindly man with big dove eyes and spider legs. One of six children, he grew up in a color-blind neighborhood in Brandywine, Maryland. His tight-knit Baptist family moved to New Orleans in 1970 and posted a sign in the living room about the Golden Rule: Do unto Others as You Would Have Others Do unto You. Like Brothers Neariah and Amri, Leonard had once been a promising athlete, a nationally ranked karate black belt with a reputation as one of New Orleans' finest practitioners. His opponents said his ax kick felt like a ton of bricks falling on their heads. But after winning several national competitions, Leonard began drifting away from his family. "Searching," his sister Michelle explained. He joined the army reserves and dabbled in drugs and the teachings of Malcolm X. He stopped going to the gym and ended up in a psychiatric ward with a mild breakdown. New Orleans Hebrews, coveting his karate skills, chatted with him in the hospital and sold him a Star of David necklace and a Yahweh T-shirt. They were reassuring. Leonard's parents may not have understood him, but he thought the Hebrews—and God—did.

Leonard's father, sick of arguing about the trip, finally agreed to lend his son two hundred dollars for the bus. Leonard packed a blue fold-up bag with some blue jeans, a sports coat, his black belt, and his white robes. The messiah had begun to teach that if they

154

wore white robes, they would have the power to rule over their destiny and usher in the kingdom of God.

"Sheets," Leonard's daddy called them.

Leonard said good-bye to his family.

"Take care of Mama," he told his sister. He kissed her good-bye and said he'd be back in two weeks.

He had no idea what awaited him in Yahweh's kingdom.

22

Like Leonard Dupree, Amtullah Raheem of Chicago was a babe in Yahweh's kingdom. Unlike him, she didn't plan on going back home. She excitedly packed her quilts and her sewing machine, giving her Frigidaire to a niece. She wanted to meet this messiah before she died. Amtullah, age seventy-five, was studying to be an Amway saleswoman. As a girl, she plowed with a mule on a hard-scrabble farm and had never gone to school. She had felt sluggish, lazy, without purpose, before a young Hebrew elder named Daniel knocked on her door earlier in 1983. He showed her *You Are Not a Nigger!* and an hour later, "I was shouting, I was crying, I was asking him to forgive me for being so stupid."

It was autumn. "I can't be playing because I'm too old and I'm going to soon be dying," she thought. "I'm going to have some kind of sign that I've worked for my God while being on this earth." So she called the messiah, just before Tabernacles. "Sir? Amtullah Raheem from Chicago here. Sir, I'd like to come home.

"The sun's goin' down," she explained. "I got to hurry."

When she arrived in Miami, the Hebrews put her up in the warehouse. Unruffled by the spartan living conditions, she marked off a little space with chalk and slept on the floor. She didn't need a telephone or magazines or a lot of food. All she needed was a blessing from her messiah. One day, he saw Amtullah standing behind the door as he was making a tour to kiss and sanctify his babies. Her knees were rocking, and her body shook. He made her feel like a young person, just as much as she made him feel like Abba. He loved uncomplainers like her. His spirits soared. "Emah" (mother), he directed. "You behind the door. Come here. Come, baby."

And then he blessed her. He ordered the Hebrews to find her a real room, and he gave her the name Amtullah Bat Yahweh, mother of Yahweh's kingdom.

156

"You can see I'm in love! Everybody can look at me and see I'm in love!" she would say in rapture. "Look at him! He's smiling at me!"

But the Hebrew Israelites weren't smiling at Leonard Dupree. When he arrived in Miami, they immediately passed the word that he seemed weak-minded, in his own world. Whenever he had come to class in New Orleans, he stared blankly into space. The messiah made a point of reminding Brother Samuel, the New Orleans elder, to shepherd Leonard at all times—to sleep with him, go to classes with him, work with him. Samuel didn't take the order literally, and five days before Tabernacles, he was out passing literature in Liberty City. Leonard was walking around the temple alone, checking out his new surroundings. Yahweh University was in session, and the children were chanting and showing off their knowledge. Men and women were dusting, cleaning, painting, making sure everything would be perfect for the feast. Sisters were mending robes and draperies in the sewing room. Other Hebrews were eating a hearty meal in preparation for the Day of Atonement fast at sundown. It is the Holy Day when Jews around the world ask forgiveness for their sins.

It was midafternoon. The messiah and Sister Judith had just left the temple when her oldest son came running after them in the parking lot. The strange one from New Orleans had started a fight. He'd pinned a brother up against the wall. They ran inside, where about fifty people had gathered near the sewing room. Word swept through the temple that the karate star had grabbed a pair of scissors. A seamstress named Zipporah tried to stop him, and Leonard supposedly called her a bitch. Thinking he was about to stab her, Zipporah screamed to Yahweh for help.

A man who heard the profanity ran over and tugged the scissors from Leonard's hand. A swarm of Hebrews managed to wrestle him to the floor in a full nelson.

The angry crowd mumbled that Leonard must be some sort of Uncle Tom spy, maybe an FBI informant, or possibly a Black Muslim infiltrator. They had sent him from New Orleans to kill the messiah.

"We can't have that happen!" someone cried.

What Leonard Dupree was, was just a confused kid from New Orleans, looking to walk closer to God.

They lifted Leonard up to stand before God.

"Do you want to hurt me?" the messiah asked.

"No," Leonard replied. "I just want to kiss your feet."

"So you think you know karate?" the messiah said. "We got brothers here who know karate." Elder Amri, the temple's karate expert, stepped forward to protect the sect leader. The crowd formed a circle.

"You want to challenge me?" the messiah persisted. "Challenge me and my brothers?"

"No," Leonard said.

"Kill him!" a spectator yelled. "He's the devil!"

Leonard tried to break free as the messiah moved out of the way. Amri stepped into the ring and squared off with Leonard, who delivered two or three quick jabs to the challenger's face. Amri fell to the ground. He never got off a punch.

"Get him!" the messiah's followers heard him say.

Several men tackled Leonard. Brother Job, the master barber, grabbed a metal object, possibly a car jack, and cracked his skull.

"Lock the doors!" someone screamed.

They continued to tear at him, even after he was helpless. They pulled down his pants, hit him in the groin, poked out his eye with a broomstick.

A horrified woman ran from the room. Brother Amariah hauled her inside.

No one, the messiah said, was allowed to leave the room. He told every man, woman, and child they were to beat the body and that way they would prove their love for God. All of them would be in on the murder. No one could become a witness. "Everybody take a hit," he said.

One by one, the blows shattered Leonard's skull, his ribs, and his bones as a rabid, shrieking pack bathed its hands in his blood.

Brother Jeremiah, Judith's fourteen-year-old son, grabbed a broken broomstick handle and struck Leonard four times. "I hit

him wherever I could because I wasn't the only one hitting him,"
Jeremiah recalled later. "There was a lot of blood, you know, from
his head and his skull cracked right here, and his body was bruised
up because as he got beaten. They took, kind of ripped his clothes
off and stuff and bruised up, you know, and his head was cracked
and blood everywhere and stuff. . . . I was a strong believer . . . and
if I didn't help out, you know, chip in, put in a little bit, I would be
looked at wrong and maybe confronted. . . . I did it because I thought
I wanted to do it."

Jeremiah's older brother, Solomon, landed just one blow to
please the messiah, because he didn't want to be looked at as an
outcast. "It was torture," he said later. "I can't remember vividly
if he made noise when I hit him or not. . . . I just did it because he
said it."

Deborah Vashti, the messiah's sister, stood just two or three
feet from her brother, then moved in to hit Leonard in the leg. "I
was told to," she explained. "If I didn't do it, then I would have—
he said we would all end up the same way. So if I didn't—I tried
to run out, it would be the same could happen to me. I would be
afraid not to."

Leonard Dupree's clothes were shredded and his mutilated
corpse was beaten with the broomstick, a chair, maybe even an
ironing board, for twenty minutes or more. It took time for him to
die. As followers waited for their hit, they watched the violent spasms
of death. A thirteen-year-old girl holding a baby saw Leonard's
contortions and heard his screams. Many of the children—up to a
dozen—hit him, along with everyone else—everyone except the messiah and Sister Judith. He was so sure of her loyalty she didn't have
to strike the body.

When it was over, people rejoiced and praised Yahweh. A few
stood quietly, ashamed. Later, they would break into tears over their
black brother.

Some of the disciples went to get rags, disinfectant, and water,
to wash blood from the walls and floor. A man drove a Ford pickup
to the back of the compound. The truck belonged to Brother Ahi-

nadab, a thirty-two-year-old Dade County sewer worker once known as Ernest Lee James, Jr. Someone ran to the food co-op for large plastic bags, and then they carried Leonard's body to the rear exit, rolled it in carpet, and wrapped it in the garbage bags. They tied the package with nylon rope and loaded it onto Ahinadab's truck.

After removing diadems and Star of David necklaces, four or five disciples became what the Hebrews called the disposal team. They shaved off an Israel bumper sticker from the rear of the pickup. They loaded fishing rods and a tackle box, to make it look as if they were going fishing. They put the body in the truck bed and headed off to look for a burial ground. One or two Hebrews sat in the truck bed, legs propped on top of the fishing rods and Leonard's body. Joseph Ahab, the former Willie Swift, would later tell the authorities that the disposal team stopped several times, driving for what seemed an eternity. As the sun went down, they came upon a wooded area with soft white sand, at the edge of a canal. There, they dug a long, narrow grave. Some people said that they burned Leonard's body or sliced off his head. Nobody but the disposal team knew for sure. And they would never say.

Back at the temple, Brother Joshua and other Hebrews went through Leonard's belongings. Everything—his wallet, his ID, some Muslim literature, his black belt—was burned.

At sundown, they stretched out to the east and prayed. The Day of Atonement had begun. The messiah would later gather his flock and remind them of the Azazel and the wilderness where the biblical scapegoat, laden with Israel's misdeeds, was sent on the Day of Atonement. The goat was a guiltless man who bore the sins of his people. Through his wounds they were all healed and forgiven.

"The Day of Atonement," he'd say, "is not just about lying down, stretched out to the east for twenty-four hours. It's not just about fasting and praying and asking Yahweh to forgive us. Yes, we do all of that—fast and pray and ask Yahweh to forgive us of all our sins for the past year—and then we grab the devil who caused us sin and share a goat. . . . Yahweh is so powerful he'll give you the goat. The Book says Yahweh requires blood sacrifice. Blood. And what can be better than the goat?"

160

"Don't have pity on the goat!"

"No, sir!"

"Don't say the goat look pretty!"

"No, sir!"

"Don't say, 'Ain't the goat cute!' "

"No, sir."

"The Book say the goat must be killed!"

The Feast of Tabernacles, the holiday celebrating autumn, came five days later. It was a happy time of confusion, reminding the Hebrews they were temporary pilgrims in America. By day, they shopped at the Yahweh grocery store and boutique, gathered for fellowship at the barbecue pit, and toured Miami's riot zones. Yahweh weathermen forecast America's latest floods and disasters. At night, they attended classes, dined lavishly at multicourse banquets of lamb and quail, and celebrated their messiah's divine mind. His children rushed toward him with open arms, almost sweeping him off his feet as they surrounded him in a magic circle of care. His mother, from Oklahoma, played the piano, and he formally introduced his biological kin—his mother, his sister, his children. And then he revealed more about himself.

"Did you know me when I was a Christian?" he asked. "Did you know me when I was a Buddhist? Did you know me when I was a Hindu? Did you know me when I was a whatever? . . . You never knew me. People who came out of my mother's womb don't know me yet. . . . They know there's something strange about me. They all know there's something peculiar about me. All who came from my mother's womb, all know that I'm a special child, I'm a holy child, the number one child, born first holy, given to God."

When he was born, he said, "They took me straight to the church and gave me back to God. I was dedicated. Yahweh put it in their hearts to do it." He was natural, he said, perfect, circumcised in his mother's womb and never cut by a doctor. "My mother wrote me a letter. 'You are my Jesus.' She said it."

The crowd, up to a thousand people, cheered wildly. Amtullah Bat Yahweh, mother of the kingdom, danced, sang, and shouted with the young people as the New Jerusalem Band played remakes of tunes by Stevie Wonder and Kool & the Gang. "This is Yahweh night and the feeling's right. Oh, what a night!"

Amtullah, the messiah's adoptive mother, didn't know anything about killings, about hunger, about beatings in the Temple of Love. She knew only she had found the messiah—and a home—in the slowly setting sun of her existence.

"He is my life!" she'd shout to the world and to heaven. "He is my life!"

23

The execution bound them together as never before. Finally, they were a real "blood family," chained to one another not only by word but by deed. "I'm your mother, I'm your father, I'm your sister, and I'm your brother," he had always told them. "We are one."

Mothers and fathers, not eager to make "gator food" of themselves or their children, buried Leonard's memory in a collective sea of guilt and forgetfulness. If the police ever unraveled the secret, the messiah could find fifty witnesses to testify that the bloody murder near the temple sewing room never happened. It was a lie, a vicious episode imagined by raving racists who wanted to perpetuate old myths about human sacrifices, about the frenzied killing methods of natives, of black men.

As Leonard Dupree's family and friends searched for him in vain, the messiah's appearances grew more royal and Christlike. A temple tailor sewed him an assortment of white robes made of fine linen and satin, bedecked with jewels and gold epaulets. His turban was held by a gold clasp. His adoring multitudes conformed, wearing gold medallions and white robes, plainer than his, sometimes embroidered with the letters YAHWEH.

When they gathered for class, the announcer warmed up the crowd. "Our savior is not only coming but he's here! The one who has put all Uncle Toms out of business, who set all black leaders down, who has put the preachers out of business. . . . An intergalactic phenomenon, the one who did it all . . . the king is here!"

To a thunderous roar, the warrior king with the keys to heaven strode briskly onto the stage. He seized the title Yahweh Ben Yahweh—God, the son of God—and announced a new recruiting drive, a formidable, twenty-two-city tour through Babylon, mother of harlots. Like the biblical Joshua, his followers would march around the walls of America, quietly at first, warning black people that the messiah had come to rescue them in a life raft. He would save them from personal turmoil, from crime and riots, from cops and bigger guns, from a cocaine culture that had grown so bizarre it produced its own television show. "I am the Heaven," he'd rant. "I'm right in time, on time, at the end of the white man's rulership, the beginning of your rulership!

"By the time we finish marchin' around the walls of Jericho and scream Yahweh loud enough the whole wall's gonna be tumblin' down! . . . The walls of America are gonna come tumblin' down! The walls against Yahweh shall come tumblin' down!"

It was June 1984. Favored followers arranged the logistics for the tour. They rented auditoriums, arranged for $25 million in insurance, and allotted $250,000 in expenses and leasing fees. The rank and file conditioned the temple's growing fleet of tractor-trailers, vans, trucks, diesel buses, cars, and a limousine, all valued at $2.8 million.

When the big day finally came, a caravan of two hundred Hebrews in white robes rumbled from the temple's parking lot, led by the savior in his white limo. They blew horns and yelled out the window, "Yahweh! Yahweh!" but the buses started breaking down just at the Miami city limits. Yahweh Ben Yahweh later joked how his wheels—even his own wheels—had rebelled against him. Mechanics fixed the buses, but there would be no quick fix for the human breakdown up the road.

As they crisscrossed Florida, stopping in West Palm Beach, Tampa, Orlando, and Jacksonville, the Hebrews streamed through neighborhoods with products and literature. Every night, they returned to the buses, their faces gleaming with sweat. A supervisor handed them the day's meal, usually a bag with an apple, an orange, and a pear—if they met their twenty-dollar quota. By the time the caravan reached Richmond, Virginia, Yahweh's nephew, Joshua, had become so desperate for the money that he grabbed a woman and took it by force. "She was scared," Joshua reflected later. "I guess I looked real rough. I had my head wrap on and my braids and

164

things were hanging, and she gave it to me and then I took off."
Five minutes later, the police arrested the teenager for strongarm
robbery. His mother came to the courthouse to help him, but Yahweh
Ben Yahweh exacted judgment. Leave him there, he told his sister.

They rolled on without Joshua, but the crowded conditions took
a greater toll. Hebrews slept in the grubby, aged buses, one so unsafe
that it would later drift off a California freeway, careening into a
light pole and leaving three people dead. At rest stops, the faithful
washed in sinks. Husbands, irritated by the celibacy rules, begged
women to get biblical in the shadows or in the trucks. The gossip
wires hummed with talk of "temple whores" hooking to bring in
the quota.

Everywhere along the way, the travelers tried to hide their grievances. For many, it was their first chance to see the United States,
and they radiated pride as they explained their self-love beliefs to
local reporters. Yahweh Ben Yahweh's entourage leafleted the cities,
placed ads of his upcoming lectures in newspapers, and positioned
the bus fleet in crumbling neighborhoods with double-locked doors
and iron gates. His Circle of Ten checked each auditorium for guns,
bombs, and listening devices, then stationed a white-robed member
at the door. In mosques, convention centers, and sports arenas, the
Hebrews danced and sang, and their celebrity prophet appeared as
a voice for the voiceless. "I am here to separate all of you!" he'd
bellow. His orations attracted audiences of thousands—professionals
and cops, street people and teachers—and across the country motorists and pedestrians would stare in utter amazement at the sea of
white robes. Police cars drew up to observe, but the cops had nothing
to do except avoid the challenging stares.

The longer the excursion lasted, however, the more the facade
cracked. Hebrews lied, cheated, and committed carnal knowledge
as they plodded through Raleigh, Washington, Philadelphia, New
York City, visiting satellite temples. All over the empire, discipline
was breaking down. Extension temples were ruled by elders who
thought they were Yahweh Two. Intoxicated by their out-of-town
power, they were skimming money, dressing in crassly commercial

clothes, and building Houses of David with many wives. Worse still, some elders were ignoring the messiah's taped messages—"leaning to their own understanding," just as the murdered hypocrites had three years before.

Newark was an especially turbulent spot in the firmament. The first elder, twenty-four-year-old Yehudah Israel, had gambled away his job in Atlantic City. He made a Jersey disciple pregnant, ran up a six-hundred-dollar telephone tab to Miami, and accepted a gift, a pair of silk underpants, from one of his lovers. Yehudah had become a gifted seducer of women and a self-professed Junior God. His fall from grace came in May 1984, after he and several worshipers, wielding brass knuckles, knives, and guns, tried to ward off an attack against their small storefront temple. Now, the same temple on South Orange Avenue was run by Neariah Israel, the one-time pro-football player fresh out of prison, again. Neariah preferred combat fatigues and expensive leather jackets to his white robes. He dipped into temple coffers to buy marijuana, smoking it in front of his congregants. By night, Neariah cruised New York City streets, speckled with porn theaters and prostitutes. His Jersey disciples whispered that a white wino had been sacrificed under Neariah's command in honor of Yahweh's recruiting trip. The messiah busted Neariah off his post and onto the tour.

With Yehudah and a third man, named Gabriel, Neariah formed a clique that became known as the Three Stooges. They distributed mangoes and cash to hungry followers. They chased women, went to movies, made their own money, did drugs, and, in bitter open defiance, ate pizza and other fast foods. One day in Atlanta, the last stop on the tour, the Stooges were eating Big Macs and french fries when suddenly Neariah shouted, "There goes Yahweh!" It had become a running joke on the recruiting drive: What would happen if the son of God caught them breaking his laws?

"Sure," Yehudah said and laughed. Neariah ran behind a Ronald McDonald poster. Gabriel, a handsome man with a silver tongue and a yearning for cocaine, hid behind a brick wall. Yehudah stood there, frozen, with a sundae in his hands. As he looked out the

McDonald's window, he saw the messiah in his limo, staring. It was too late to run.

When the caravan pulled into the temple parking lot in Liberty City, the weary travelers rushed for reunions with children they had left behind. "Oh God," Yehudah thought, as he hugged his four-year-old girl and eighteen-month-old boy. "They have potbellies like the kids in Ethiopia."

Many temple children were emaciated. Yehudah complained bitterly to the messiah, but he was like a hardened piece of clay that couldn't be reshaped. "It's not my fault," he said.

He proclaimed the tour a victory. Out-of-towners gravitated to Miami in record numbers, and satellite temples were established in thirty-eight cities. The FBI estimated national membership at five thousand, but the messiah knew that recruiting trips did not build a loyal, full-time following. They brought in part-timers who enjoyed the feasts and sympathizers who listened to his speeches because he said some things America ought to hear.

Still overstaffed with flamboyant and assertive men threatening his authority, Yahweh Ben Yahweh became determined once and for all to legislate mutinous conduct out of existence. Although the Bible made no provision for prisons, modern-day Israelites who were failing God sometimes were shipped to the temple in West Palm Beach, where a mean elder whipped them into a better understanding of Yahweh's commandments.

Back at headquarters, the messiah summoned his elders for a little group discipline. Jacksonville's Zerubbabel was ostracized as a playboy. He wanted to stay in Miami, to be closer to his biological family. His mother, the former Johnnie Mae Simmons, was sick. She was developing a spider body—slim legs and arms and a stomach growing so round that some Hebrews believed Yahweh had blessed her with a divine pregnancy. Johnnie Mae, long one of the temple's biggest contributors, was suffering from a malignant stomach tumor. "You're still an elder," the messiah said, ordering Zerubbabel to his knees. He said he was switched, alongside an elder from Chicago.

The Temple of Love was sliding into anarchy. The process of

167

keeping backsliders in line had turned into a spiral of violence as Hebrews, deflecting blame from their messiah, directed their anger toward one another. "Good people" and "bad people" were caught up in a kind of musical chairs game. Even small children were ordered to the prayer room to await Yahweh's lightning.

Enforcers pressed butter knives on the cuticles of "bad children" until they screamed. Parents tried to keep them from crying, for crying was a sign of weakness. There could be no weak link, not even a tiny one, in the Temple of Love. "I guarantee you, when we come out of the prayer room, you'll have control of your kids," the messiah warned mothers and fathers. "I used to hear prayer changes things. Now I KNOW prayer changes things."

The prayer room became known by many names: the pain room, the blue room, the room of understanding, and, from Ezekiel 37, the valley of the dry bones.

In New York City, children who ate too much or who didn't make collection quotas said their parents made them hold heavy books and kneel for hours. Sometimes, the grown-ups beat them with religious statues. After roddings, they snapped scissors in front of the kids' genitalia or rubbed pepper sauce into their wounds.

In Miami, Yahweh Ben Yahweh presided over the punishment sessions, though he didn't participate unless his family was involved. After accusing his teenage niece Bathsheba of adultery, he brought her before seventy-five congregants. She was stripped of her shirt and bra and made to turn around in front of the congregation. "And then he began to whip me with a stick . . . with a hook on it," Bathsheba testified years later. "Then I had to turn around and face him and be beat with a paddle."

He reserved his harshest treatment for his hungry granddaughter Athaliah, about nine years old. She had a history of taking oatmeal. One day, a classmate reported her for swiping a pencil from a school box. Yahweh strapped her to a whipping post in the cafeteria and left her there, depriving her of food for several days. "He got this big old like green stick," the girl's cousin Dinah later told the police, "and beat her across the head, you know, and everywhere else with it, and she wouldn't cry . . .

168

"He done starved her. . . . When he let her go, he tried, you know, like to plump her up because the feast was coming and her mother was coming down, but it still didn't help. She still had marks and bruises on her."

Parents were traumatized by the floggings, but they rationalized the treatment. They convinced themselves that it was God's way of building character and self-discipline. Dinah Israel's mother must have understood the emotional damage of marriage on her fourteen-year-old daughter. Dinah was scared. She told her mother she didn't want to have sex with the man. But fearing Yahweh, the mother told Dinah to do as told. "I got pregnant from the man and I was around three months," Dinah said, "And I lost the baby, [for] which I was glad." She wanted to leave Yahweh, but she couldn't see living without her mother. Many of her teenage brothers and sisters faced the same problem. They had grown up in the temple, receiving an option every day: work for Yahweh or be beaten with a rod, obey or get kicked out, and every day, driven by the threat of pain, they chose to work harder than the day before.

But by 1985 the first generation of temple children was coming of age. The summer tour had given them a taste of the real world, and the mean streets didn't seem as bad as Yahweh Ben Yahweh had said. They no longer believed in his miracles or his threats of disasters. The teenagers wanted out, even if it meant defying Abba.

24

Brother Solomon Israel, Sister Judith's oldest son, had provided the spark for the teenage rebellion. By the spring of 1984, he was sixteen and keeping secrets from Yahweh Ben Yahweh, secrets about what he ate and smoked, whom he touched and where. He was tired of getting punished for every little thing he did, fed up with panhandling and working for free. For years, he'd run the temple printing press, producing twisted hate literature and recording Yahweh's angry sermons on tape cassettes. He watched Brother Love turn from a humble servant into an arbitrary God with no taste for limits.

It was supposed to be the Temple of Love, Solomon said, "but you don't feel very much love there. . . . I don't feel loved."

Solomon knew a little of the outside world—what he learned in Yahweh, and what he could remember from his hazy, distant life before. So one day about eight months after the karate homicide, he called his grandma in central Florida. Without going into a lot of detail, he said he wanted to leave.

"If you're tired of it," she told him, "you can come and stay with me."

Quietly, Solomon slipped out of the temple and reclaimed his slave name, Freddie Gaines. He set his sights on a real education, a job, a little money, and some hope.

To Yahweh Ben Yahweh and Sister Judith, Freddie was a troublemaker, his defection no big loss. But it made his temple friends feel braver and wiser, and they formed secret alliances to compare notes on temple life.

Fourteen-year-old Gad Israel tried not to mix with the defiant teens. He kept to himself, studying, stamping prices on groceries, and avoiding open signs of disloyalty. Then, a few months after Freddie left, Gad called a relative. Send an airplane ticket, he said. "I'm coming home."

Gad was a light-skinned youth, only 4 feet 11 inches, 100 pounds. He wanted to be a track star and worried that his small stature and lack of skin melanin came from poor nutrition. "I missed growing up," he said five years later.

On January 29, 1985, a Tuesday he'd never forget, Gad waited for the guards to change shift. Leaving his mother, a sister, aunts, and cousins, he hitched a ride to the airport. He caught a flight to Denver and into the arms of waiting relatives.

"I'm free," he said.

Gad Israel was no ordinary temple teenager. He was Yahweh Ben Yahweh's grandson.

His defection sent shock waves through the temple. True believers tried to keep it quiet, but the resistance gathered momentum. Men joined the ranks of adolescent boys challenging hypocrisy in the compound. Among other things, they questioned Yahweh Ben Yahweh's sexual habits. Who was he to order them to lead a life of abstinence when he could have an unrestrained sex life with young girls?

In the beginning, his female followers had thought it was a tribute to be "chosen" by him. As one woman would tell the FBI two years later, he had come to her room for a massage, dressed in a robe with nothing underneath. She felt honored to be among his special favorites. She said the female disciples he picked for sex received special privileges, including lavish meals.

But as the women got younger and word of his flirtations spread, a few teenage girls who had sacrificed everything to him started to wonder aloud if they had sacrificed too much. For years, Sister Judith's daughter, Sarah, had hidden an ugly secret about her childhood in the temple, but now she told a small group of friends: she had been having sex with Yahweh Ben Yahweh since she was ten and a half. He showered her with jewelry, shiny shoes, and satin and silk clothing. She said he took her to the Hotel Alexander on Miami Beach, the pastel-pink corporate home of *Miami Vice*. At first, she unquestioningly followed him. The first sexual encounter had occurred after a midwife class, she told temple confidants and later the police. Then known as Moses, he ushered her to a private place in the temple. She said she had sex with him once a week or so for years. He told her it was their secret. He explained that as God's messenger he was supposed to teach women how to have sex. Assuming it was OK, she didn't tell her mother, a teacher, or any adult.

As she got older, though, Sarah felt pulled in two directions. By 1985 she was fourteen. She didn't want to betray Yahweh or her mother, but the pressure for sexual intimacy had begun to frighten her. "She got emotional, you know," Brother Joshua said later. "She started crying because she was afraid to tell me."

Sarah Israel was pretty and down to earth, and everybody liked her. As her story got around, rebellious members were thrown into a tizzy. Sarah's older brothers, Freddie and Kelly, came to the temple one day and confronted her. Tears streamed down her face as she told them. At her brothers' urging, Sarah finally mustered the courage to tell her mother. Publicly at least, Sister Judith said she didn't believe her daughter. Sarah refused to take it anymore. She became Lydia Gaines again. Kelly, the former Jeremiah who had left a few months before his sister, felt such revulsion for the cruelty of his adoptive father that he would agree to wear a body bug in the temple. For a series of FBI payments totaling thirteen thousand dollars, Kelly would wear his Yahweh necklace and pose as a true believer. He didn't feel he had much choice. It was either turn informer or kill Yahweh Ben Yahweh.

Years later, the messiah would flatly deny the abuse allegations, but at the time he didn't feel he had to dignify innuendo with any response. They didn't judge him. Only God judged him. He tried to give each defection swift action, but even his blood family began to betray him.

His nephew Joshua had become an unofficial leader of the brat pack, as loyalists called the angry teenagers. After coaxing Sarah to share her secret, Joshua started interrogating her girlfriends. One fourteen-year-old told him about a trip to a hotel with Yahweh and Sarah. After sending Sarah from the room to get something, the messiah summoned the other girl. "She told me she kissed him," Joshua related in a sworn statement. "Then he said, 'Now I want you to kiss me how you really kiss.' And she kissed him again. And then he said, 'Now I want you to kiss me how you kiss one of your little boyfriends.' And then after that he proceeded to put her up on the bed and have intercourse with her."

Tired of his uncle's lies, Joshua grew more outspoken and seditious every day. Almost seventeen, he sneaked out to malls and acquainted himself with the street life. He began to notice that people who looked like drug dealers were driving to the temple in fast cars, flashing gold jewelry, and tithing wads of cash. The drug culture "semifascinated" him.

In the spring of 1985, Joshua told his friends he was getting out. No way, he said, was he going on another summer tour, not after his uncle left him in a Richmond jail for a month, a day, and six hours on the first trip. Yahweh Ben Yahweh caught wind of the plot. The day Joshua was to leave, he was summoned to the prayer room with several co-conspirators. One boy had been planning to escape with Joshua. Three others knew about the plan. They were ordered to their knees.

"You can't leave, and if you go out you can't come back," Yahweh Ben Yahweh warned them. He lectured for a while, and as the speech wound down, he approached the plotters one by one. "He was putting his hands around their necks and choking them and then throwing them on the floor," Joshua said. "Then when he got to me, he put his hands around my neck and I was a little heavier than anyone else, and I did not realize he was trying to push me down, and he looked at me and said, 'Do you want to rise up against me? Stand up against Yahweh? . . . I will have your head cut off right now.' "

Joshua rolled on the floor and pretended to be dead. He and his friend Daniel waited in silence for three weeks, and then they fled.

Their escape offered a glimmer of hope to disenchanted grown-ups, who slowly realized their only option was escape. Having been ridiculed for excessive phone bills and sexual promiscuity, Yehudah Israel had run away for one day. But fearing the real world too much, he returned. He was demoted to bottle washer, banished to the warehouse where men and women slept in separate barracks, and barred from seeing his wife, Marlcah. She stayed in the temple with the couple's two children. Marlcah, Yehudah was now convinced, was one of Yahweh Ben Yahweh's wives.

One Saturday, Yehudah wised up in the room of understanding. He spent a few hours on his knees, slumped over crying, accused wrongly, he said, of stealing Yahweh's money and products. "He can't be God," Yehudah thought, "because he's telling us that the white man is the devil, that we're God's chosen people, and the dollar bill is no good and all this kind of negative thing. And yet they're gonna punish me because I don't have this white man's almighty dollar to give him? I'm a sucker."

Yehudah later went to pass the Word. He collected a little money, but he knew that to meet his quota he'd have to steal. He didn't like the idea of breaking into people's houses and stealing stereos, as he had once done. He came back to the temple, kissed his kids good-bye, and walked out as Lloyd Rodney Clark. He tossed off his turban, patted down five years of hair, and, hoping to find his father, wandered eight miles to his old house in Carol City. The house was vacant. Weeds were waist high in the yard. He went to his in-laws' house in Opa-locka, but they didn't offer him a place to stay. He slept in an abandoned car, and the next morning, he dialed his old number. His father had left a new address. Not knowing what to expect, Lloyd went there. When his father opened the door and hugged him, Lloyd was unable to restrain his tears.

A short time later, Johnnie Mae Simmons died. She was the mother of Zerubbabel, Lloyd's best friend, and like a mother to Lloyd. For years, she had suffered silently while the cancer spread. Lloyd went to her funeral. He was enraged that no one from the temple, not even Zerubbabel or any of her children, attended the service. "No one sent a card," Lloyd said.

When he told Zerubbabel over the phone about the funeral, he was grieved to his heart. Although Yahweh had taken Johnnie Mae to the doctors, Zerubbabel became convinced that his mom's tumors hadn't been treated properly. He held Yahweh responsible for her death. "One of these days we're gonna come to blows," Zerubbabel told Lloyd. "I'm gettin' ready to blaze."

"Brother," Lloyd replied, "give me a call when you're ready to split and I'll come get you."

Zerubbabel would eventually renounce the faith—four years after he had helped decapitate the Jamaican Aston Green.

Yahweh Ben Yahweh suggested to his flock that studs like Yehudah and Zerubbabel were worthless homosexuals or "doodoo brothers." How could they leave him? Why were they making it so hard on him? he would ask his followers. "I'm the Word," he raved. "I've taken you and made you something."

But more people left or dreamed of leaving. Sherah Israel, the girl from Yahweh Ben Yahweh's hometown, the one who had been overwhelmed by his supernatural powers, knew she'd get out one day. But now, with no one waiting for her on the outside, Yahweh was her only hope, and the cause of all her fears. She had a vague memory of the time he'd first approached her, during the temple's grand opening celebration in 1981. She was fourteen or thirteen. Sherah later told the FBI that Moses asked her if she liked older men. "Yahweh," Sherah quoted him, "made everything to have a pussy." He told her she had one year, but then, she'd have to give herself up to him. When the time came, she said he entreated her to watch as he had sex with her teenage roommate. Don't be jealous or scared, he told her. Since her roommate was enjoying it, Sherah would find it gratifying too. She had intercourse and oral sex with him and the roommate, and then the liaisons became a ritual. But on the summer tour, she had begun falling out of love with the messiah and in love with someone more her age. He was a nineteen-year-old former high school football star named Michael Mathis. His Hebrew name was Aushalom, and he served on the Circle of Ten. "He was the most handsome, physically appealing man in the temple," Sherah said. When she told the messiah she wanted to marry Aushalom, the lord of love was mad at first, though he later reluctantly blessed the union. Sherah would cling to Aushalom, as she had clung to Yahweh, for five years.

As betrayal threatened to tear apart the temple, Deborah Vashti

Israel sat through Yahweh Ben Yahweh's classes, so blinded by love she couldn't see the truth. For decades, she'd kept her brother's sexual secrets. She remembered when she was growing up in the wheat fields, the times he had violated two of his biological sisters. She also recalled the way he had molested one of his own daughters, long before he started his new religion. Everyone else in the Mitchell family denied the incest had occurred, and none of the incidents was ever reported to the police. But now, in the Temple of Love, there was even talk of her brother with her daughter. Old memories and more recent ones began to eat at her. More than two years had passed since Deborah went along with the mob, hitting the karate expert. Her brother's words still rang in her ears: "The ones that love me do that."

She still loved him, but she missed her family—her son, her daughter, her niece, her son-in-law, her husband, all of whom had abandoned her there. She listened as Yahweh Ben Yahweh called for curses on them. "You pray death upon someone," Deborah thought, "that means you want them killed."

Weeping in front of the congregation one day, Deborah Israel promised her brother she would never leave him. Two days later, she was gone. Her defection would turn out to be the biggest crisis in the temple's history.

25

After six turbulent years, the temple seemed to be collapsing under the weight of defection and death. Its Liberty City neighbors just assumed it would go the way of so many religions, which blazed across the landscape like comets, giving off a lot of heat and then disappearing as quickly as they came. But just as Yahweh Ben Yahweh was losing the monumental battle on the inside, he declared a miracle on the outside. He said he had become the most powerful voice in Miami's black community. Having succeeded so grandly in phase one of his revolution, he was escalating to phase two: he wanted to conquer white Miami.

Yahweh needed the establishment to survive. For not only was he facing internal rebellion, he was running into recruiting limits caused by the very same hate doctrines that had helped his tiny Miami commune grow into a national organization. The rumors of violent indoctrinations and steady run-ins with the cops were spreading across the country. They frightened off most black Americans, who thought that guns and swords were a lot less likely to bring on the black millennium than to bring on a pogrom.

So, anxious to expand his base, the messiah set out to carve a new image as a humanitarian savior. Bit by bit, he renovated his house. After stripping dissident men of power and title, he replaced them with more malleable followers. At headquarters, amicable, long-gowned female administrators, known as supervisors, were put in charge of secular departments from wine to telecommunications to the Yahweh school. Answerable to Sister Judith, the supervisors passed down orders to the rank and file and kept careful records of all their secular activities. Female angels began to join men in other domains. For example, they were spotted with increasing frequency pulling guard duty, standing at the temple front door with babies in their arms. It wouldn't take the women long to put a new, gentler face on Yahweh's kingdom. As they learned to make small, day-to-day decisions that the messiah had once made alone, Yahweh Ben Yahweh proceeded with his mission to gain acceptance and respect from the people he condemned: Miami's power structure.

How could the son of God—a mysterious, whiskered vision, aglow in head wrap and white robe, a hatemonger and possibly a murderer—even think about turning white Miami into Yahweh territory? It sounded impossible, but Yahweh Ben Yahweh, dissatisfied and supremely confident at the same time, was exactly the right leader in the right city at the right time.

For this was an age when a person didn't need a lot of respectability to become respectable in Miami. Along Brickell Avenue, bankers competed feverishly for the business of the most shady characters. Sometimes tellers counted their money on high-speed machines. And if they didn't have time to count it, they simply weighed it. Real-estate brokers sold million-dollar homes to people who paid with cash toted in cardboard boxes. Dealers sold fleets of luxury cars to phony corporations. Clothing salesmen peddled hot suits, discounted by a very modest ninety percent and still carrying pricey tags from Bloomingdale's, to a statewide corruption prosecutor, among others.

As the character-eroding flood of cocaine reached into all levels of society, south Florida had become the site of entrepreneurial business gone crazy in a swamp of money, crime, and corruption. People like David Paul, whose giant CenTrust tower dominated Miami's neon skyline, held forth at high-society cocktail parties, even though Paul's excess, greed, and shoddy management were driving his thrift into ruin. Miami was home to Miguel Recarey, Jr., a reputed organized crime figure turned Medicare swindler. By flashing cash, Recarey received invitations to gatherings at the Reagan White House. And it was home to Willy Martinez, a ponytailed boxing promoter who shuttled politicians and cops around in a Rolls-Royce with a mink floor mat. Willy's ultramodern, bay-front mansion was used as a set for *Miami Vice*. All of this, even while Martinez, a big-time doper, was committing Miami vice.

Yahweh Ben Yahweh saw no reason why he shouldn't be allowed

178

to soar with the Paul-Recarey-Martinez crowd. To gain entree, he
enlisted the help of gray-suit respectable Floridians. Among others,
he hired a white Jewish broker named Wally Lazarus, who recruited
his son David, fresh out of law school. Yahweh, it turned out, had
an uncanny knack for making white authority figures feel even more
comfortable than black ones. Never mentioning they were impostors
from the biblical synagogue of Satan, the son of God charmed Wally
and David with his personality and his pocketbook.

A short, friendly man, David began attending temple feasts and
enjoying himself immensely. He never saw a hint of violence or
negativity. The Hebrews even baked him a cake on his birthday. To
David, Yahweh Ben Yahweh seemed like a neighborly, agreeable
fellow, a guy next door. "There was nothing overbearing or fearsome
at all," the attorney said. "He's a fine man. He's honest. He's forth-
right. He's dedicated to the community. . . . The man is doing
incredibly good works."

David's main temple contact was Sister Judith. He found her
warm and funny, a champion of family values. She always kept her
word. "Very bright, on the ball," he said of her. "I can't imagine
her ever swatting a fly."

The attorney and his broker father advised the temple on commercial matters. They helped the Hebrews scour south Florida for
blighted, bargain-basement real estate. His minions passed out a
leaflet: Praise Yahweh Ben Yahweh, they said, for uplifting society's
blind, deaf, and dumb failures and instilling in them integrity, morals, and values. With Washington cutting funds to the cities, with
families and foundations strapped, churches broke, and government
in crisis, south Florida was hungry for a black messiah, someone
who could whip the ghetto into shape.

In October 1984, the Hebrews sealed their first big real-estate
deal, a rundown apartment complex in Hallandale, north of Miami.
A Soviet immigrant sold them the property for $135,000, the same
price he'd bought it for. He lost nothing except the headache of
maintaining property in the slums. The Yahwehs found a gold mine.
They quickly improved the apartments, gaining friends in the neigh-

borhood, and a short time later the temple locked into a bigger deal. In one of Liberty City's largest private sales ever, the Hebrews paid $975,000 for a ramshackle, four-story church. After changing into dead clothes, they began to caulk the windows, tile the floor, and install door frames, toilets, and a new roof. The messiah's landscapers planted flower gardens. His artists painted the building a celestial white from foundation to roof. The only ornamentation was the Tetragrammaton, the four Hebrew letters in heavy black paint that transliterated into Yahweh. In the ravaged neighborhood, torn by years of crime, fear, and neglect, the church stood out like a virgin's wedding gown. The Yahwehs renamed it the Yahweh Education Center.

The school was a landmark on Yahweh Ben Yahweh's road to respectability. The educational curriculum expanded as more teachers were drawn from the rank and file. Children got new schoolbooks. They still had trouble reading them, but the kids in the whitewalled classrooms provided Yahweh Ben Yahweh with the good image he needed to counter the bad. His tour guides shuffled business leaders through the school where dozens of children, sitting in neat rows, recited the alphabet for them: "aleph, bet, gimel, dalet." Small voices in singsong unison would chant the names of 152 nations in alphabetical order.

Yahweh was their shining prince, older and wiser than the sun, the moon, and the stars. "Super!" an eleven-year-old at a desk bellowed. "Yahweh Ben Yahweh is super!" It didn't seem to matter what was beneath the shell. One white landlord from Broward County would gush over the adorable, smiling, chanting, clean, well-behaved black children. They looked like little angels in their white robes and turbans, as they queued up for class, played in the school playground, or cheerily harvested vegetables from the temple's lush garden. This was the ghetto moneyed Miami hungered for: a docile, disciplined, unquestioning supply of labor whose leaders loved capitalism.

In sermons to potential business converts, Yahweh Ben Yahweh said he was turning the children into industrialists, hotel managers, and high-tech geniuses. He preached an anticrime message, complained about the wastefulness of welfare, and stressed the need for thrift and hard work: a pull-yourself-up-by-the-bootstraps gospel, à la Ronald Reagan. Yahweh heaped special compliments on Cuban Miami, whose brotherhood and entrepreneurial spirit made the Cubans rise above his people—black people—the "walking dead, zombies," he called them. The Cubans, the son of God said, came twenty years earlier with nothing, pooled their resources, and managed to buy Miami. On the other hand: "My people look like they're the lords of the trash pile. . . . They're sitting on crates and in the midst of garbage, like this is a wonderful kingdom. . . . It's amazing. And they walk so proud with no shoes on. They just wear anything. . . . They'll kill anybody who gets in the way."

The more the Yahwehs flexed their financial muscles, the more people at the conservative margins publicly praised the son of God's professed self-help philosophy. Even the KKK praised Yahweh. "We just want to let you know we've been reading your literature about Yahweh, the Hebrew Israelites," a Klansman told a Hebrew in Atlanta. "We agree that all black people in America should return to their own God."

Yahweh Ben Yahweh's magnetic effect, though, went far beyond white conservatives. Miami's most visible establishment black leaders, too, fell victim to the messiah's special methods of persuasion. In 1985 funeral director Athalie Range, a longtime activist/politician, praised the group's financial achievements and its orderly and disciplined efforts to clean up the ghetto. "Progressive," she called Yahweh Ben Yahweh's philosophy. Range never mentioned it, but her name allegedly appeared on a Yahweh hit list. No one in Miami, black or white, was ever quite sure if the black man or woman sitting next to him or her was a Yahweh. There were Yahweh police, Yahweh social service workers, Yahweh bankers, and Yahweh customs agents. Everybody would just as soon keep quiet about the rumors of head taking.

Barbara Carey, then the only black member of Dade's County Commission, put a positive spin on the Yahwehs' indoctrination techniques. "I don't think we [black people] do enough of that," she'd say. "You can't control everybody in an organization . . . I kind of admire him. . . . They're pooling their resources and working for black economic empowerment."

Support from black politicians helped the Yahwehs to survive. But an even more crucial backer was Sonny Wright, president of Miami's only black-owned bank. Reportedly, the Hebrews so impressed him that he personally arranged for a $409,000 loan so they could buy the school building. No payments were due for a couple of years. Wright kept his dealings with the Yahwehs strictly confidential. He would never comment publicly on the curious payment schedule or why, despite questionable finances, his Peoples National Bank of Commerce gave the group other perks, from immediate credit on thousands of personal checks donated to their very own banker.

In time, the Hebrews would boast that they owned Wright's bank. "We're getting rich!" Yahweh told them. "They better hurry up and get us out of this country before we just buy up Miami. . . . We buyin' up the vacant land in Liberty City now—not sayin' a word; just buyin' it."

With the police, selected businesspeople, and politicians behind him, Yahweh Ben Yahweh looked to the next level—clearly beyond paradise. He strengthened his stronghold on foreign soil with a worldwide communications system and postal service. Through this international network, his followers dispatched their messiah's writings and tape-recorded miasmas. His postal service could respond to tens of thousands of pieces of mail a year, and eventually the group would claim a circulation of five million sympathizers in hundreds of American cities and dozens of foreign countries. The wastelands of Ethiopia, the jungles of Guyana, and the American air bases in the Philippines proved to be rich recruiting grounds. Even a few white people started attending temple feasts. "One day," he said, "we'll have Yahweh's airlines."

In the fall of 1985, Yahweh Ben Yahweh ended years of secrecy and summoned a reporter to the compound. If he was aware of the rage still building inside the temple, he didn't let on. He cared about only one thing: he wanted the world to know of his rising fortunes. The Hebrew Israelite movement, he told *Miami Herald* reporter Susan Sachs, controlled fifty million dollars in assets.

His empire had become so far-flung it aroused the curiosity of the FBI, which opened a domestic terrorism case file. The feds suspected, among other things, the misuse of welfare funds, but they couldn't look to Yahweh Ben Yahweh for answers.

The son of God, with a master's degree in economics, claimed not to know the details of temple finances. He attended to spiritual matters, he said, and received no salary. His 18-karat Rolex was a gift from a devotee. He kept nothing in his name—no stocks, no bonds, no cash depositories, no bank accounts in America or offshore, numbered or unnumbered. Yahweh said he left money matters to Sister Judith, who shed almost as little light on things as her boss. Only a fraction of the temple's assets was held in the corporate name. Records for what Judith said was the group's only bank account suggested that the Yahwehs barely made enough money to cover their debts and expenses. Judith claimed the Hebrews survived on one million dollars a year in contributions, but she refused to reveal revenues from other Yahweh businesses: real estate, manufacturing, publishing, wine, grocery stores, and so on.

As more money rolled in, the financial picture grew cloudier. A federal district court judge declared the Yahwehs a bona fide religion, giving them an extra religious cloak that further insulated them from scrutiny. Inside the temple, insurgents like Brother Joshua had planted the idea of drug connections. A few Hebrews began to wonder if narco-disciples might be tithing dirty cash to the temple.

True believers wanted Yahweh to be rich.

"You don't want a poor God, do you?" he'd ask his flock.

"No!" they screamed.

"You want a poverty-stricken God?"

"No!"

They showered him with a treasure trove of jewelry and, as for themselves, they believed if they worked hard, God would reward them with a new apartment in a sect-run property. After renovation of Yahweh Education Center, the prayers of a few privileged families were answered. They were reunited in tidy apartments, and their children began to receive heartier meals. But property acquisitions didn't keep pace with Miami's Hebrew population, which the neighbors estimated at about five hundred. Of those, more than a hundred followers still vied for space in the Yahweh warehouse or under trees. About fifty trusted disciples lived in the temple with Yahweh. And around the fortresslike compound, the transportation fleet, which had advanced to fifteen diesel buses, five tractors, nine trailers, limos, and a host of vans, cars, and motorcycles, housed dozens of defrocked Hebrew men.

They removed bus seats, laid carpet, installed wood paneling, and hooked lights to generators. The men lived three or four to a bus. "If I had to go to the bathroom," Abyah Israel later explained, "I had to get up out of the bus and walk across the park." Abyah would soon be demoted from his elder's post. He would start to pull guard duty and condition the buses. Like other men stripped of power, Abyah fought to stay awake, make production quotas, and escape the messiah's erratic temperament, rarely saw his wife or kids and began to feel like an outcast. "It was just like I wasn't there," he said.

If zoning people, health authorities, or fire marshals questioned the unorthodox living conditions, the messiah was ready with a stock reply: before they criticized his housing, they should do something about America's homeless situation. In Miami, the homeless were camped under highway overpasses and in crevices known as Underbridge and Mudflat.

"At least we have a roof over our heads, at least we are warm and well fed," Yahweh once said, "but America has millions that she refuses to take care of."

Yahweh Ben Yahweh agreed to do what America wouldn't. He helped feed the masses. As an example of his new philanthropy, he dished up two free dinners for the whole city, but he still scolded his followers for eating too much bread.

His public charity, though, was helping to lift him into a higher orbit, and in October 1985, Yahweh Ben Yahweh celebrated his fiftieth earthly birthday in a cloud of heavenly achievement. For his second half-century, he had even bolder plans. He announced an interest in politics. For years, he had condemned "the white man's corrupt politics," saying "votes equals slavery" and calling presidential contenders like Jesse Jackson "false leaders." But Yahweh Ben Yahweh knew that having a little cash handy in a shoe box would make it easy to get politicians to embrace him. In Miami they'd take money from just about anyone, and it was OK because almost everyone did it, and there was no official law against it. And that was exactly what the Hebrew Israelites had in mind when they sent out a leaflet declaring they could swing a close election in Miami. "We have earned our right to exert power," they wrote. "It is a fact that Yahweh will decide who will be elected into political office. . . . The only way to be a winner is to stand on the side of Yahweh. . . . If you reject Yahweh, he will set up base men over you." Saying they owed an enormous debt to Miami, the Hebrews were willing to deploy on a moment's notice for whomever Yahweh supported, for whatever task his son dictated. They'd distribute campaign leaflets, lick envelopes, go door-to-door in slave clothes for votes, for free.

In their clumsy first attempts at politics, they invited two mayoral candidates—one a black educator named Marvin Dunn, the other, a Cuban-born banker named Raul Masvidal—to vie for the messiah's endorsement. The candidates later told similar stories about their campaign trips to the Temple of Love.

When they arrived at the compound, Sister Judith greeted them and gave them copies of Yahweh literature. They got a glimpse of the temple and the school. Masvidal thought the whole setup was tightly controlled and "very suspicious." Dunn, who had a degree in psychology, felt he could see through the children's smiling facade. Empty-eyed, they never made a peep. "They're neat and disciplined," Dunn thought, "impressive in the same way you'd be impressed by a Nazi youth camp."

After the tour, Judith walked each candidate to her office. "We would like to make a contribution to your campaign," she said. A gift from Yahweh Ben Yahweh.

She opened her desk drawer, pulled out a shoe box full of cash, and thrust a wad at Masvidal. The first thing that went through his mind was that he was being set up, caught in the act of accepting an illegal cash contribution.

"We can't accept cash," he blurted out.

"Oh," Sister Judith said. "I'm sorry. We didn't know that." She wrote a check for five hundred dollars, but then, as Masvidal headed back to the bank in his limo, he started reading Yahweh Ben Yahweh's lessons. He turned to his campaign adviser. "Luis," he said. "This stuff calls for the elimination of white people." Masvidal returned the check the next morning.

Dunn, who had a similar moment of reckoning, said he wouldn't take money in any form from a group peddling hate. "Blatantly racist," he called the Yahwehs. "Antiwhite."

Both Dunn and Masvidal lost the election. The winner, Xavier Suarez, would eventually go on his own campaign trek into the Temple of Love, the lair of Yahweh Ben Yahweh.

26

Emboldened by success, Yahweh Ben Yahweh issued new propaganda statements demanding that God's enemies bend their knees to him. In March 1986, he thundered from the pulpit about a man in the Bible who became king over the objection of his enemies.

"Whoever does not want me to rule over them, those are my enemies," he railed. "And if you are my enemy, you must die."

"Must be killed. . . . I want to see it. . . . I want to see your head come off personally. I want to see the blood seep from your vein, you know that jugular vein. I want to see it."

He made a gushing noise. "You won't be able to see it seep, but you'll feel that sword when it bites your neck. I can't wait to see that. What a pleasure! All my enemies killed with a sword." He called himself the executioner. His army was "Yahweh's killing machine."

When they weren't fixing roofs or toilets, the young soldiers on the buses studied the Bible. They pulled guard duty, rescued drug addicts on the streets, and took down tags of suspicious cars. They tried to interpret Yahweh's easily misunderstood—and sometimes not misunderstood—words. The men hung close together, gagging down peanut butter sandwiches at "Jesse's place," a trailer parked on the side of the compound. Jesse, the former James Louis Mack, was a former marine who took enemy rounds in Vietnam and now led Yahweh's royal guard. He limped around with a big stick, but he always smiled at strangers.

The messiah would sometimes appear on the porch and sit with the men. He promised to break open the seals of Revelation, the last book of the Bible describing an angry God who defeats the persecuting powers. Having breathed new life into them, he talked to them in a kind of hieroglyphics. He said he was leading them into new doctrines and rituals, and they waited patiently for him to solve the riddles of secret biblical words, symbols, passwords, grips, and initiation rites. Some of the men at Jesse's place came to believe his cryptic language was code for an ultrasecret suborder of favored warriors. They called it the brotherhood.

Aushalom Israel, the Circle of Ten member married to the girl from Oklahoma, thought back to an incident in 1985 when Yahweh Ben Yahweh made his soldiers go "under the sword." He had a disobedient brother on his knees, begging for mercy. Someone placed a sword at the man's neck, then pierced his skin. "Son, your life is in my hands," the messiah told the doubter. After sparing his life, Yahweh made Aushalom and every other man strip down to their underwear and walk under the sword. Aushalom wondered if it was a loyalty test for initiation into God's secret group. "It was said by Yahweh Ben Yahweh from that day on that we were some form of a brotherhood," Aushalom said. "We was not to speak about the incident whatsoever."

The men at Jesse's place, eager to prove they were apt disciples, sharpened their machetes with rocks. They called the knives their gardening tools, but most people in the neighborhood knew to get the hell out of their way. On occasion, a mugger or a thief would try to challenge one of them, and some of the Hebrews didn't hesitate to fight back. Mostly, though, they just talked—about women, dumb-dog preachers, and biblical blood sacrifices. Talk of spilled blood fired the imagination of Neariah Israel, always chasing girls, sometimes AWOL from his roofing job. "Anything that came out of his mouth was supposed to be the Word, it was God," Hasadiah Israel recalled. Neariah later said that to qualify for the brotherhood, a Hebrew man had to prove himself willing to execute Yahweh's laws, not only by spirit but by human flesh. They had to "show thyselves approved" by killing a white devil.

On a Sunday in April 1986, Liberty City's lawmen were put on alert after the body of a white drunk was found near the temple. Six days later, Neariah Israel decided to test his mettle for the brotherhood. After slipping into dead clothes, he wrapped a twelve-inch samurai sword in a jacket and went to hunt some devils.

It was a Saturday night. The bars in Coconut Grove were alive with yuppies, gay people, and bohemians. Neariah stalked them, waiting for one to drift apart from the crowd, in a parking lot or a dark alley. Finally, as he sat on a bus bench, he noticed a man staggering across the street—white, drunk, smiling, probably gay.

Neariah followed the man to the center of a three-story, U-shaped apartment complex. When he stopped at apartment number 9, Neariah walked up behind him. He felt invisible. He stood close while the man, fidgeting for his keys, unlocked the door.

The stranger stepped inside and turned to close the door. Startled, he stared into the cold eyes of the tall, calm black man.

"What do you want?" he asked.

"I'm an angel of Yahweh," Neariah replied, drawing the sword from its sheath. "I'm here in Yahweh's name."

There was a second man in the apartment, and bolting toward the bedroom, the man Neariah had followed cried out for his friend. The second man, in the bedroom, was putting on a pair of pants over his bikini briefs. He was skinny and balding, older than the first man.

Neariah rushed the older man, grabbing him and thrusting his knife once, twice into his heart. He screamed and stumbled, falling backward onto the bed. The younger man screamed for help, but none came. Neariah pinned him against the wall, stabbing him in the chest, in the stomach, until he stopped moving. Neariah placed the younger man, his keys still in his right hand, facedown on the bed, next to his friend. Neariah wondered if he should chop off their heads, as Yahweh had preached. But he knew he couldn't ride the Metrorail carrying a head. He wiped his sword on the bedsheet, stuck it back into its scabbard, and walked into the kitchen to get some napkins. He cleaned his fingerprints off the door and left. When he got back to the temple, he turned his bloody clothes in to the laundry, where the stains were washed away.

With the sun up, Neariah did not regret what he had done. He said he went to show Yahweh Ben Yahweh the killing sword. The messiah had often chastised Neariah for his arrogant and violent personality, but Yahweh didn't turn him in to the police or toss him out of the temple. That spring, the messiah's actions became more puzzling, his moods more bedeviling, and his rhetoric more volatile. He seethed with anger after police in New York City raided two Hebrew residences and accused the occupants of torturing children. How could white America possibly judge his people on the word of tiny blasphemers? he asked. Weren't these the same "monkey" lawmen who mercilessly ignored crimes against black victims and let the white suspects loose? Racial episodes stirred him to the depths. In New York, a white devil bragged to the world that he had shot four brothers who asked for five dollars. In Newark, the police killed a teenager. In Atlanta, elderly women were preyed on with impunity. "Let a black man shoot four white devil teenagers," Yahweh had told his flock, and "I don't think the black brother will escape indictment. And if another black man shoots some black youth because he said they were trying to mug him, they'll turn him loose."

As the days passed, Yahweh Ben Yahweh faced more indignities from within and more aggressions from without. In the poor and working-class neighborhoods where his big, white buses rolled every weekend, he believed drug dealers and haters of God's law were brutalizing his Hebrew saints. One female angel had been cut by an old lady with a rusty machete. Why was it that the police persecuted him, but when a "black snake" or a drug dealer harmed one of his righteous in a neighborhood dispute, they never took his followers' side? He was hemmed in on all sides by Yahweh's enemies. "Why do you hate me?" he'd ask.

At Jesse's place, Yahweh's soldiers were spoiling for a fight. The courageous Neariah quoted Yahweh's law on killing as a religious experience. If the brothers stabbed a devil from behind, in the kidneys, it would send him into instant shock and paralysis. It would make him easy to finish off. Rumors of a holy war began to circulate: a house bombing in Detroit, a stabbing in Albany, New York, a decapitation in Tampa, a phony worshiper sliced into 360 pieces and dumped into a garbage bin in Chicago. None of the out-of-town reports could be verified, but something, something big, was about to happen to make "the abominable and murderers and whore-mongers and sorcerers and idolators and all liars" bend their knees to Yahweh. All that the men had to do now was to wait.

27

On a Sunday afternoon in May 1986, the messiah's prophecy was fulfilled. The shaky truce between Yahwehs and unbelievers ended in a bloody clash in the little town of Delray Beach, Florida. South of West Palm Beach, Delray Beach is mostly middle class and white, with a growing pocket of poverty and crime. About a dozen Hebrew panhandlers were making their rounds there, on a street forgotten in the shadows of Interstate 95, when a thirteen-year-old neighborhood girl swiped a bottle of cologne from a missionary's pouch.

As the angry Yahwehs gathered, youths ran to the girl's aid. Swinging sticks, bricks, and two-by-fours, they encircled the outnumbered Hebrews and chased them, robes flapping in the breeze, down the street. Older residents, tired of the brazen young crack dealers overrunning the neighborhood, saw the fight. They sympathized with the Yahwehs.

"Stop, stop, stop," one resident shouted, as the kids attacked a seventeen-year-old Hebrew. "You're going to kill him."

Catherine Hendrix, a food service worker, called the cops. Alphonso Bonaby, a short, stocky carpenter and neighborhood pioneer, rushed to comfort several bruised and bloodied Yahwehs. When the paramedics arrived, they slapped on a few bandages, but the Hebrews were upset because they didn't think the authorities took their injuries seriously. The cops, who liked to avoid this part of town, were slow to investigate.

A Hebrew supervisor asked to use a neighbor's phone. "I'm calling my God," she said. She dialed the temple and allegedly told Yahweh Ben Yahweh, "We've been attacked."

The messiah told the supervisor to write down the address where the violence had broken out. After doing what he said, she gathered the flock and turned to the kind lady who let her use the telephone. "We'll be back," she warned.

At the temple, Yahweh Ben Yahweh waited for the bus carrying his injured children. No one had been seriously hurt, let alone killed, but the incident gave them the proof they needed. Real enemies *were* out to destroy them. "There was no justice done," said Michael Israel, who suffered bruises and a broken tooth. When the bus arrived about 9:30 P.M., temple midwives doctored the wounded with bulky bandages, big casts, slings, neck braces, and crutches. They rolled out wheelchairs. The media sensationalized and staged events, so they could too. A photographer shot pictures to show the world how Yahweh's chosen people had been persecuted and abused.

Yahweh Ben Yahweh summoned his followers for a briefing. Teary eyed, before dozens of congregants, he vowed punishment on the sinners. On a blackboard, three of his followers later testified, he drew a route to the neighborhood where the melee had occurred. Yahweh was no sissy God, he told them. It was time to keep the law. Delray Beach would perish in flames for its crimes, like Sodom and Gomorrah.

The messiah and his warriors talked over specifics. They would burn the whole block. They would check out the area, line up in front of the houses, get a signal from the platoon leader, and toss firebombs. The explosion would occur at three in the morning, the time of greatest rapid eye movement and deepest sleep. Anyone who tried to stop them would be killed. Abyah Israel recalled Yahweh making some sort of slitting gesture with an imaginary sword. "It meant to use it," Abyah said.

Ahinadab, the slightly slow-witted water worker who had helped dispose of Leonard Dupree's body, was tapped as the operation's leader. Ahinadab had a lively debate with Brother Neariah over the bomb recipe: the proportions of kerosene and diesel fuel to be mixed.

His avenging angels left to get some rest, and the next night, May 19, 1986, about fifteen men, in dark dead clothes, gathered with machetes and swords. Someone passed out latex gloves from Job's beauty shop, so no fingerprints could show up. They loaded the weapons and Bic lighters onto the floorboard of a light-colored van, along with ingredients for Molotov cocktails: a canister of fuel, white cloth to make wicks, and empty Yahweh wine bottles.

The men climbed into the van and a dark-colored Plymouth. The car had a temporary license in the right corner of the rear windshield. Paper tags were hard to trace. They drove north on the highway to Delray Beach, stopping in a secluded field near a cemetery, about seven blocks from the street they were going to bomb. Four or five men got out and started making the cocktails. After filling each wine bottle with a caramel-colored mixture of gas and fuel oil, they stuck a rag in the mouth of each. Suddenly, a police cruiser approached without siren.

"Shut up, shut up!" a Yahweh whispered, as the men in the van ducked.

Officers Craig Hartmann and Theresa Bradley, on their way to a low-income housing project, crept to a stop behind the two vehicles. They beamed flashlights onto the bearded black men in ski caps. "Jamaicans or possibly Rastafarians," Hartmann surmised. Maybe a drug deal going down. The black men gave the cops a dead stare. The officers began to pull away. It was Tuesday, 1:41 A.M.

Hartmann and Bradley drove half a block or so, then turned around, approaching cautiously. They noticed that the hood of the Plymouth was up. As they climbed from the squad car, they smelled gasoline. One of the men stepped from the shadows and greeted the officers. Yahweh Ben Yahweh always had taught them to smile in the face of the devil and say nothing.

The Hebrew explained they were having car problems. They'd run out of gas or something. Another man, tall and muscular, turned to Officer Bradley, a rookie just out of the academy. "Do you have a funnel?" he asked.

Hartmann asked whose car it was.

"It's mine," someone replied. He was about 6 feet 2 inches, two hundred thirty pounds, with a beard and a wool cap. He picked through his pocket and handed Hartmann a New Orleans car registration with the name Alvin Murphy. He said he had just moved to Miami and wasn't sure of his new address.

"What are you doing in Delray at this hour?" Hartmann asked, jotting down the tags for the car and the van.

"Visiting friends," Murphy replied.

Who? Hartmann persisted.

Murphy couldn't remember their names.

Hartmann reached for the radio on his belt and gave the dispatcher Murphy's name. He asked for a check on 260 DXT—the van tag. Suddenly, he heard a noise from inside the van. It sounded like metal clanking, as if someone had dropped some tools or something. Hartmann shone his flashlight on the van and realized there were more people inside, maybe three, four, or five, plus the men standing outside. When Hartmann stepped forward to get a better look, two of the Hebrews drew near him.

He was nervous as hell. Here he was, a white cop in a high-crime black neighborhood, with one white rookie female, up against at least eight big black guys, with no backup. Delray was short of patrolmen that night. What if they got into a pitched battle with machine-gun-wielding Rastas? "We were a little outnumbered with .38 revolvers," Hartmann explained later.

The officers decided the best thing to do was to get out of there. Hartmann handed Murphy his ID. "You're free to go," he said.

Neariah Israel couldn't believe how lucky they—or the cops—had been. "If that white officer would have touched the van," he said, "he would have been knifed."

The men studied the maps and, under the cover of night, made their way to the mission. It was about 2 A.M., and the street was dead. They parked, checked for drug sentries, and fanned out in front of the small, concrete-block houses, about ten in all on both sides of the street. They lit the wicks, and at a signal, hurled the bombs. Glass shattered. Bedroom curtains burst into flames. The Hebrews strode fearlessly from house to house, pitching bombs. Screaming residents jumped from flaming beds.

"Let's go! Let's go!" a Yahweh hollered, as several houses exploded into flames, crackling and spewing smoke into the street. A couple of the bombers walked calmly to the getaway vehicles.

Others ran frantically. One dropped his sword. They almost left another man behind. They praised Yahweh as they made their escape. The only problem was, they had bombed the wrong block. Instead of striking at the hoodlums who had beaten them, they torched the homes of the good people who had come to their rescue. They were one block off.

Catherine Hendrix, the woman who had called the cops when the Yahwehs were attacked, heard the explosions and saw flames licking at her bedroom window. As she leaped from bed, she looked over at the crib of Marva, her nine-month-old girl. It was on fire. A Molotov cocktail had landed right in the middle of the crib, splattering Marva with burning fuel and broken glass. The mother was sure the girl was dead.

"Grab the baby," she hollered to her husband, Marvin. After snatching Marva from the crib, he ran to the next room, where his two older girls were screaming. The room was on fire. "Run through the fire," the mother commanded her fourteen-year-old daughter.

With Marva in his arms, Marvin walked through flames to save his middle girl, curled up in terror on the side of the bed. He cried for her to jump through the fire. She couldn't. She was too scared.

Finally she jumped, right into the fireball. Her father reached into the flames and picked her up, smothering the fire on her legs.

Together, the Hendrix family crawled to the front door and out of the inferno. Marva, the most seriously injured, had burns from dimpled face to pudgy thighs. They watched as fire gutted their home of eight years.

Down the street, a Molotov cocktail had exploded next to the head of Alphonso Bonaby, the man who ministered to the Yahwehs when they were attacked just days before. His house was now in flames. After helping his wife and seven kids get out, he grabbed a garden hose and tried to douse the fire. But almost everything he owned was engulfed by fire and smoke.

In the burning street, people huddled in their nightclothes, tempers flaring. They knew who did it. "They came back," one woman said.

Engine and rescue trucks pulled to a stop on Southwest Fourteenth Avenue and First Street. They choked blazes in four houses and a couple of front yards as paramedics worked on the Hendrix children. One of the first cops to arrive was Craig Hartmann. "My God," he thought. He walked up to Sergeant Robert Brand, thirty-seven years old, known on the force as Pop.

"Hey, Pop," he said. "I think I had the people who did it. They were on Tenth Avenue about an hour ago."

While rescue workers evacuated the block, the detectives returned to the spot where Hartmann and Bradley had earlier confronted the black men in ski caps. Investigators took samples of gasoline from the sandy soil, and at the fire scene they collected thirteen Molotov cocktails, three charred Bic lighters, and a two-edged ceremonial sword with fish and serpent markings.

A police check revealed that the van was registered to a Levi Hubbard, a Hebrew elder in Saint Petersburg, Florida, also known as Leviticus Israel. And Alvin Murphy, the man who had presented his ID to Officer Hartmann, was a former New Orleans lawman. After quitting his job, he'd become a full-time investigator for the Temple of Love.

People in the bombed neighborhood waited for a second attack that never came. With no insurance, they camped in Red Cross shelters. Sympathetic friends rallied to ensure they were not alone.

The Hendrix girls' burns would heal, but cherished parts of their childhood—family photos, school rings—were lost forever.

Alphonso Bonaby, unable to forget that harrowing night, went to the temple to talk to Yahweh Ben Yahweh. "Do you know who burned down my house?" Alphonso asked.

No, the son of God said coolly, he didn't know anything about it.

Shortly after the bombing, Yahweh penned a letter to the Bonabys and the Hendrixes, enclosing a five thousand-dollar check to each family. "Because of your past support," he wrote, "I must do what I can in your time of need. Our private investigators have discovered that the people who attacked us are known drug addicts, thugs, and hoodlums who have victimized many people in the Delray area before attacking us, and nothing was ever done about it. We have learned that the same people who attacked us are responsible for firebombing those of you who came to our rescue while being attacked in that block. . . . We will do all we can to help you and all of our people across America who are being destroyed by the evil and wicked people of this earth. If you would be so kind as to give us the names of all the people on 14th Street whose homes were damaged, we would be very happy to come in and help them rebuild and paint and restore their homes to a better condition than before it was bombed. Yours in peace and love, YAHWEH BEN YAHWEH."

He was back in the headlines again, staunchly disavowing any connection to the bombing. In a tiny, yellow frame hideaway fifty miles south of Delray Beach, Yahweh's defectors heard about the firebombing on the evening news. All the old demons came snarling back.

28

For months, recovering Hebrews had congregated in the yellow safe house belonging to twenty-four-year-old Ricky Woodside, the former Zerubbabel Israel. Brothers met sisters they once cajoled into sex. Men exchanged sad looks with boys they had beaten. They tried to avoid talk about the Temple of Love. Some ex-Hebrews quickly snapped out of their hate-the-world mind-set, but for many of the people at Ricky's house, the journey back wasn't easy because all the things they'd left behind—families, faith, guilt—were still out there.

To fill the gaping holes in their lives, some defectors turned to Jesus, some to Allah, some to Pabst Blue Ribbon. For Sister Judith's sons, Freddie and Kelly, a religious addiction spun into a crack-dealing habit. With opportunities faint, limited education, no job, no money, no Big Brother, no parents to fall back on, no social service agency or child psychologist laboring to keep them out of harm's way, it wasn't surprising that ex-Hebrew teenagers flirted with street crime and drugs, which drifted over Florida in the 1980s like an Oklahoma dust storm.

Ricky tried to rescue his confused teenage brother. "Learning," Ricky said later, "how to love all over again." He boosted the spirits of other defectors and helped them financially. "I don't know how to deprogram myself," he explained. "After being brainwashed for so long . . . it's almost like you have—you're not a person. You have no heart. And I had to bring myself back to life, you know."

He tried singing, but the tears kept falling. He kept thinking about what a "likable person" he once was. Ricky had never hated white people. His had been one of the first black families on the block, and they always got along with the neighbors. Now his wife and a baby boy were out of reach in the temple. His older brother and younger sister had important roles in Yahweh. Ricky was confused, angry, and lonely. Nothing made a man feel lonelier than murder. In his eyes, it was Zerubbabel Israel, not Ricky Woodside, who helped slice off the head of the hypocrite Aston Green. When news of the firebombing broke, Ricky froze at the familiar MO. The terrifying image of that fall afternoon in the east Everglades raced through his mind. The Yahwehs had not changed at all, he thought. Ricky had made Molotov cocktails in Yahweh, and so had his former frat brother Lloyd Clark.

After Yahweh, Lloyd hadn't turned to drugs; he had become a possession junkie instead. In the thirteen months since leaving the temple, he'd bought clothes, stereos, even love, simply because he could. He had tried to save his children from Yahweh because he feared they were suffering a world of problems, like kids growing up in war zones. He didn't want them to be like the eleven-year-old Hebrew boy who drew apocalyptic pictures of tornadoes lifting blasphemers to heaven. Or like Yahweh Ben Yahweh's granddaughter, the girl he had locked up. Out of Yahweh, Athaliah Israel wouldn't cry for a long time. She would tell stories about bodies stacked in the temple. Lloyd tried to kidnap his little girl Keturah, but he brought her back to the temple because she had cried for Emah, her mother. Lloyd had received threats, but he tried not to let them bother him. Except for his children's, he never wanted to see another white turban again. He studied nursing, read books about cults, and began to fall in love with a student nurse, a white woman.

Then came the firebombing. Old feelings for his wife and kids surged back. He felt guilty about the burned baby girl. He had nightmares about what happened to the affectionate Aston Green. At the least, Lloyd had watched a near-fatal beating, and done nothing. Didn't that make him just as much a murderer?

He knew he had committed other indictable offenses, but implicating himself didn't seem to matter anymore. Lloyd would have preferred to see Yahweh Ben Yahweh dead. But seeing him in jail would do.

"Fuck this," Lloyd thought. "Somebody has to say something and put an end to this shit."

Days after the arson, Lloyd drove down to the windowless FBI headquarters on Biscayne Boulevard. He turned to the receptionist. "I need to speak with an agent."

"What's it in reference to?"

Lloyd hesitated. He realized he didn't trust the feds. "Yahweh," he finally said.

As he thumbed through a magazine, Lloyd's mind flashed back to what people on the street had told him: that the lawmen had never gone after Yahweh Ben Yahweh because he was either a government informant or in the pay of politicians using him to whip up support against black people.

About ten minutes later, a black man, about 6 feet 6 inches, in his mid-thirties, came to the waiting room in a three-piece suit. "Cute," Lloyd thought. "They sent a brother."

Before saying anything, Lloyd had a question for the fed. "Does Yahweh work for you?"

Special agent Herbert Cousins, Jr., who'd been working on the case for six months, smiled. He wanted to know what Lloyd had heard.

"Someone told me Moses Israel had some ties to the FBI or the CIA," Lloyd told him. "They knew he was talking militant—kill the devil, kill whitey talk—and somebody, the CIA, somebody, wanted to get some powerful black man who talked that talk to round up all the so-called militants in Miami so that when something broke out they would know where these militant people are, and they'd corner them off and keep them at bay."

Cousins, a former basketball star on Panama's Olympic team and a rising star in the bureau, assured Lloyd that Yahweh didn't work for the FBI. The two men walked into a freezing interrogation room. There, for four hours, Lloyd tried to explain his bizarre life of terror in the temple—how in five years he had changed from a vulnerable teenager seeking a spiritual niche into an angry warrior in God's army, spewing violence. He talked about murder, assault, child abuse, rape, fraud, slavery, and hate, in an understated way, not at all in proportion to the horrors he described. Minimizing his involvement, Lloyd said he feared for his life and his children's. He named names of Yahweh strongmen primed to kill. Before leaving the bureau with a code name, El-Indio, he warned that if Yahweh wasn't stopped, the bloodbath was going to get worse. And it did.

As the FBI's domestic terrorism squad reactivated its probe, Yahweh Ben Yahweh died again. He chucked his social security number and officially changed his name to God, The Son of God. He presented his followers in forty-five cities with an account of mortal death angels flying forth to cleanse the cursed world in preparation for New Jerusalem. God, he said, had rained firebombs on a neighborhood of sin, and now was raising up angels on the streets with guns. In a missive entitled "Yahweh Kills Blasphemers," he told of an unbeliever who shouted "Yahweh sucks" in front of the temple. When he grabbed his private parts, a gunman suddenly appeared. "The last thing the blasphemer heard was 'You don't talk about Yahweh like that.' POW! POW! POW! POW! POW! POW!" He was "shot in the neck and his penis was shot completely out," Yahweh wrote. "They shot all of his private parts out and killed him. . . . After he was killed, voices rang out of thousands, 'That's what you get for talking about Yahweh like that.' "

The killing happened in broad daylight, and the angel went free. "Yahweh has angels everywhere," he said. "We serve the true and living God. If you don't like Yahweh, say nothing, or Yahweh will cause one of his angels to kill you."

And he did. Bodies showed up on Biscayne Boulevard, once Miami's main drag, now a collage of cheap motels, drive-by crack houses, and comfortless hangouts for scam artists. The first victim, Clair Walters, was a Vietnam vet suffering from Agent Orange. The night after the Delray Beach firebombing, he had been sleeping in the abandoned, graffiti-scarred Aloha Motel when someone sliced his throat. The killer took nothing but the vet's left ear. Beside him was a Bible, a toothbrush, some clothing, seventy-two cents, and the remains of his last supper: an empty can of potted meat and a gallon of grapefruit juice.

One month later, just a few blocks away, an Indiana drifter was stabbed in the back. James Lee Myers, age thirty-one, stumbled through weeds and grass, trailing blood, pleading for help. He never got it. He fell dying, with his head against a palm tree. A male hooker, working the low-rent side of paradise, heard James's whimpers and called the police. They were just a few minutes late. The cops noticed slice marks on James's right ear, but the Dade Medical Examiner's Office didn't make much of either homicide. Bodies came in there every day, bloated, burned apart, and a whole lot just quietly dead. Dr. Joe Davis, one of the world's leading experts on serial murder, was so occupied with other bizarre deaths that the lawmen joked about him doing autopsies with one hand while eating lunch with the other.

Yahweh's angels, it seemed, had expanded on the biblical eye for an eye. At Jesse's place, a few men witnessed ears, one in a plastic bag, another in a little jar. Neariah concluded that to win admission to the brotherhood, a warrior had to bring back a white devil's ear as a sign of a confirmed kill. The sect leader himself, Neariah later testified, presided at the brotherhood meetings, where the killers told their stories. Abyah Israel, who had reluctantly participated in the Delray Beach firebombing, was working at the manufacturing plant one day when the messiah himself, flanked by two men, dropped by with a piece of evidence.

"Hey, son, come here," the messiah said, summoning Abyah from the mechanic's shop. "Looka here."

Abyah said he saw Yahweh holding a small brown bag. He opened it and pulled out something. "You see this?" the messiah asked.

Abyah just listened. He didn't ask any questions.

"See this hairy sucker here?" Yahweh repeated.

It was an ear, a white ear. "Just a normal ear," Abyah thought. "A devil's ear."

"Oh," Abyah said, sort of astonished. He didn't know what to say. Yahweh Ben Yahweh thought his apostle hadn't acted grateful enough. The messiah told him he was supposed to rejoice.

Abyah, fearing they might turn against him, pretended to enjoy the sight because Yahweh obviously did. "Well," Abyah said, "praise Yahweh!"

Yahweh put the ear back in the bag. Abyah thought he heard him tell a follower, "Burn it."

Abyah decided then that it might be time to leave Yahweh. He knew things weren't right, and he'd come to the point he was even willing to leave his family. But Yahweh, who had eyes and ears everywhere in the temple—after all, he could see through walls—found out about Abyah's plans. He stayed on and kept his mouth shut.

Yahweh couldn't stop talking about white devils. In August, he channeled his anger onto paper again. He lionized Neariah Israel, who was shot in the thigh one Thursday night by faceless white terrorists. "The whites of America are challenging our God Yahweh to show forth his power to protect us against the black man's common enemy," he wrote. He quoted Jeremiah, the radical prophet of the Bible: "For this is the day of Yahweh, god of Hosts, a day of vengeance, that he may avenge him of his adversaries. And the sword shall devour and it shall be satiated, satisfied, and made drunk with their blood."

Neariah was invincible, proof of Yahweh's superhuman envoys. He cultivated a following, sharing books about Masonic rituals with his brothers and explaining that God wanted them to change their MO. If they cut a tongue, instead of taking a head or a finger, the police would think the Mafia had done it. Then, as Metro-Dade detectives joined the FBI in a widening Yahweh murder investigation, the holy war shifted to the Miami River, but this time the victims weren't missing their ears or any other small appendages. One victim was a homeless Cuban refugee with a tattoo of a flower-draped casket, the second a street corner preacher wearing a Star of David T-shirt. Lyle Bellinger, a Jews for Christ convert who'd been trying to cleanse his life of the evil spirits he'd worshiped for twenty years, was stabbed through the star, in the heart. If Biscayne Boulevard was Miami's Sodom and Gomorrah, the river was its hell on earth, a five-and-a-half-mile crime scene that in 1986 was home to dopers, rusting freighters, and headless chickens left over from Santeria ceremonies. Just as prostitutes found a niche on the boulevard, young bandits in hooded sweatshirts preyed on drug dealers working the river. Even some of the cops patrolling the river were crooked.

The good police were finally catching on, not only to the bad river cops but to the excessive number of poor white men getting stabbed in Miami. The police couldn't figure out why. They called homicide victims living on the fringe "rickets" or "disposables." Usually, they got killed for one of three reasons: money, sex, or fear. The cops ruled out money and sex. That left fear. They put out a call for the street life to report any unusual happenings, but in the summer of 1986 even the bums and the hookers were frightened.

On Saturday, September 6, one drizzly morning after the Star of David murder, a patrol cop radioed from the parking lot of the Tepee Lounge in South Miami: "We got a homicide; the guy's missing an ear." In fact, Raymond Kelley, a sixty-one-year-old master mechanic, was missing more than one ear. He was missing one and a half ears. His body was sprawled across the front seat of his Chevy Malibu, next to some miniature bottles of Jack Daniels and Smirnoff vodka. His spectacles were on and his Timex was still ticking when a crime-scene officer looked down at the pavement. He saw what looked like the ear. He got excited and summoned his fellow officers, who all leaned over to get a closer look. Homicide Detective Danny Borrego placed the ear in a little paper bag and handed it to another detective. "Maybe we can lift some prints off of it," Borrego said, only half-joking.

As the police pressed the search for a serial ear killer, possibly a deranged Vietnam veteran collecting trophies, money mysteriously flowed into the temple at a faster and faster clip. Under the watchful eyes of federal lawmen, Hebrews made deposits and withdrawals of up to $250,000 a month, handling almost three times as much in cash donations as before the murder spree. Prosecutors wondered if some foreign government might be encouraging a U.S. terror spree.

The FBI in Miami, meantime, was host to another ex-Hebrew, Ricky Woodside, who turned himself in at the urging of his buddy

Lloyd Clark. As the defectors healed, they were growing bolder. "I am afraid," Ricky said, "but I think that right is right and wrong is wrong." Without a lawyer present, he confessed to a role in the murder of Aston Green. He also admitted he was one of three men who tried to kill Eric Burke in his Liberty City apartment. Ricky knew he could face some jail time, but he was more afraid of the secrecy and guilt that had imprisoned him for five years. "I don't think the fear will ever cease," he said. On a Friday afternoon in September 1986, Ricky met FBI agent Cousins and Metro Detective John King at a Holiday Inn on Biscayne Boulevard. He led them to Aston's decapitation site, a dead end on the fringe of the Everglades. The area had been transformed by five years of housing growth and an invasion of alien melaleuca trees. Downplaying his part in the killing, Ricky blamed two accomplices and Yahweh Ben Yahweh. "Anybody who brings harm to Yahweh or his servants deserves to die," Ricky quoted the messiah. "Go buy a sword and cut the bastard's head off."

Ricky also told the investigators he heard about a plan to kill five black leaders should something ever happen to Yahweh Ben Yahweh. Among the people on the hit list: the Reverend Jesse Jackson, the Reverend Louis Farrakhan, and Athalie Range, the local politician who claimed to be a big Yahweh admirer.

The lawmen had Ricky dead to rights on a homicide charge, at least as an accessory, but they didn't lift a finger. They saw a bigger picture, and before deciding what to do about him, they wanted more evidence against other Hebrews. What the police were looking for fell right into their laps nine days later. It was another ear case.

Death angels cut the right ear off a hot-tempered garbage man named Cecil Branch. He had blasphemed a Yahweh girl soliciting at his mother's house. Big Man, as the 258-pound army vet was known in his neighborhood, shoved the girl and chased her and some other Yahwehs down the street. She took down what she thought was Big Man's license number and gave it to the temple authorities. Two weeks later, the killers drove to Big Man's one-room cottage in Coconut Grove and ordered him on the floor.

"Well, I'll do what you tell me to do," Big Man said as the

killers turned up the TV and rolled him on his back. "My mama didn't raise no fools."

They gagged his mouth with a floral pillowcase, bound his hands and feet with the matching bedsheet, and stabbed him twenty-five times.

Unlike the other ear victims, Big Man was black, but then, on October 2, an ear killer returned to Biscayne Boulevard to stab a sixty-eight-year-old white man. His name was Harry Byers. He'd been sleeping on a park bench. "That makes five ears that we have," Detective Borrego said. "We have something here."

Dr. Joe Davis put together a chart showing similarities down to the minutest detail, even to the Benson & Hedges cigarettes found at two of the crime scenes. But instead of telling the public, the cops thought it best not to say anything. The tourism board always worried about the effect of murder on tourism. In the hot and humid summer and fall, there weren't a lot of domestic vacationers in Miami, but the weather never stopped Europeans or thrill seekers, who thought being shot at in Miami would be an adventure. Nor did it stop refugees from Port-au-Prince getting the chance to earn two dollars an hour.

A week after Harry's body turned up at the morgue, a young man named Hezion Israel appeared at a hospital in North Miami. His bloody hands were wrapped in homemade tourniquets. He explained that a crazy man waiting for a bus had tried to cut him for no apparent reason. The knife-wielding man, Hezion said, was dirty and didn't speak good English. Hezion told the police he grabbed the knife in self-defense and thought he might have hurt the man. The explanation left out a few details. Hezion had stabbed him eleven times, in the chest, the back, the side. He thrust the blade in with such force that it cracked five of the victim's ribs. "Overkill," the medical examiner called it.

Hezion suffered deep lacerations on his fingers, but he had no other injuries. It looked as if he'd gripped the knife so tightly that his hands slid down the blade while he plunged it into the victim. Surgeons called such wounds "pumpkin fingers."

Hezion, the former Brian Lewis, was an honors college student.

He gave up a chance to go to law school for his new religion. He came from a loving home, was a talented saxophonist, and a bright person almost nobody forgot. The victim, Reinaldo Echevarria, was a man few people remembered. A skinny divorcé in his mid-forties, Reinaldo came to the United States on a 1965 freedom flight from Cuba. A onetime bank clerk, he sometimes slept in cars. He had a rap sheet for petty crimes, and the cops found him a nuisance. At his funeral, there was only one spray of flowers, and his relatives told the Dade County state attorney's office they didn't care if the murder was pursued or not. So, overlooking the eleven holes in Reinaldo's body, prosecutors closed the case. Justifiable homicide.

The son of God and his holy executioners had risen above the law.

"Who's our president?" he asked.

"Yahweh!"

"Who's our governor?"

"Yahweh!"

"Who's our mayor?"

"Yahweh!"

"Who's our leader?"

"Yahweh!"

"And who do we follow?"

"Yahweh!"

He had come to believe he ruled over a sovereign city-state called the Nation of Yahweh. It was a theocracy, with laws superior to those of the United States and other nations. He told his followers he was the Omnipotent One who created the seed in his mother's womb, the alpha and omega who originated the heavens and the earth, the one who gave life and took it away.

America, he proclaimed, was a cursed land, a divine place of exile for Yahweh's enemies, who would all burn in a nuclear lake of fire. Just a week after Reinaldo's killing, Yahweh Ben Yahweh stumbled upon his next flashpoint, a place called the Dirt Road apartments. It was a pastel-colored complex squatting on Northwest 131st Street in the star-crossed city of Opa-locka, the suburb of

Miami with modest homes and streets named for the *Arabian Nights*. But in the fall of 1986, there was no magic in Opa-locka. The downtown minarets were in disrepair. City hall operated from a trailer. Although the murder rate was lower than in Miami, Opa-locka had its first on-duty cop killed in more than fifty years. The town tossed through sleepless nights after another officer gunned down a drug suspect, Willie "Junebug" Spikes, Jr. His death, in front of a coin laundry on a crowded corner, almost ignited a riot. "Murder!" Junebug's friends cried. "This is murder."

This was Yahweh territory. Nowhere in Opa-locka were people more concerned about security than at the Dirt Road apartments. The complex consisted of 129 tenants in five two-story buildings set in a row. There were eight apartments in each building, all littered with beer bottles, glass vials from crack cocaine, and rats not even the least bit afraid of the daylight. Up and down the street it was bragged that a drug den operated openly at the complex. The dealers used the apartments for shelter and to enjoy one another's company. They met in the alleyways between the buildings to distribute drugs and stolen goods. They trained young apprentices, paying five dollars to ten-year-olds to be whistling lookouts from apartment balconies. The police staged midnight stings and arrested suspects, but the dealers kept coming back in larger numbers. The tenants figured the cops were paid off to help the dealers.

Filth, disease, rot, sin, Yahweh Ben Yahweh said of the Dirt Road apartments. He would cleanse them. "Buy beautiful apartments," he thought, "and fix them up into a heavenly state."

29

Most of the Dirt Road tenants were single mothers living with their children on month-to-month leases. The landlords, three French Canadian investors, were led by a bearded, portly man named Roger Martin. Martin once boasted of owning a banana plantation in Haiti. When he bought the Opa-locka complex, his dream was to get rid of the drugs, the junk, and the rats, and to fix the broken locks and leaky ceilings. The landlords told the tenants they were sinking money into the complex, but living conditions got worse. Defective plumbing left residents without water for cooking and bathing. Kids frolicked in polluted, knee-deep water where a playground was supposed to be. After thieves broke into a meter box in Denise Broussard's building, the mothers at the complex started having electrical problems. Denise, age thirty-four, was fighting like hell to change things. She lived with three kids, a niece, a nephew, and an on-and-off boyfriend in apartment number 19, a two-bedroom unit. She worked part time at a jai alai fronton and struggled to pay the $310-a-month rent. Her friends called her Neesie. Tired of exorbitant bills and ruthless landlords, she took the tenants' grievances to city hall. The politicians promised to make the owners bring the complex up to code, but a political promise in Opa-locka didn't mean much. Like officeholders elsewhere in the county, some of Opa-locka's incumbents had other problems to worry about. The mayor, for one, was facing a heated reelection campaign with accusations of bribe taking, among other things. City hall didn't act quickly enough, and on a Monday in September 1986, a six-month-old girl, playing with a lighter, burned to death in apartment number 6. Her mother, a crack-cocaine addict, was charged with neglect. The landlords lost their liability insurance.

Martin and his partners decided to cut their losses. Portraying themselves as losing combatants in a war against drug-dealing and

210

gun-toting tenants, they sent out a letter stating that occupants had nineteen days to get out. Instead of fixing serious electrical defects, power was cut to one whole building. Tenants started taking in their displaced neighbors. Leaving her furniture and clothing, Neesie and her children moved in with her sister, who lived in another building at the complex. Neesie's brother, Rudy, a tall, thin father of two and a sometime marijuana dealer, lived right below his sister in the building where the power had been disconnected. Neesie complained to Opa-locka mayor John Riley. "We're getting illegally evicted," she said. The tenants had no place to go.

Riley, believing the eviction notices were improper, agreed to call legal services on behalf of the tenants. On a Thursday in October attorney Barbara Malone Goolsby filed a lawsuit to correct "slum conditions" and to stop the illegal eviction threats. The depiction of the tenants as bad people, Goolsby said in her court papers, was a smokescreen that emerged after the landlords were cited for code violations. Some people staged a rent strike, infuriating the owners.

The mayor called a special meeting to review the situation. Landlord Martin, speaking quickly and passionately, told of being threatened and beaten by drug dealers. He offered to give away the complex, even handing the mayor a deed to the property. But Opa-locka wasn't interested. Taxpayers would have had to assume the $480,000 mortgage.

Yahweh Ben Yahweh read a newspaper account about the problems, and shortly thereafter Martin received a message on his answering machine: the Hebrews wanted to buy the complex. Sister Judith explained that they wanted to make the property "an oasis . . . a heavenly place for our people to live."

The landlord was delighted. If anyone could put a stop to drug dealing, it was Yahweh Ben Yahweh. "If they take control," Martin told himself, "I don't have to worry." He hopped in his car and headed to the temple.

Yahweh Ben Yahweh told him, "They have to pay their rent or else they're going to get evicted. No one will have a free ride."

The Yahwehs inspected the complex and agreed to make a

$14,000 down payment. The sales letter called for immediate possession. The son of God gathered his flock to announce the good news, informing them at morning prayer that they had inherited a paradise in Opa-locka. They needed to cast out the vermin from the buildings in time for the upcoming feast.

On Tuesday, October 28, 1986, at about 11 A.M., at least four white buses and a van pulled up to the Dirt Road apartments. About 150 Yahwehs spewed from the vehicles. Yahweh Ben Yahweh climbed from his limo and surveyed his new kingdom. "Totally destroyed," he said. "Burned out."

He stayed for only a few minutes, and then his soldiers started knocking on doors, telling the tenants that they had to pay up or move. Neesie Broussard was on the telephone with the legal services people when she heard the commotion. She rushed over to see what was going on. Neesie knew the Yahwehs. She used to buy their hair grease. She walked up to the man who seemed to be in charge, Elder Gideon, the soul singer. "What are you doing here?" she asked.

Gideon smiled at her. "Yahweh owns these apartments now," he said politely.

"What does that mean?" Neesie persisted. The tenants, she explained, had a court case against the landlords. Why should they have to move without a court order?

Gideon tried to be diplomatic, but he wouldn't back down. The Yahwehs were going to renovate the apartments, and everybody had to get their belongings out by noon the next day or the Hebrews would get them out for them.

"You just can't come in here with your white sheets, knocking on doors and telling people to leave," Neesie insisted. "I'm not getting out until a judge says so."

Mothers began telling the Yahwehs they had nowhere to go. They asked to see eviction notices, some proof they had to leave. At the least, they wanted their security deposits back so they'd have money to move.

Anthony Roosevelt Brown was angry. "If Yahweh Ben Yahweh comes back to these apartments," he said, "some tenant might kill him." Anthony, age twenty-eight, was a tall, hulking man known around the complex as Pudley. He had a beard, a mustache, and the horoscope sign Virgo tattooed on his left biceps. Pudley had been staying with his younger sister Kasha Briggs and her three children, contributing to the monthly rent. From time to time, he painted people's houses and worked on cars, but the cops suspected Pudley's real occupation was drug dealing. He told his sister not to move, not to worry.

By the time people arrived home from work, the Yahwehs had fortified the complex. They staked out vacant apartments and stood around silently, staffs of life in hand. Tenants called Mayor Riley to complain. The mayor and the legal services people called the police. The cops, thinking the Hebrews would bring order and discipline to a place with almost none, didn't respond. "I don't anticipate any problems with the Yahwehs," Chief Floyd Reeves said.

That night Neesie Broussard tried to ease anxieties. She carried a pitcher of ice water to some Yahwehs after another tenant refused to. It didn't help. The situation grew tenser when a new shift of white-robed guards arrived. They stood at the stairways of each building, seeming to block entrance and exit. They shared guarded moments, prayers, and chants about Yahweh. "It's like living in a prison," a woman tenant said.

Wednesday brought a fresh complement of Yahwehs, with cleaning equipment, rags, and an eighteen-wheel tractor-trailer to get rid of the dirt. They started removing soda cans, empty cigarette packs, bubble gum wrappers, and pieces of old tires. They slowly graduated to the bigger items, hauling furniture and clothing from vacant apartments and from the deserted building where the power had been out. A Hebrew shone a flashlight into a woman's bedroom window as her son put on his pants.

"We're going to paint the buildings white!" a Yahweh announced. "Today is Yahweh Day!"

The commotion woke up Kasha Briggs, who hurried outside. "Why do you want to paint the buildings white?" she asked.

"We're not here to make anybody feel uncomfortable," the Yahweh told her. "This is all about love."

"Love?" Kasha said. "Come on. You are invading people's

houses. You're standing around our homes. You're making us feel uneasy. Our kids are afraid. We're afraid. The average person around here's a woman trying to take care of kids by themselves and you're saying you're about love? You don't know anything about your people. We don't know what you're coming to do."

Kasha had a funny feeling. She called her workplace to say she'd be late, and she asked her father to take the kids for the day. Then she began to play gospel music as the situation at the Dirt Road apartments went steadily downhill. Solemn, authoritative, the Hebrews stood with arms crossed, lips sealed, holding stare-off contests with the tenants. A few carried walkie-talkies. A cluster of Hebrew women balanced video cameras on their shoulders and took pictures of the occupants. It seemed a form of intimidation. TV news crews arrived to film the picture-taking Yahwehs. When Pablo the ice-cream man tried to get through the yard for his daily visit, a Hebrew waved him off. Children cried. They loved Pablo, because he gave them free ice cream.

Someone scrawled a message on the door of apartment number 28: "You have to go."

Suddenly, the Yahwehs began removing some of Rudy Broussard's stuff, along with a refrigerator from Kasha Briggs's front porch. "That belongs to us," she yelled. Kasha ran to tell her brother Pudley, who confronted the Yahwehs. "Hey, man," he said, "that's my apartment and I ain't moved out."

Kasha insisted that the freezer was stocked with soda and frozen cups for the kids. The Yahwehs claimed Pudley stored beer and crack cocaine in it. As they hauled it to the tractor-trailer parked at the gate, Kasha ran to tell Neesie that they were taking Rudy's dresser. Someone called the police to report a burglary in progress at apartment number 19. Neesie warned the Hebrews not to mess with her stuff, and minutes later Rudy made a beeline to the trailer to retrieve the dresser. He'd recently suffered a gunshot wound and had a cast on his left arm. Pudley climbed up to help unload the stuff. "No goddamn Yahweh," he muttered.

The tenants rallied, shouting at the Hebrews to stop stealing things from occupied apartments. Hoping to attract attention, Pudley sprinted to a back alley and pulled a gun from his striped shorts. He fired into the air—round after round. "This isn't for you guys," he told the Yahwehs. "It's just to get the police here."

At about 11:35 A.M., the cops finally showed up, and so did Sister Judith. As the Hebrews melted to the edges of the property, Opa-locka officer Charles Jones began filling out a report that accused the Yahwehs of burglary. Officer Emily Crawford buttonholed a sect woman and asked her for a written eviction notice, some legal proof they owned the building. The woman couldn't produce it. "If you cannot show me your ownership, and I know by basic patrolling that these people live here, I can't order them off that property," Crawford said. Aware of past "violent behavior" by the Hebrews, she felt the situation at the apartment complex was a ticking time bomb. She told the Yahwehs they were trespassing and would have to leave. "I felt there would be a retaliation," she said later.

An assemblage of important people arrived, including Police Chief Reeves. Sister Judith insisted the Hebrews were simply cleaning vacant apartments, and the brass ordered the patrol cops to back off. But after seeing the chaos for himself, Mayor Riley told Judith that the group had until 3 P.M. to produce ownership papers or another legal document giving them authority to be there. Otherwise, he would order the police to kick them off the property.

The politicians and the tenants congregated around the TV cameras. With the bare-chested Rudy standing nearby, Pudley told a reporter for WTVJ-TV that he wasn't budging. "I'm gonna stay here until I get an eviction notice," he said, nestling his one-year-old girl in his arms. "I don't care what they say 'cause they ain't going in. Just as simple as that. Right, fat girl?" Pudley said, tickling the child's chin.

"F--- Yahweh."

Back at the temple, Yahweh Ben Yahweh watched the events unfold on TV. "Profanity," the messiah called Pudley's remarks. "Profane words directed toward Yahweh, his name." How could a drug dealer who hadn't paid his rent tell the chosen people, as the new owners, that he didn't have to leave? How could the tenants who tore apart the complex think of filing a lawsuit against the good landlord? Why was the establishment persecuting his people when they were doing a job the politicians wouldn't do?

That afternoon Yahweh Ben Yahweh met quietly with two of his soldiers. The 3 P.M. deadline slid by, but the eyeball-to-eyeball confrontation between the Yahwehs and the Dirt Road residents continued. As night fell over Opa-locka, only two squad cars patrolled the entire city. Dozens of men with sticks ringed the apartments, hovering like pale ghosts in hallways, on balconies, and on sidewalks. When Mayor Riley drove by the complex at 10 P.M., he felt pure terror—a scene that seemed as if it should be taking place in Beirut, not in America. "Like an armed camp," he thought. "Where are the police?"

Rudy, Pudley, and Neesie sat in the kitchen, wondering how rich folks would have reacted. "What would they say if men in white robes came to their door?" Neesie said. They were having dinner, hamburgers and french fries, but Pudley seemed in a hurry to go. He said he had to take fat girl home to her mother. Rudy kissed his sister good night. She was exhausted. She hadn't gotten much sleep the night before and she wanted to take a shower.

It was cool and dry outside, completely silent. No more cries of children asking about the men in robes. No gunshots. No streetlights. Just a blanket of black clouds above a sea of white robes. About an hour passed. Neesie heard a knock on her window.

"Praise Yahweh!" a voice said. "Yahweh is God!"

"Oh, God," Neesie thought. This was it. The Yahwehs had come to kill her. The men outside kept chanting. Neesie thought one of the voices sounded familiar.

It was Pudley, standing outside with Rudy, their faces mimicking the frozen blank stares of the Yahwehs. A terrifying practical joke, a little prank to slice the tension of the night. They all broke into laughter. Neesie handed Rudy a cigarette through the window. Then the two men said good night again and headed home. A few seconds later, a green Plymouth pulled to a stop. Several white-robed gatemen came to greet the car.

"Praise Yahweh!" someone said.

"Yahweh, brother," a man in the car replied.

Two men stepped from the Plymouth. Both were in dead clothes. Amri Israel, the onetime Opa-locka elder, was the senior guard that night. He was wearing white. All of Yahweh's soldiers who lived on the buses respected Amri, who had previously received an invitation to the secret brotherhood.

The Yahwehs began to scatter as a tenant named Sherry drove up. A mother of four, she'd just gotten off her shift at Long John Silver's. As she backed up to park, she saw three to five Yahwehs in the darkened corridor. They stepped from the shadows and knocked on a door.

"She hit your car," a Yahweh called to Pudley. He looked through the window, then came outside. Sherry's car lights were still on. Rudy watched from the litter-strewn walkway bisecting the buildings. Pudley walked over to Sherry. "How bad did you hit it?" he asked.

"I didn't hit your car," Sherry said.

As Pudley started to walk away, a man in street clothes suddenly grabbed Rudy. He tried to pull away, but someone forced him to his knees.

"I didn't do nothing, man," Rudy said. "Don't hurt me."

Pudley tried to get away, but a man in street clothes grabbed him and backed him up against the wall. "I ain't goin' nowhere," Pudley said.

There was a pause, followed by a gunshot.

"No, no, no!" Pudley yelled.

Sherry screamed and stepped on the gas. Neesie heard the shot and ran into the living room to get her kids on the floor.

Hit an inch above his eyebrow, Rudy fell at the foot of the stairwell. Blood trickled from his nose. A spent .45 casing lay between his feet.

Pudley bolted free and took off. "I won't say anything," he said. "I won't tell nobody." The gunmen chased him.

"Why you running if you some tough bad ass?" an assassin shouted, firing as Pudley rounded a sharp corner. He made a quick turn around the back of the last apartment building as a barrage of gunshots, some louder than others, rang out. Two men on the street ducked.

Hit in the arm, Pudley tripped on a garbage can. He regained his balance, crawled through a fence hole, and made a hard left toward the main street. He kept screaming for help.

Neesie, in her nightgown, ran to the front door. "Are they shooting out there?" she asked. "Who are they shooting?"

"Yes, yes, they're shooting," a man replied. "Come on around and see."

A desperate woman telephoned the police: "This is where we have the problem. This is where the Yahwehs are. We have some shooting going on. I'm not going out there."

Despite everything that had happened, the dispatcher was skeptical. "How come you think they're shootin' somewhere?"

Pudley, still running for his life, stumbled. A gunman ran up and tackled him, grabbing his left ankle.

"Don't shoot!" Pudley cried. "Don't shoot me!" He put his hands over his face.

A second assassin stood over him. "Shoot the motherfucker."

A hitman aimed his .45 at Pudley's forehead and squeezed the trigger once, then again.

Mayor Riley, at home just four blocks away, heard the shots and knew the worst had happened. He tugged on his clothes and dashed out the door.

Neesie grabbed her robe and ran out in the yard. Pudley's sister, overwhelmed by grief, came toward her. "It's Rudy!" Kasha Briggs wept. "Rudy's shot!" Kasha didn't know her own brother had been shot too.

Neesie rushed around the corner to the stairwell. Her brother lay on the ground with a hole over his left eye, hemmed in by Yahweh men. One of them muttered something over his radio.

Rudy was breathing shallowly. Neesie grabbed his limp body, hugged him, rocked him in her arms, and began breathing into his mouth. "What happened?" she asked.

He was too weak to answer.

Neesie looked up at the Yahwehs hovering over them. "What did you do to my brother?"

It was a robbery, one of them said coldly.

A crowd began to gather. A tenant tried to comfort Neesie, gently tugging her away from Rudy. She held him tighter. She was terrified that they would cut off his head. "I'm not going to leave my brother here," she sobbed. "They done already hurt him. I'm not going to leave him."

Neariah Israel, in blue jeans, a T-shirt, and a knit cap, tossed a gun to a Yahweh in white robes, then hopped into the green Plymouth. As he drove down the street, a police cruiser rounded the corner, no lights, no speed. Neariah looked into his rearview mirror. The cop car was going slow. Lights were flashing, and people were screaming. The squad car stopped. Neariah flinched. There was no time to find his brothers.

He ditched the car and took off running. He headed toward a field, then tripped through the tall weeds, making a lot of noise.

"There he is, there he is," a tenant from the apartment complex yelled.

Corporal James Smith, the cop in the cruiser, shone his high beams right at Neariah. It was 1:42 A.M. Smith, who had been off duty, radioed for canine officers. Smith, known as Bowlegs, began driving through the field.

Neariah, hiding in the underbrush, stayed perfectly still. "Where are my brothers?" he wondered.

Smith's high beams got brighter, then dimmer. The squad car began to move away. Neariah waited until he couldn't see it, then got up and walked briskly toward a dirt road. Again, the cop car approached. Neariah hit the dirt.

Bowlegs didn't see him. Neariah lifted himself, jogged toward the road, then fell into a ditch. He tossed a pair of latex gloves on the ground and laughed to himself. He was just twenty feet or so from the road and could see his getaway. "If I make it to that street,

219

I'm gone," he told himself. All of the excitement made him want to relieve himself.

He rolled over on his side, and suddenly dogs were barking. Flashlights were bobbing. Buddy, a German shepherd drawn by the smell of urine, came straight at Neariah. Pinned down by dogs and floodlights coming from all directions, Neariah hugged the dirt as hard as he could, praying that he would become an invisible angel.

"Don't even think about it, pal," a canine officer said, ramming the barrel of his gun into Neariah's back.

Bowlegs pulled Neariah to his feet. The officer's .38 was cocked, aimed at the suspect's chest. "What are you doing here?" Bowlegs asked.

Neariah said he'd been in a fight. "I was chasing a tall black man."

Bowlegs patted him down. He reached into the pocket of Neariah's blue jeans, crusted with dirt, weeds, and spurs, and removed cartridges from a deuce-deuce, a .22 pistol.

"Let's go," Bowlegs said.

As the police hauled Neariah to the Opa-locka station house, paramedics at the housing complex lifted Pudley into an ambulance bound for Jackson Memorial Hospital. He had two through-and-through head wounds. Rudy, age thirty-seven, was dead. The tenants covered him with a yellow blanket, and forty to fifty people began hurling obscenities at the politicians who'd gathered at the scene to pay their respects. "They didn't have to shoot him!" cried Pudley's brother Glenn. "Why?"

Mayor Riley, standing inches from a pool of blood, didn't try to defend his city. "It didn't have to happen," he said. Opa-locka had sat on its hands as the landlords and the Yahwehs engaged in a "conspiracy" to get rid of the tenants. The police chief had seriously misjudged the situation. So had the mayor and every member of the Opa-locka city commission, the city manager, the county housing authorities, everyone who had acquiesced or failed to speak out against the possibility of violence at the Dirt Road apartments. The government had broken down, but this time it wasn't a callous white rode atop a fire truck. Dade County state attorney Janet Reno walked the route, occasionally stopping to shake hands. But hours after the parade, Miami's hopes for a little good PR went up in flames. For the fourth time in a decade, rocks and bottles rained down on paradise, this time after a Colombian-born officer shot and killed an unarmed black motorcyclist. The motorcycle careened head-on into an oncoming car, killing a second black man, the passenger on the motorcycle. It was Monday, January 16, 1989. An angry mob tackled cameramen searching for a pregame Super Bowl angle. From high-rise suites in the Omni Hotel, Cincinnati Bengals watched the fires in the heart of Overtown, which was again feeling the mist of eye-stinging tear gas.

As the smoke cleared, the Reverend Al Sharpton rolled into town from New York. He had gained notoriety for his involvement in the case of Tawana Brawley, a young black girl who claimed she had been raped by several white men. Miami's black establishment did not welcome Sharpton, who, in turn, called it "a bunch of funky, bourgeois politicians."

The son of God? He had been called a lot of things, but never bourgeois. Yahweh Ben Yahweh took credit for bringing calm to the streets. Not only did his followers not riot, but they rescued white people being dragged from a car by an enraged throng. During the looting and mayhem, Yahweh said he'd been busy working for "positive" change, providing hundreds and thousands of jobs. "I'm the man who holds the key to the prosperity of America," he declared, "because I'm prepared to employ all of the unemployed blacks in this country." Riots, he warned the power structure, could erupt at any time, but if America blessed him, he would bless America.

Yahweh Ben Yahweh's transformation into Miami's black messiah was complete. He was the total solution, the rags-to-riches antidote to social unrest, the ruling elite's foil. Civic leaders needed him. Rarely would he talk about the Apocalypse anymore. Now Miami was his Promised Land, his jihad, his City of Yahweh. Cruising the steamy streets of Overtown in a stretch limo, he said he felt like the king of Israel.

administration ignoring black people. Opa-locka's administration was predominantly black.

The Yahwehs huddled under a stairwell.

"Anybody know what happened?" a cop asked.

They shook their heads.

"Who's in charge?" a female officer asked. Again, the response was a wall of silence.

Officers searched the green Plymouth, its engine still running. Inside the getaway car was a Yahweh robe. Under the passenger's bucket seat was a white canvas gym bag with a black gun holster and four knives. On one twelve-inch blade, police saw what they thought was dried blood.

At 2:10 A.M., Detective Rex Remley of the Metro-Dade homicide bureau arrived to take over the investigation. He chatted briefly with the Opa-locka cops, then received a report at 2:35 A.M. that Anthony "Pudley" Brown was dead. As word spread through the complex, the tenants grew more enraged.

Remley, fearing a riot, asked an officer to get the names of the Yahwehs and to make them gather their things and leave. The mothers of 131st Street, with their kids, left too, driven in minibuses to a Red Cross shelter on Biscayne Boulevard, not far from where Yahweh's holy war had begun. The Red Cross set up cots, fed them, and bought five hundred boxes of Pampers for the babies. But the women still worried about being marked for death by a quiet white-robed Yahweh with a portable video camera. In the next days, the city would condemn the Dirt Road apartments. Thieves broke into the unsecured property and carted away everything. The tenants moved from house to house, waiting for news of where they would go next. "Sometimes I just cry for nothing," Kasha Briggs said. The cops dropped by to give Neesie Broussard's mother Rudy's effects—$26.28 and a cracked Timex wristwatch, stopped forever at 12:30.

30

The morning after the homicides, the Temple of Love was under siege, deluged by reporters' requests for interviews with the mystery man within the walls, buzzed by aerial photographers shooting pictures from helicopters. Holed up in the compound, Yahweh Ben Yahweh would sputter indignantly about a planned assault. "I told you to be aware, I told you Satan would come like this, I've warned you for some time!"

The Hebrews blanketed the streets with a pamphlet proclaiming Neariah Israel a victim of a police frame-up. Yahweh Ben Yahweh said he could produce three to five alibi witnesses who would testify the victims were wicked scum, destroyers of black motherhood. They lived violently and died violently in a dope rip-off after profaning God's holy name on TV. "I want to say that whoever killed them, they did a righteous thing [for] Yahweh in killing a blasphemer."

An armed assault never came, but an onslaught of bad press made Yahweh realize that he needed a lawyer, a good criminal lawyer, to repair the legal and political headaches caused by the incident on 131st Street. In south Florida, where good criminal lawyers are as plentiful as palmetto bugs, one of the most famous was Ellis Rubin. A white conservative Jew with silver hair, Rubin fancied himself a tough law-and-order man. More important, he had a national reputation as a master of legal pyrotechnics and trial by microphone. His roster of hero-villain clients included Watergate burglar Frank Sturgis, astrologer Mickie Dahne, and nymphomaniac-prostitute Kathy Willets, who eventually made it all the way to the Donahue show. Rubin also brought the world the "TV intoxication defense" of fifteen-year-old Ronnie Zamora, accused of murdering an old lady after he watched too much *Kojak*. Though the lawyer's actions sometimes provoked skepticism among fellow members of the bar, Rubin knew how to defend himself and his clients in ten-second sound bites—in sharp contrast to Yahweh Ben Yahweh, who tended to run off at the mouth.

It was Rubin who cleared a Miami man after his homemade booby trap electrocuted a would-be burglar. Rubin never let the case go to trial. He tried it on the *Today* show, making Prentice Rasheed, the trapper, a household name, the little man who fought heroically against urban predators. The grand jury ruled it self-defense. Prentice Rasheed recommended Ellis Rubin, who got a call one day from the temple: Would he like to be interviewed for the job of Yahweh house counsel? The messiah noted that Rubin had been sent by God. According to the Bible, Rubin was a high priest from a different lost tribe of Israel. "What would it be like," the lawyer wondered, "to negotiate a retainer with the son of God?"

Rubin's advice would cost the Yahwehs plenty, more than they had dreamed of spending. "It's gonna be hard to tell him what to do," the lawyer decided, " 'cause he's God and I'm just a high priest."

The temple's choice for house counsel raised eyebrows and sent cackles through Miami. "The religious sect had been preaching hatred of white people," the black-owned *Miami Times* wrote, "but when they got their round ones caught in a vice in that Opa-locka shooting, guess who they sought out to defend them? It sure wasn't Jesse McCrary or H. T. Smith" (two prominent black attorneys).

In a matter of weeks, Rubin became an unofficial power behind the throne, lecturing Yahweh Ben Yahweh on doing away with racist doctrines. "You can't exist by preaching hatred of the white man," the lawyer told him. "You've got to stop the inflammatory language. It just exacerbates the attacks against the temple." In effect, Yahweh would have to rewrite his official beliefs as a defense to legal problems, sort of like putting out the burning bush because Smokey Bear says no to forest fires.

From a criminal lawyer's perspective, Yahweh's 250,000 minutes of tape-recorded sermons and his five hundred written articles, with all their angry words about white oppression and retribution, could be incriminating. If Yahweh Ben Yahweh knew his tirades resulted in one inadvertent homicide, he could probably say it wasn't his fault. But if it happened a second time, a third time, and a fourth time, any prosecutor would say Yahweh was intelligent enough to deduce that his language was being misunderstood and resulted in violence. And what if a prosecutor concluded that Yahweh Ben Yahweh ordered the homicides? The messiah had to stop taking the Bible so literally, the high priest of law advised.

Rubin's advice went beyond doctrinal change. As far as conduct was concerned, the Yahwehs had to gussy up their community image in a highly public way. "You have to open up your religion and let the media see what you're all about," the attorney said. "When the mystery dissolves, the fear will disappear."

And so the son of God set out to transform himself and his followers into symbols of hope for Miami's black community. The reversal process began just three weeks after the Opa-locka homicides, when Yahweh Ben Yahweh opened the temple to dozens of reporters and photographers. They toured the sewing shop, the ice-cream parlor, two cafeterias, the first-aid room, the vegetable garden, the grocery store, and the Hebrew school. In the beauty shop a patron in street clothes had her hair styled while reading page 324 of the unabridged dictionary.

Sister Judith requested that journalists not interview the Hebrews, who floated through the crowd smiling. Some stood behind a table offering their guests glazed kosher donuts and coffee from a silver pot. Judith read a litany of denials, from murder to child abuse to racist teachings. Then, with Ellis Rubin beside him, Yahweh Ben Yahweh welcomed the visitors in a honey-sweet voice. "I'm sure that you will discover with great surprise that I come with a message of peace," he beamed. "My message is of morality for all people." Quoting from the Book of Matthew, he said a tree is known by its fruit. "So I hope you have enjoyed tasting some of my fruits today!"

Over the next months, Yahweh elaborated on his new official beliefs in a series of national interviews and media extravaganzas orchestrated by attorney Rubin. Claiming the Miami media had gotten it wrong for years, Yahweh told the *New York Times*, among other publications, that he always taught peace, brotherhood, charity, industriousness, prayer, and love. There was hardly a mention of race—not a hint of anti-Christian, anti-Jewish, or antiwhite feeling. "I don't believe in black supremacy," he'd say. "The skin color game is the creation of those who are enemies of peace and love in this country and on the earth."

A few designated followers came out of hiding for media opportunities, to contrast their former dull lives in the dead world with their new religion. Yahweh Ben Yahweh, they said, had given them order, wonderful new identities, and hope. The Yahwehs were the family they never had. Elder Gideon, promoted to prince, summoned local reporters to his temple in Hollywood. The bathroom reportedly had gold-plated fixtures and a throne in the tub. To one interview, the singer wore rhinestone-studded sunglasses. To another, he had on two gold rings and three gold bracelets on his right hand, a diamond ring, a gold watch, and two gold bracelets on his left hand, and around his neck he wore four chains with what looked like five gold charms. He sucked on a foot-long candy cane. Gideon became evasive when interrogators asked where he got the jewelry, but he was effusive about the God who'd taught him goodness and righteousness. "The world," he proclaimed, "has got the wrong impression of Yahweh Ben Yahweh. They think they have to give up everything to join Yahweh, when, in fact, we share happiness and everything we do. . . . We just enjoy each other being here. It's all legal and legitimate."

To avoid any appearance of illegitimacy, the rank and file stopped carrying staffs of life. They got birth certificates for their kids and took full-time jobs in the dead world. And those who couldn't find private-sector employment began showing up en masse to clean up abandoned apartments in Liberty City and rat-infested motels along Biscayne Boulevard. The death angels had disappeared, but the panhandlers and hookers still solicited between the elegant palms. Yahweh Ben Yahweh, like Donald Trump, purchased properties for a little down and a lot of borrowed money. His construction crews unclogged the toilets, sterilized maggot-infested cabinets, and trashed refrigerators loaded with the by-products of crack cocaine. Then he rechristened the motels with names like Yahweh Resort Villas and Yahweh Economy Inn. Their color-coordinated rooms, costing between twenty-six and sixty-five dollars a night, came with air-conditioning, free Home Box Office, twenty-four-hour security, and a telephone system with automatic wake-up. The lobbies were conspicuous for their absence of bulletproof glass. In the hotel parking lots, Hebrew guards conducted visual shakedowns. In the lobbies, receptionists in white screened the guests. They had to sign a moral code agreeing not to be naughty—no prostitution, no drugs, no smoking, no drinking, no unmarried couples.

The code was part of Yahweh Ben Yahweh's new family-values doctrine. "We've had some obvious prostitutes try to check in," the son of God explained at one of his regular press conferences. (Ellis Rubin had shown him the way.) "We don't allow it, we turn them away. We won't compromise our principles for a dollar."

With Rubin's help, Yahweh Ben Yahweh met important people in town. One of his best contacts was a mysterious hotelier named James Angleton, who ran the Biscayne Boulevard Chamber of Commerce. Angleton knew the politicians at city hall and seemed eager for Yahweh to meet them. After taking out a $395,000 mortgage on one of Angleton's properties, the son of God began appearing at chamber gatherings and other business functions. Sometimes he'd show up with a cellular phone and his docile, smiling women retreating into passivity and silence. Holding out the fig leaf of cleaning up decrepit neighborhoods, Yahweh told his multilingual audiences he would heal the sick. He promised to give scholarships to the poor, food baskets to the hungry, and lodging to the homeless. He would open grocery stores around the country, stocking the shelves daily with fresh bread, chicken wings, and collard greens, often at lower prices than at their mom-and-pop competitors or twenty-four-hour chains.

If anyone felt queasy about a man with a terrorist-pocked past, Yahweh Ben Yahweh calmed them with jokes and a 14-karat smile.

"I have heard that the Yahwehs do not like white people," a businessman once said to him. "Is that true?"

"Impossibly not true," Yahweh Ben Yahweh replied. "If you look in my eyes and see the blue, the green, and the gray, you know that's always been impossible."

The messiah supplied volunteer Hebrews for various business projects, and no one seemed to care if anyone other than a few of his close associates were actually getting a check, or hospital insurance, or even decent food. Yahweh claimed to vigorously support the Urban League Push Out the Pushers (POP) program, in which city inspectors combed deteriorating neighborhoods for building violations. At the same time, the inspectors condoned code violations at Yahweh's school, which was operating not only without a permit but with obstructed exits and missing smoke detectors. Again, no one spoke of the irony.

Among Miami's corporate elite, Yahweh Ben Yahweh seemed to touch a nerve almost no one else could. Finding him charming, smart, courageous, aggressive, and wealthy, they granted him membership in good standing to the Chamber of Commerce, the Better Business Bureau, the Convention and Visitors Bureau, the NAACP, the American Hotel & Motel Association, the Urban League, and the Japan Society.

By attending their meetings, Yahweh Ben Yahweh began to experience another epiphany. He learned to modify his speech, depending on the audience he faced and the response he got.

Meanwhile, particularly in noncorporate circles, there were still those lingering images of dead tenants and the man accused of killing them. Not even the prettiest picture of a smiling Yahweh could erase them. Something more was needed.

31

Neariah Israel sat in solitary, studying verses from Exodus. He had no image makers or makeup men. He tried to convince himself that the homicide suspect he kept seeing on TV was a character in some sort of Grade B gangster movie. "He just looks like me," Neariah thought.

For homicide detective Rex Remley, the pieces of Neariah's criminal life had fallen together quickly. Not only did gunpowder residue show up on his hands, but blood appeared to be on his blue jeans. Tenants from the Dirt Road apartments identified him as the taller of two, or possibly three, hitmen. But Neariah's homicide trail went far beyond Opa-locka. A .38-caliber revolver, found by police near the Opa-locka getaway car, had been reported stolen. The owner was Raymond Kelley, the master mechanic stabbed to death seven weeks before the 131st Street shootings. He was ear case number three. When Remley made the ear connection, his eyes lit up. He and his partner Danny Borrego had interviewed Ray Kelley's friends, delved into his marital situation, his finances, and his drinking, but they could never come up with a reason why anyone would want him dead. Then the clues fell into place. Neariah Israel's partial palm print, it turned out, was on the driver's window of Ray's Malibu. Another print belonging to Neariah, of his left index finger, was on the door of Big Man's house. Big Man was the garbage collector stabbed to death after kicking the hysterical Yahweh panhandler. He was ear case number four.

With physical evidence to support them, state prosecutors filed four first-degree murder indictments. They announced they would seek the death penalty against Neariah.

In the meantime, other lawmen, both local and federal, had rounded up new Hebrew witnesses. The most compelling were members of Yahweh Ben Yahweh's blood family. Accompanied by an FBI agent, Detective John King had paid a visit to Oklahoma to

228

interview Yahweh's sister, forty-three-year-old Jean Solomon. Out for more than a year, she had been trying to forget everything that happened, hoping to come to terms with her experience privately. When the law officers first asked her questions, the answers eluded her. But slowly, as they pushed Jean to think about her reasons for leaving, the answers exploded in a series of frightening images: the beating of her niece; the death of her infant granddaughter; the burial of babies without ceremony; the murder of the karate expert; her own near-starvation on a rice-and-bean diet; the sex. Jean portrayed her brother as a control freak with a sexual obsession dating back to adolescence. She gave the lawmen the names of five Hebrew girls who might talk. After leaving the temple, Jean had come to realize that her brother had maximum control over his followers' actions, including homicide. "He may not say, 'Go do it,' but he takes the mind that way," she said.

Jean gave a full accounting but she begged that her statement be kept confidential. She feared that if she turned against her brother, her mother, father, brothers, and sisters could turn against her. Jean's son, Anthony, was less reticent. After his mother's interview, he walked outside with the lawmen. He told them he had almost perfect recall of long-ago events and direct information tying his uncle to murder. He said he remembered in detail the conversation in the cafeteria between Moses Israel and the men who killed accountant Carlton Carey.

Anthony was eighteen. Like the lives of other defector teenagers, his had taken a rocky course. When the school system tried to place him in the seventh or eighth grade, he dropped out. He applied for a job as a maintenance helper, but they refused to accept his Yahweh diploma. Anthony began experimenting with a drug called premo, marijuana laced with cocaine. Soon he would be driving a fancy car as he worked his way up to a big-time Miami-Oklahoma coke connection known on the streets of Enid as Big A.

His life in flux, Anthony agreed to fly to Miami and go under cover to spy for the government against his Uncle Junior. The FBI outfitted him with a beeper.

The legal attack against Yahweh was coming from other directions, too. After hiring attorneys, the mothers of 131st Street had begun to press a spate of civil lawsuits. Among the defendants were Yahweh and the Temple of Love Inc., the old Dirt Road landlords, the savings and loan that held the mortgage on the apartments, the elected officials, and the police. The tenants knew there were criminal suspects besides the lone triggerman charged with killing Rudy and Pudley. They charged the city of Opa-locka with reckless disregard for human life, complete indifference toward it. The Yahwehs, they said, never should have been allowed on the property (for a $14,000 down payment) in the first place. It was like throwing a match in a pool of gasoline. What's more, according to one lawsuit, the city had been irrational, negligent, and discriminatory because, although knowing the tenants' plight, elected officials and the police took no special precautions.

Besides negligence and wrongful-death cases, the tenants filed another, more unusual claim. It accused the Temple of Love Inc. of a "terrorist occupation" in the Dirt Road siege. The lawsuit, identifying the tenants as John and Jane Does, was based on violations of the federal RICO statute, the Racketeer Influenced and Corrupt Organizations Act enacted by Congress in 1970 to stop organized crime's infiltration into legitimate business. Over the years, federal prosecutors and private citizens had been using the statute to attack a broadening list of defendants, among them antiabortion protesters, S & Ls, white supremacists, and even a weekly newspaper. A private person filing a civil RICO lawsuit has to prove that an enterprise has engaged in a "pattern of racketeering." The law defines a "pattern of racketeering" as the commission of two or more criminal acts (such as murder, kidnapping, arson, extortion, drug dealing, securities fraud, mail fraud, and bribery) within a ten-year period.

Legal services attorney Barbara Goolsby, enlisting help from two private lawyers, accused the temple of extortion, assault, and murder under RICO. According to the lawsuit, paramilitary Yahwehs occupied the Dirt Road complex, went into tenants' apartments uninvited, removed their belongings, tried to terrorize them into moving, and finally succeeded by executing Rudy and Pudley. If the temple was found guilty, it could be subject to heavy penalties: triple damages, lawsuit costs, and attorneys' fees.

After the racketeering accusation, it was clear that Yahweh Ben Yahweh had more than an image problem. He had to stave off the law. Sensing informers were looking over his shoulder, he shocked Sister Judith's son Kelly Gaines by asking point-blank one day, What had he told the FBI?

"I didn't tell them anything," Kelly lied.

Yahweh praised God. "Those who oppose Yahweh will be dealt with in the end," he said. In the temple of Yahweh, Kelly knew that could mean losing his head.

Intimidating and discrediting defectors became part of the sect's legal game plan. Hebrew witnesses and potential criminal defendants received new names or one-way tickets to new cities. Savoring the thought of a public fight, Yahweh Ben Yahweh issued a challenge to the media. "Go gather all my detractors together," he said, "and let's have a battle like Elijah did with the four hundred false prophets."

It was Thursday, May 14, 1987, 3:15 P.M. God, the son of God, was summoned to Ellis Rubin's office in downtown Miami to lay out his defense for the first time. The Opa-locka tenants had subpoenaed him, and in front of Sister Judith and an assemblage of lawyers, he affirmed to tell the truth. Then he explained his metamorphosis into a mighty God through the normal process of revelation. "I know that I am the genius by definition," Yahweh Ben Yahweh testified. "I am not *a* genius, I am *the* genius."

All his rantings and exhortations to kill devils were similar to allegories in the Bible, never meant to be taken literally. If they could hold him guilty, then they could hold the pope of Rome guilty. When he told his followers to "bring me a head," he was speaking figuratively. When he told them he believed in the sword, he meant the two-edged Word of God, so sharp that it cut coming and going. When he told them to kill, he meant for them to kill off their bad personal attitudes. When he said he would reach out and smite his enemies, he didn't mean kill them. "I have been smiting all over the earth ever since I have been here," he said. "Every time I teach to stop smoking cigarettes, that has smitten the tobacco industry. It has smitten the doctors and the hospitals and cheats them of treating people for lung cancer. It hurts their pocketbook. When they no longer walk a mile for a Camel, orthopedic surgeons don't have any reason to excise corns from people's feet.

"That's a scriptural and spiritual understanding. When I teach righteousness, morality, that smites the wicked and the evil."

And how about ears? Did he tell his followers to bring him ears? How silly, the son of God replied. "I hear perfectly well. What could I do with someone else's ears?"

Neariah Israel—the man Yahweh had once promised to protect, the one he said was innocent, the brave soldier canonized for standing up against the white persecutors—was left twisting in the wind. He had told Ellis Rubin everything, and now Yahweh Ben Yahweh stopped taking Neariah's telephone calls. Visits from his temple loved ones, including two wives and two babies, ended. Rubin encouraged Neariah to plead guilty, or innocent by reason of insanity. Rubin, Neariah said later, even told him to act nuts and drool on the table in the courtroom.

"No way," Neariah said, as it dawned on him that no angel in white was swooping down to save him.

32

On Tuesday, June 9, 1987, Neariah called the temple's tele-communications office and demanded to speak to Yahweh Ben Yahweh. His loyal assistant, Abishag Israel, said no.

The next evening, as Neariah watched the news from his nine-by-six cell, the face of Yahweh Ben Yahweh appeared on the TV screen. Ellis Rubin was beside him.

With a flick of a black Magic Marker, Yahweh crossed Neariah's name out of the *Lamb's Book of Life*. Declaring him a "black devil," Yahweh told the TV audience of the telephone call from his former disciple. He said Neariah had threatened to tell sect secrets to the prosecution if he wasn't given a new lawyer. His excommunication, the messiah explained, was not a statement of Neariah's guilt or innocence, but a reaction to the threatening phone call, which Yahweh called blackmail and extortion.

Neariah Israel would be known henceforth as Bobby Rozier. He was booted from under the umbrella of God's love. Bobby Rozier, superstar athlete turned petty con man turned religious fanatic turned holy executioner, was pissed. Who in the hell did that rag-headed son of a bitch think he was, stabbing him in the back for doing his will?

Bobby's banishment was part of the legal counteroffensive, paving the way for Yahweh Ben Yahweh to complete his latest incarnation. As word of the temple's economic achievements spread, Hebrew supervisors began to process a growing number of requests from struggling landlords eager to be rid of drug-infested real estate. The owners offered the properties at bargain-basement prices and usually held onto the mortgages. Wherever the Yahwehs went, they seemed to do wonders for the crime rate. Although police in Miami could never corroborate statistical drops in assaults or burglaries, the Hebrews still sent out waves of good vibes along Biscayne Bou-

levard, in the areas of their motels. "They cleaned up my neighborhood," said a boulevard streetwalker named Martina Mish. "I'm
a prostitute and I know they wouldn't even let us in their hotel.
. . . They made the hotels look better. They're cleaner. Even though
I do drugs, they don't let it around the place. . . . They didn't let
no trouble happen. . . . And they ain't giving me nothing to say it."

For crime-weary small businesspeople, the Hebrews were good
for the pocketbook as well as the spirit. They were a dream come
true—a private security force, working free of charge, adding nothing to their tax bills—amiably doing anything asked of them so
quickly it was hard to believe. "Here's a place where you had all
rats, scum, people living there at night," Martin Johnston told a
reporter, describing a mustard-colored drug den transformed by the
Yahwehs into a white oasis of hope. Johnston owned an office furniture store a few doors down. "This is a godsend."

The Yahwehs' self-esteem was infectious. As their properties
rose like a phoenix from the ashes and burned-out crack dens of the
inner city, a renaissance seemed to take root. Hoping to duplicate
the success, black Christian churches began painting their buildings
white. Not even the media were immune to Yahweh Ben Yahweh's
seduction. Sick of bad-news stories that alienated advertisers and
tourists, news executives ran upbeat accounts of the temple's economic accomplishments.

With his metamorphosis into a humanitarian businessman,
more political clout flowed. The messiah's vote machine began to
grow into a sophisticated block-by-block ward system, coveted by
every politician in town. No longer did Sister Judith thrust wads of
cash into the hands of aspiring officeholders. God, the son of God,
didn't court the politicians anymore. Now they courted him. They
streamed to temple feasts—judges, commissioners, police chiefs—
hoping for audiences with Yahweh. Frisked for weapons at the door,
they were filmed by white-robed cameramen in pictures and videos
later to be used as sect propaganda. Drawn by curiosity or the
prospect of votes, or sometimes for reasons that remained a mystery
even to those who went, political hopefuls agreed on one thing: When

they shook Yahweh Ben Yahweh's hand, it never had a trace of blood on it.

After his pilgrimage, Victor H. De Yurre, a young real-estate lawyer, heaped praise on Yahweh's "Godlike" stature. "They take care of business," said De Yurre, son of a former mayor of Havana. He thought the Yahwehs could deliver the black votes he needed to win a seat on Miami's city commission. De Yurre also claimed to be a true believer in a little Charles Bronson vigilantism, in a city awash in crime. "Whatever tactics they use, they work. If you mess with us, we're gonna mess with you—I don't have any problem with that."

In time, Yahweh's political reach extended across racial, ethnic, and party lines. He nuzzled up to Dade County commissioner Joe Gersten, a white Democrat who later skipped the country after allegedly cavorting with a hooker in a crack den. And Yahweh found a steady, reliable supporter in Arthur Teele, Jr., a black Republican who would eventually replace Gersten as the king of Dade County politics. Undeterred by the ongoing homicide investigations, the politicians put Yahweh volunteers to work on their campaigns. Teele introduced Yahweh Ben Yahweh to prominent black businessmen around the country, always praising the sect as a shining example of black achievement. "Absolutely more successful," Teele said, "than any other group I've seen in the United States today."

The crowning moment of Yahweh Ben Yahweh's political success came in the fall of 1987, just a year after the Opa-locka murders. Xavier Suarez, the city's first Cuban-born mayor, faced a tough reelection battle. A GOP moderate, Suarez didn't seem like the typical Miami politician. He had a reputation as clean, both in deed and dapper clothing. Not only had he managed to keep himself relatively unpolluted by the corruption swirling around city hall, but he looked good, too. The creases in the Harvard grad's pants could slice onions, and a speck on his loafers would have died of loneliness.

James Angleton, the boulevard hotelier, suggested that Suarez meet Yahweh Ben Yahweh. Angleton had become a frequent visitor to the temple, claiming to understand the messiah as well as, or better than, any establishment person in town. Angleton assumed the group could swing two thousand to eight thousand votes. The mayor saw salvation. What harm, he thought, in trying to win the support of a deity who was not only fixing up buildings, but also imposing discipline in turbulent neighborhoods? Suarez always had been personally alert to his city's violent reputation. Thieves once broke into his car, stealing a Beretta from his briefcase. The mayor got a new gun. (Later, he had to flash it at intruders who held his wife at gunpoint in the family room.)

Suarez, Angleton, and an attorney named Vince McGhee went to the temple, and for once the Yahwehs didn't search their visitors. During the interview, Suarez spotted a black Madonna on a shelf behind Yahweh Ben Yahweh's desk. When the mayor asked about it, the son of God professed a deep respect for the pope. Though Yahweh had once prophesied that John Paul II would revive the Roman Empire by force, he now praised the Holy See's positions against birth control, abortion, homosexuality, and oppression of the masses. The mayor, a devout Catholic, was impressed. Yahweh didn't seem at all like the hate-mongering fanatic that Suarez had read about in the *Miami Herald.* "They do inculcate a certain lawfulness and discipline in their members, which is admirable," the mayor said later.

The audience lasted forty minutes. Suarez said he left with no commitments—no cash, no contributions, no promises offered or accepted. Then, on election night, two dozen white-robed disciples filed into the Hyatt Regency ballroom for Suarez's victory party. They stood conspicuously apart from the cheering crowd in business suits and *guayaberas.*

The mayor and the messiah posed for pictures together, and Yahweh told a reporter he had thrown four thousand votes in Suarez's direction. "There's a small problem," the son of God said. "I can only endorse one man on earth. Yahweh."

After the election, Yahweh's reputation as a black kingmaker grew from coast to coast. He befriended a Who's Who of African-American leaders—from civil rights activist Benjamin Chavis to Hollywood actress Marla Gibbs to Atlanta mayor Maynard Jackson. Philip Michael Thomas, *Miami Vice*'s Tubbs, showed up at a Passover feast dressed in white.

With political stardom came the spoils. With few questions asked, Yahweh's shadowy organization obtained loans and tax breaks, defying economic realities that stifled so many legitimate businesses in poor neighborhoods. When the property appraiser's office denied the Yahwehs an exemption on real estate, raising questions about the group's finances, the sect leader turned to an old admirer, Dade County commissioner Barbara Carey. A board including Carey promptly reversed the decision and granted the exemption. "I would have done the same for anyone in the community who I thought was honorable and decent," Carey explained.

All the nightmarish images from the past—the siege at Opalocka, the accusation of head taking, the allegations of child abuse, slave labor, fraud—were being forgiven, blotted out by orderly white facades in the ghetto. It didn't matter to the establishment where he got the money to finance his ghetto empire. Questions about basics, such as Yahweh's background and family life, as well as the group's size and budget, were routinely deflected. If anyone asked, Yahweh said the money came from contributions by mayors, commissioners, lawyers, doctors, and a host of "incognito" sympathizers, pooling their resources. Ellis Rubin never pressed him. "I think it's a miracle," the lawyer said.

Yahweh Ben Yahweh added more miracles, more jewels of praise to his promotional crown. The Urban League of Greater Miami, a powerful establishment organization pushing for economic advancement of local blacks, bestowed upon him a Whitney M. Young, Jr., humanitarian award for economic development. The league's T. Willard Fair, a future candidate for Miami mayor, praised Yahweh's leadership, style, demeanor, imagination, altruism, vision, and common sense. Just two years before, the FBI had cautioned Fair that he appeared on a Yahweh hit list.

Then came the ultimate achievement, Yahweh Ben Yahweh's biggest-ever acquisition: a $1.85 million, 106-room resort on sun-baked Sunny Isles, north of Miami Beach. Reported to be the first black-owned public facility on the Florida coastline, the hotel catapulted Yahweh into the role of richest black businessman in Miami. His followers, awed by his growing power, called it the New Yahweh Sun City Motel. Across the street, the rabbi from the Young Israel synagogue remained skeptical, but Yahweh Ben Yahweh and his white Jewish lawyer had a solution. They announced that the Temple of Love's rank and file would go on synagogue patrol, to prevent acts of anti-Semitic vandalism.

The temple went into the tourism business, gracing its travel brochures with pictures of smiling white patrons. "The tropical resort of the joys that vacation dreams are made of," one advertisement boasted. "In ancient times, there was a prayer for the stranger within our gates. Because this motel is a human institution to serve people, and not solely a money-making organization, we hope that Yahweh will grant you peace and rest while you are under our roof. Shalom—we are all travelers. From birth till death, we travel between the eternities."

By December 1988 the new, peaceful Yahwehs were wooing visitors to Super Bowl XXIII. The tourism board expected 100,000 guests and 1,500 journalists. Here was Miami's big chance to show the world it had finally overcome its reputation as America's murder capital and to prove wrong the bumper stickers declaring "Miami's a Riot." To make the city glitter for tourists and a national TV audience, the cops rounded up vagrants, hauled them to jail, and destroyed their meager homes in parks and under bridges. Sanitation men spruced up Bobby Maduro Stadium, a baseball field that had been converted into a shelter for two hundred penniless new immigrants from Central America. As part of a beautification project, Yahweh's warriors-turned-pussycats had helped hoist Art Deco–style banners along Biscayne Boulevard. The flags, with pink-beaked white flamingos, palm trees, and a burst of sun, flapped gently against blue skies and drifting Miami clouds.

A few days before the bowl game, Yahweh Ben Yahweh and other civic leaders took time out to pay homage to the poor. During the annual Martin Luther King parade in Liberty City, Mayor Suarez

238

33

As the Hebrew Israelites achieved new power and veneration in Miami, Mary Dupree sat in church a thousand miles away. She thought she saw him, her tall, gangly, impressionable son, singing in the choir. But then her daughter would take a harder look and gently tug her mother back to reality.

"Mama," Michelle would say, "that's not Leonard."

Mary and Lartius Dupree lived in a small brick house on the Mississippi, surrounded by constant reminders of him: three-foot trophies of his karate days; photographs of his army days; yellowed newspaper clippings of victories in his short life. More than a year before, in the spring of 1987, Detective John King had turned up on their doorstep. He had bad news. He asked for dental records and photos of Leonard. King couldn't say for sure, but Leonard was probably dead, killed at the hands of religious fanatics in the Temple of Love. He couldn't tell them a lot, and he couldn't find the body. Without a corpse, King claimed, they couldn't prosecute.

Leonard's body wasn't the only missing link. Lawmen suspected the Yahwehs had gotten rid of other evidence—the vehicles in the Delray firebombing, knives in the white devil stabbings, the big silver .45 used to shoot Rudy and Pudley. Physical proof that the police did collect—the knives found at the foot of Eric Burke's stairwell, the green carpet linking the temple to Aston Green's beheading— were destroyed or lost without explanation. Witnesses and suspects turned up missing or dead by the time investigators got around to talking to them. And sometimes they were impossible to find. When Bobby Rozier told his new court-appointed lawyer, Jeffrey Weinkle, about Amri Israel, Isaiah Solomon Israel, Aher Israel, Seth Adam Israel, and more than one hundred people named Israel who knew about what happened at Opa-locka, the lawyer had a problem: What do you do with a subpoena when everyone has the same last name?

Weinkle asked Ellis Rubin how to reach all the Israels. Rubin sent back a curt reply: "We do not know aliases or current addresses."

Weinkle, a former public defender, had sniffed a cover-up. Upon his coaxing, process servers swooped down on the temple to serve all the subpoenas. Many simply didn't show up for depositions. Those who appeared, including the messiah himself, had convenient memory lapses on many topics of recent history, such as their names, the state, country, or continents on which they were born, the number of children they had, the names of their spouses, their occupations —but, most important, the circumstances of Yahweh homicides.

"Do you think there are any drugs in the food you eat that would prevent you and the Yahwehs from having normal memories?" Weinkle asked one Obadiah Israel.

"Not to my recollection," Obadiah replied.

The attorney's conversation with one Yoel Israel went like this.

"State your full name for the record."

"Yoel Israel."

"Have you ever been known by another name?"

"Yoel."

"Has anybody else ever called you by any other names?"

"Yoel."

"What other names have you been known by?"

"Yoel."

"When you were born, is that the name your parents gave you?"

"Yoel, that's my name."

"That's not my question. Have you ever been known by any other names? Have you answered to any other names?"

"Yoel is the only name I have ever answered by."

"Let me try this one more time. I understand that you presently answer to the name Yoel. Has anybody—have you ever answered to any other name besides Yoel?"

"Yoel."

"Do you have parents?"

"Yahweh is my parent."

"Do you have flesh-and-blood parents?"

"That's my parent."

"What are their names?"

"Yoel."

"Is that your mother or brother?"

"You asked me my name and I told you my name."

"I'm asking you the name of your biological parents."

"Yahweh is my biological parent."

"Are you talking about the God Yahweh or Yahweh Ben Yahweh?"

"Yahweh."

"Are they one and the same?"

"Yahweh."

"Do you have a slave name?"

"I'm born a free man."

"Let me try this one more time. Tell me the name of your two biological parents."

"It's Yahweh. . . . I believe in Yahweh. . . . I believe in Yahweh."

Despite the witness problems, Weinkle had managed to cast doubt on the murder allegations against Bobby. He pointed out sloppy police work, inconclusive physical evidence, and flawed eyewitness testimony. One eyewitness had told the police the assassin was clean-shaven. Bobby wore a thick beard. Some witnesses said the shooter was five feet ten inches and weighed 150 pounds. Bobby was almost six feet four inches and weighed at least 210. One witness who identified Bobby as "the taller killer" said he wore short gray pants. Bobby wore blue jeans. Some witnesses described Bobby's gun as a small, .22-caliber pistol, consistent with the .22 shells the cops found in his pocket, but inconsistent with the murder weapon, the missing .45.

The tenant eyewitnesses simply weren't sure of what they saw, and what they did see, they were too apathetic, or too scared, to say. One woman, after looking at a police lineup for several minutes, said her pastor told her not to identify any pictures of homicide suspects. Yes, she admitted, one of the six photos was the killer. But if she were asked in a court of law, she would deny recognizing anyone in the lineup.

One day at a court hearing, with questionable physical evidence and tainted lineups against Bobby about to be suppressed, prosecutor Don Horn asked Weinkle if they could sit and talk. The state wanted to offer Bobby a deal: If he agreed to sing, they'd let him plead guilty to four counts of second-degree murder, meaning twenty-two years in prison. If he took the deal, Bobby would elude the electric chair four times.

That sounded pretty good to Bobby. In the state system, with good time, it meant a sentence of eight years or so. He could do that standing on his head. With his attorney's help, Bobby put together a report called a proffer, a sort of résumé for criminals, to tweak the lawmen. It was a thirty-three-page description of twenty-seven alleged homicides, leaving blanks where the killers' names were supposed to be written later. Bobby knew how to work the system. Before filling in the blanks, he had four demands. Number one: He wanted a get-out-of-jail card, a complete walk, on every homicide he had committed that the state didn't know about. Number two: He wanted to serve his time in a nice federal prison where the U.S. marshals could protect him. (Inmates with Yahweh stenciled on their prison garb had the run of the Florida jails, and Bobby was afraid of them.) Number three: He wanted to go into the federal witness protection program. Number four: When he finished his sentence, he wanted a little cash to help him on his feet.

Bobby's requirements had to please the state of Florida, or at least the Dade County state attorney's office. Ever since losing the McDuffie police brutality case in 1980, State Attorney Janet Reno had faltered in the pursuit of controversial cases like the Yahwehs. Overwhelmed by an exploding street-crime problem, handicapped by a close working relationship with potential targets, Reno had, at best, a mediocre record of putting brutal cops, corrupt politicians, and politically influential people behind bars. When a potentially troublesome case came along, it was the U.S. attorney, not the state attorney, who usually went after it. Who could be more of a political headache than a black messiah? Going after a black leader in Miami was hard enough. Going after a black religious leader who'd befriended almost every politician in town could be downright career ending.

Denying any political motive, Reno asked the feds to handle the Yahweh case—a decade's worth of largely unprosecuted allegations of homicide, child abuse, and fraud. She cited three factors:

- If the feds did the case, they could make use of the IRS to trace the Yahweh money.
- Witnesses would be better protected through special federal programs.
- Florida's rules on pretrial "discovery" would make it tough to convict Yahweh Ben Yahweh under state law. ("Discovery" is an accused's right to know evidence that prosecutors plan to introduce at trial. Florida's discovery rules grant defendants far more latitude than federal law does.)

There was one hitch: The U.S. attorney's office didn't want the case either. "Why should we handle Janet Reno's garbage?" one federal prosecutor asked. But upon the insistence of the FBI, the U.S. attorney's office reluctantly agreed to take over the case. State prosecutors and local detectives would help, if needed. Bobby signed a twelve-page plea agreement and quietly went before circuit court judge Ellen "Maximum" Morphonios. She had earned her nickname by handing out mean sentences, and she always was the court system's stuff of legends. Though she denied it, legend had it she once ordered a rapist to the bench, and as two bailiffs held him by the arms, hiked up her black robe to flash her legs and snarled, "Take a good look at these, because this is the last time you'll see 'em for a while."

Bobby, wearing white robes, got a break in his sentence, but he didn't get a look. Morphonios quickly sentenced him to the prearranged jail term, amounting to about 3.1 years per murder, less with early-release credits. U.S. marshals whisked him out a side door for the twenty-four-mile pilgrimage to the Metropolitan Correctional Center, south of Miami. There, in a hundred hours of debriefings, Bobby talked about killing as if it was as easy as drinking a glass of water. As Detective Remley, FBI agent Cousins, and attorney Weinkle scribbled notes, Bobby recounted his seven murders—one for himself and six, he said, for his ex-boss. Yahweh Ben Yahweh, Bobby said, gave holy kisses to his warrior killers. Once, the son of God tossed around someone's ear like it was a Frisbee. Another ear, Bobby said, quoting Yahweh, looks "like a pig's ear." After the killers played games with the ears, they wrapped them in newspaper, poured gasoline on them, and burned them in fifty-five-gallon drums.

Bobby filled in the blanks of his ex-comrades. Huram Israel, he said, drove a filet knife through someone's chest so violently that the blade broke. Yahweh scolded him for leaving behind the evidence. Bobby described the way he and other soldiers used to stalk innocents—old people, University of Miami frat members—before deciding if they should knife them. Bobby also said he heard about a plan to have female followers, working as domestics, poison the food of their suburban employers. Once, Bobby said, he and his friend Aher were going to kill an older couple with car problems, then left them alone when a tow truck came to help. Another time, they saw a man with a German shepherd. They didn't want to bother with the dog, so they left the man alone. They stumbled upon a bespectacled man sleeping in his car. "Neariah, is he black?" Aher asked, according to Bobby's testimony. "And I said, 'I don't know. Let me see.' I walked and looked at him, and I couldn't tell. It was dark so I leaned over, grabbed him by his shirt, pulled him toward me into the light, saw that he wasn't black. . . . I reached up, pulled my knife out, and started stabbing him. When I stabbed him the first couple of times, he woke up and tried to grab my arm. I grabbed his arm with my other arm, continued to stab him. Aher pulled out his knife, stepped to my right, moved me over a little bit, and centered his knife in the middle of his chest, pulled all his weight down, and the knife went all the way into the chest, and he died. He had been laying on top of a gun, and it hit the ground and Aher stuffed it in his pants, took his knife, cut off the man's ear, removed his glasses first, cut off his ear, put his glasses back on, and said, 'Damn, I dropped it. Do you see it?' And I looked under the car, and we couldn't find the ear. So then he removed the glasses again, cut the other ear off, and put the glasses in place. We shut the door, wrapped the ear up, and left."

The lawmen munched on candy bars and potato chips as Bobby told his stories. During breaks, he read *Playboy* magazine. He offered details of methods, circumstances, and as best he knew, locations, so the police could check his information. For example, Bobby said, a Hebrew stabbed a drunk white devil on a park bench. The victim was wearing a suit, no vest or tie. Hoseah Isaac, the Yahweh guard Bobby implicated, returned to the temple and showed off an ear in a bottle of alcohol. Another time, Bobby said Isaiah Solomon told him about two Yahwehs who attacked a white devil on Biscayne Boulevard. The victim fell to the ground. Isaiah Solomon mentioned how the man had been stabbed from behind, in the kidney, because Yahweh Ben Yahweh taught that was the proper method of assassination: it caused people to go into immediate shock. So the killer was surprised when it didn't work; the victim got up and began walking away. The Yahwehs had to flee before they could amputate the man's ear.

Bobby talked about the killing of the man wearing a Star of David T-shirt. As best as Bobby could remember, Aher, the alleged assassin, mentioned that the victim had very short hair. Aher couldn't take any body parts because the victim's body may have fallen into a body of water.

After the debriefings, Detective Remley went to work on Bobby's information. Every one of his stories matched a dead body found in Miami in 1986, and every one of them was still unsolved. But despite Bobby's skein of leads, the federal case against Yahweh Ben Yahweh, like the state case before it, started to slip away before it even began. In the corridors of justice, prosecutors and FBI agents bickered among themselves about self-serving leaks, insufficient resources, bungled subpoenas, missing welfare records, and case strategy. Yahweh bank documents piled up in an FBI field office, unanalyzed, collecting dust. "Why aren't you guys doing anything?" defector Lloyd Clark would ask the feds. For almost three years, he had been carted around like baggage from one grand jury to the next. "What the hell is going on?" Confusion and inertia that had sabotaged state homicide prosecutions had now turned into what federal prosecutor Dave DeMaio called "willful neglect . . . a managerial f-----" on a federal level.

By 1989 the FBI and local police had identified ten witnesses who gave statements about Leonard Dupree's homicide. Willie Swift, a former elder on the run, couldn't forget how he'd helped ditch the karate expert's body. The dead man, Willie told investigators, was buried in a field in Dade County. But by the time he led search parties to the site, there was no trace of the corpse. No blood, no hair, no weapon.

Six years had passed since Leonard left home, lured to a lonesome place by the promise of salvation. In New Orleans, Mary and Lartius Dupree still badly wanted to believe that their son was alive. The pain and fear of seeing a loved one murdered was bad enough; not seeing him one last time, if only in a casket, made it impossible for them to close the book on that part of their life. The Duprees, like most families of Yahweh victims, didn't know much about courtroom finagling or the games police and lawyers played. They just knew that when someone was killed and the police knew who the killers were, there would be justice. This was 1989, not 1959, and murderers were not supposed to go free.

34

··

In April of 1989 the mothers of 131st Street finally got their day
in court. Bobby Rozier, escorted by armed marshals, came out of
his federal hideaway to be their star witness. Without offering many
specifics, he testified publicly about the white devil killings for the
first time. He said the messiah ordered him and a second Hebrew,
Aher Israel, to kill the two tenants who so boldly resisted the Yahweh
takeover at the Dirt Road apartments. A third gunman, Seth Adam
Israel, helped chase Pudley Brown. Seth Adam had since died in a
street shootout. Aher was on the run. Other Hebrews, including Sister
Judith, had known about the plan. Bobby claimed the messiah had
wanted them to kidnap the men at gunpoint, take them to a field,
and decapitate them as a message to all drug dealers that Yahweh
was God. But the plan went sour. Bobby testified he didn't fire one
fatal shot at Opa-locka. He was angry with Yahweh Ben Yahweh
for scapegoating him. "This one man has to be stopped," Bobby
said. "He is destroying hundreds of people's lives." As he testified,
FBI agent Cousins and prosecutor DeMaio sat in the back of the
courtroom, scribbling more notes.

At the trial, Yahweh trumpeted his innocence. "All we have,"
he said, "is a record of peace." But the eloquence of his denial didn't
sway U.S. district judge James Kehoe. In a blistering, eighteen-page
opinion, Kehoe ruled for the tenants. The Temple of Love Inc., the
judge found, had carried out a pattern of racketeering through assault, extortion, and "intentional infliction of emotional stress," ending in the murders of Rudy Broussard and Pudley Brown. Without
ruling on whether Yahweh himself masterminded the killings, the
judge ordered the temple to pay twenty-six families who were forced
to flee apartments in the bums' rush. By south Florida lawsuit
standards, it was a meager amount, $940,000, later reduced to
$646,000, to avoid an appeal. But the tenants were buoyed by the
victory. Yahweh's followers were stunned. The sect was forced to

give up property to pay off the court judgment, and disciples with no place to go began to wonder what would happen if their messiah was brought down. Denounced but not defeated, Yahweh Ben Yahweh comforted them. He would never leave them, he said. No way would he allow anyone to stretch him on a cross, hang him, and take the blood from his body. Martyrdom was not part of his plan. "I follow the script up to a point," he told his followers, "then I change it."

The "army of black devils" after him wanted to make him just a man. "I'm just not," he said. "I'm *not* just a man. I just—I cannot be just a man." Satan had no power over him, over God. "How you gonna *get* God?" Yahweh Ben Yahweh asked. "You can't *get* God."

His prophecy was coming true. Prosecutors recommended closing the federal case, and though his temple membership was dwindling, Yahweh himself climbed to yet loftier heights. He dined in elegance at the posh Jockey Club and mingled easily with pinstripes at city hall. He talked about becoming the first black yacht club owner, praised America as "the greatest country on earth," and petitioned blue-blooded Miami for moral support. He got more than that. On a sunny Saturday in April 1990, with bands blaring and balloons flapping in the easterly breeze, civic leaders bestowed upon the messiah a city-owned supermarket in Overtown, rent free— $150,000 worth of store equipment, free extermination, free lawn and freezer maintenance. About a hundred followers drifted through the crowd in their white robes as elected officials and aspiring officeholders rushed to shake Yahweh's hand. The program printed by the taxpayers hailed him as "His Eminence." Mayor Suarez strode to the podium to praise Yahweh for "improving the lives of our people through economic development, through discipline, through hard work."

A follower declared, "Out of a city of despair, now Yahweh is causing a repair. And to a people that have sat in darkness, now Yahweh is raising a great light of hope."

Yahweh Ben Yahweh hoisted his hands toward the heavens. "I thank and praise my father Yahweh for this miracle."

Twenty days after the opening of First Rate Foods, the supreme ruler climbed the steps of Miami's federal courthouse, flanked by four white-robed women and two lawyers. The Yahweh probe had gone to yet another federal prosecutor, the fourth in five years. Assistant U.S. Attorney Richard Scruggs, chief of the major-crimes unit, had been called on to prosecute some of the Justice Department's most urgent black-hole conspiracies. A forty-year-old, divorced ex-marine, he grew up in Atlanta's all-white suburbs while Yahweh Ben Yahweh was hawking copies of the Muslim newspaper on Broad Street. Scruggs still remembered the time his father refused to let Martin Luther King, Jr., buy a ticket at the family movie theater. After law school and a brief stint with the ACLU, Scruggs moved to Washington to work for Justice. He nailed KGB agents and prosecuted traitors who infiltrated U.S. crypto systems. At the U.S. attorney's office in Miami, he broke up drug corruption schemes involving an assortment of narco-terrorists, rogue cops, onetime spies, and public officials. Now Scruggs wondered how he'd ever get the Yahweh case to court. He checked with Trudy Novicki, a kindred spirit in the Dade County state attorney's office. She'd prosecuted a network of bad Miami River cops and, like Scruggs, enjoyed toppling corrupt icons. When Novicki agreed to help, Scruggs assigned the case to himself. "Scruggs thinks he can make chicken soup out of chicken shit," a lawyer in his office joked.

To prove that the government had more power than Yahweh, Scruggs had subpoenaed him to appear before a grand jury with the *Lamb's Book of Life*. The book listed his followers by both slave and Israel names. Scruggs saw it as an atlas to potential witnesses and murderers. Yahweh had always deemed the book a holy article. It traveled on the road with five sisters, and the profane were not to touch it. As he entered the grand jury room, Yahweh had nothing in his hands. He'd even left behind his cellular telephone after a Hebrew supervisor read the sign on the courthouse metal detector: NO ELECTRONIC DEVICES ALLOWED. The son of God politely fenced and parried with Scruggs for sixty-five minutes, taking the Fifth Amendment and the First Amendment, among other legal privileges. Then he went upstairs for a forty-minute chat with a judge, who ordered

250

him to turn over the book or face contempt charges. Yahweh, who saw it as another silly inconvenience, knew the government would lose this skirmish just as it had lost the ones before it. He left the courthouse smiling confidently, having given Richard Scruggs no solid information. No names, no leads at all.

When reports of Yahweh's grand jury appearance hit the *Miami Herald*, the city's lords of business rallied around him as never before. At a chic bay-front restaurant, men and women in their power suits, CPAs, real-estate developers, even county lawmen, dined on pasta salad and toasted the son of God with chardonnay. They nodded their heads with happy fervor as he proclaimed himself a worldwide attraction: "Egypt has her pyramids! India has her Taj Mahal. France has her Eiffel Tower. Rome has her pope. Orlando has Disney World and the mouse. Miami has the son of Yahweh. The world's greatest attraction is in your midst . . . I'm here!"

His image was already larger than life, but with all the glory and fame he had achieved, he believed his biggest contributions were still ahead of him. He vowed to heap great riches on his wealthy followers. He started a bus service to shuttle shoppers to and from his grocery store. But his hotel rooms remained largely vacant and his supermarket aisles empty of shoppers. All those years of an image remake, and many of his businesses were still shells with dead telephones. All those years, and the grassroots was still afraid of him. "I ain't getting on a bus with somebody who thinks he's Jesus!" one old woman said.

Miami's blessed and only potentate was incensed. He was paying a PR woman, Barbara Howard, to get people to shop with Yahweh. When she told him she needed more than twenty-five dollars a week to fulfill her assignment, he blamed Barbara for not believing more strongly in his divine power to succeed. He wasn't used to anyone questioning his salary scales. He turned to Barbara's Hebrew son, Yavin. "When I support people, then what do I require of them, Yavin?"

"Their all," Yavin replied stoically.

"That's right. And I don't mean any pussy either," Miami's model citizen said. "And I don't mean any ass, because everybody will tell you, I'm not an ass man."

Barbara left the meeting, enraged. Yahweh didn't care if the street people did not support him. His empire was worth one hundred million dollars, built on a seemingly infinite supply of money from a mysterious source that would flow no matter what. Important people were backing him. Even old enemies were coming around. On Saturday, August 4, 1990, nine thousand people packed the new fifty-million-dollar Miami Arena as Yahweh reconciled with his long-time rival, the Honorable Louis Farrakhan. The two men embraced for the first time since the 1960s, when Yahweh was the Muslim Hulon Shah. "This man is a builder," Farrakhan told the raucous crowd, praying to Allah to protect his brother. "We ask your blessing and your protection on Yahweh Ben Yahweh, for we know that the government is working to destroy him, his movement, and what he has built. As the enemy comes closer in their wicked plans, let us come closer to each other, that their plans—though they look mighty—may be brought to a naught."

Following the Farrakhan event, Yahweh Ben Yahweh's irrepressible presence popped up throughout Miami—on posters pasted on utility poles and bus benches along Biscayne Boulevard. He was planning a special motivational lecture, "From Poverty to Riches," for ten dollars a seat. To supplement the effort, the faithful had begun to compile a formidable leather-bound tome, *From Poverty to Riches: The Works of Yahweh Ben Yahweh*. The 230-page package of persuasion featured a color photograph of the son of God and black-and-white pictures of him shaking hands with his rich and powerful friends. At fifty dollars a book, the price tag seemed a little steep for anyone struggling to get out of poverty, but judges and elected officials received complimentary copies.

A new propaganda group, The People for Truth, hammered up Yahweh billboards, placed ads in newspapers across the country, and sent letters, pamphlets, and brochures to the influential at the rate of three or four mailings a month. The People for Truth warned,

"We are watching our televisions, reading our newspapers, listening to our radios, and awaiting notification by word of mouth for any sign of an attack on Yahweh Ben Yahweh. . . . If Yahweh Ben Yahweh is arrested, there will be WAR in the streets of America."

There was war, but not over an arrest of Yahweh Ben Yahweh. Miami's Little Haiti rose up after riot-helmeted police wielded nightsticks like tomahawks into a peaceful crowd of sixty demonstrators. The cops pummeled the Haitians, who had been protesting discriminatory immigration policies, for the crime of "not dispersing." The Puerto Rican neighborhood of Wynwood was preparing to riot, as six cops headed toward exoneration after fatally beating a neighborhood crack dealer. Civil rights leaders were boycotting hotels and conventions in Miami, because the establishment snubbed African National Congress leader Nelson Mandela during his summer visit. Mandela had refused to denounce Fidel Castro and Yasser Arafat, who had supported blacks' struggle to end apartheid in South Africa.

Miami's old guard was busy courting Yahweh Ben Yahweh's support on baseball bond deals and homeless shelters, buying into more of his miracles. He didn't care about the boycott, or the city's refusal to honor Mandela. Yahweh wanted them to honor him. He wanted the keys to the city or some larger token of tribute—compensation for a decade of great accomplishments, for his superior and unselfish work on behalf of the world. Forces loyal to the messiah marched to city hall to deliver a proposed text of a proclamation to Yahweh. They handed it to Commissioner Miller Dawkins, a longtime black establishment figure. Without checking the information, Dawkins approved it and sent it along to Mayor Suarez for his signature. Everybody, the mayor figured, got his day in Miami—drug dealers, fake sheiks, money launderers, even murderers. "We've given proclamations to judges who were later convicted," Suarez thought. By comparison with some of these thugs, Yahweh Ben Yahweh seemed like a terrorist emeritus.

"Whereas: since coming to Miami Yahweh Ben Yahweh has helped people establish and maintain businesses with assets of over

$100 million. All that he gives to his disciples, followers, believers and supporters, never accepting a salary for himself. And whereas: through economic development, this religious leader has raised the property value of communities by developing models of excellence throughout Miami and other major cities, such as Yahweh Sun City Motel in Sunny Isles in Miami Beach, Yahweh Economy Inn, Yahweh Motel, Yahweh Resort Villas, Yahweh First Rate Foods, Yahweh Groceries, Yahweh University, a publishing company, a high-rise hotel in downtown Atlanta, Georgia, and many others. And whereas: throughout the years his work in economic development has enhanced all the areas where the Nation of Yahweh has property, and through his experience he has shown people how to move from poverty to riches. And whereas: local authorities, on behalf of the community, salute Yahweh Ben Yahweh, one of the most respected religious leaders in our city, for his dedication and efforts in favor of the needy. Now, therefore: I, Xavier L. Suarez, Mayor of the City of Miami, Florida, do hereby proclaim Sunday, October 7, 1990, as YAHWEH BEN YAHWEH DAY in observance thereof: I call upon all residents of the City of Miami to join with me in the celebration of this important date. In witness thereof: I hereunto set my hand and cause the seal of the city of Miami to be affixed."

As his followers prepared for the Sunday poverty lecture, Yahweh Ben Yahweh went on a twenty-one-day fast for "peace and healing in Miami." Then he polished up his big speech. He saw the hand of God in the timing of the event, to be broadcast live to the world from the Miami Arena.

At 3 P.M., the arena doors opened, and by five o'clock about two thousand people—curiosity seekers, people bused in from out of town, civic leaders, undercover lawmen, and a few hundred people in white robes—had filtered into the stadium to pay homage to Yahweh Ben Yahweh. Police cars lined up outside. Neighbors gawked and darkened mustaches on Yahweh Ben Yahweh posters.

The arena resounded with prayer. Prince Gideon sang, and God's children recited their hypnotic chants. The voices resonated louder than ever. The faith was as unswerving. A sea of white robes

254

floated on a tide of passion as Yahweh bellowed, "I am the Prince of Peace, the Savior."

Then, while his icon was projected on a giant video screen behind him, Mayor Suarez's personal emissary stepped forward and officially declared that very Sunday "Yahweh Ben Yahweh Day."

He walked out of the Miami Arena on top.

Part IV

Operation
Jericho

35

He had always talked about the end of the world. Now it was here—at least for him. Two informants, one in the temple, one outside, kept the feds posted on the messiah's every movement. He had been traveling around the country, sleeping from place to place, holding hearts-and-flowers reunions with family and old friends. He stayed in posh hotels, almost as if he were afraid to go home. Now he was planning a six-week foray through the South for new blood, and that was fine with the FBI. They didn't want to go into a holy sanctuary, filled with women and children, to drag their messiah out by force.

They had to plan it right.

For six weeks, the FBI plotted the precision, predawn raids. The locals had made mistakes on past sting operations, even knocking down the wrong doors or taking the wrong people to jail. The feds did not want a fiasco like that in Philadelphia, when the City of Brotherly Love, to end a standoff with the radical group MOVE, bombed two city blocks and killed eleven people.

As prosecutor Richard Scruggs prepared the final draft of the indictment, the FBI formulated tactical strategies based partly on behavior profiles of the leader, his followers, and their relationship. Madman or con man, he was unpredictable, volatile. There was also the possibility of an unstable follower, whose love for and spiritual commitment to Yahweh would be strong enough to make the follower kill. With information that some of his devotees stockpiled weapons, the FBI prepared not only for an ambush but for a siege.

In their worst fear, they saw a mass suicide. No one wanted to wade into a temple littered with dead babies. It was hard for any nonmember to understand, but Yahweh Ben Yahweh's most devoted followers truly accepted that their highest calling, their highest honor, would be to sacrifice themselves, if that's what he wanted.

Sydney P. Freedberg

The feds assigned 120 agents to the roundup, code named Operation Jericho. They would be buttressed by local SWAT teams and state police. It would not, could not, be a slaughter. No heavy-handed tactics. But they still would be prepared, as one agent put it, to "overpower any firepower" they might encounter.

The FBI's Herb Cousins, who had worked on the case for five long years, flew to Miami to be briefed on the arrest plan. Cousins would take Yahweh Ben Yahweh first. If they didn't get him, they wouldn't take anybody.

On Monday, November 5, 1990, Yahweh Ben Yahweh flew from Tampa to Atlanta to New Orleans. He didn't know it, but the FBI was tailing him. He checked into a $390-a-night suite on the fourteenth floor of the Monteleone Hotel, the jewel of the French Quarter. The 104-year-old hotel, with a bird's-eye view of the Mississippi from its rooftop swimming pool, is a block from Bourbon Street. About fifteen disciples had arrived before him and were scattered throughout the hotel.

On Tuesday morning, November 6, 1990, two FBI tactical units set up a command post with audio surveillance in room 1455, just a few doors down from Yahweh Ben Yahweh. Agent Cousins flew to New Orleans to make the arrest.

That evening, thirty days after Miami celebrated Yahweh Ben Yahweh Day, a federal grand jury secretly returned the twenty-five-page indictment. It accused seventeen people in the Nation of Yahweh, "under the self-described spiritual leader known as Yahweh Ben Yahweh aka 'Moses Israel' aka 'Hulon Shah' aka 'Hulon Mitchell, Jr.,' and the Temple of Love Inc." of a catalog of racketeering crimes: conspiracy, murders, arson, extortion. Yahweh, the indictment charged, directed retaliation against followers who dissented from his rulership, revenge against members of the community who interfered with efforts to collect donations or acquire property, and execution of white citizens picked at random as a rite of initiation into the ultrasecret brotherhood. Yahweh also ordered beatings and sex to control his followers. If convicted on the counts, Yahweh Ben Yahweh, age fifty-five, could get sixty years.

The indictment's bill of particulars stretched from the November 1981 attempted assassination of Eric Burke to the June 1987 excommunication of Bobby Rozier. Bobby, the serial killer who cut a sweetheart deal to avoid the electric chair, would not be indicted. Ricky Woodside, who had voluntarily confessed to a role in Aston Green's decapitation, would be charged. After Ricky turned himself over to the FBI four years before, he'd become so upset about case delays, so desperate to build bridges to his Yahweh family, that he reestablished ties to the temple and recanted information given to the feds in earlier interviews.

By Wednesday, November 7, 1990, at 2 A.M., federal agents in blue jumpsuits and flak jackets had taken up positions at field offices in seven states. Each arrest team reviewed its operating orders, including photographs and a detailed description of each suspect, down to scars.

The FBI deployed its elite hostage-rescue team, a counterterrorist unit used in high-threat tactical missions. Agents arrived at Miami FBI headquarters in black Ninja suits, speaking in code and using names like Too Tall and Big Foot.

Scruggs, responsible for coordinating legal matters that might arise from the arrests, parked his car in the back lot and wound his way through the heavy armament, enough machine guns, concussion grenades, infrared aiming devices, ammo, and battering rams to wage a little war. He'd never seen so much firepower before, not even in his days as a U.S. marine.

By 3 A.M., Operation Jericho was about to begin. Miami's special operations center teemed with feds and local cops manning fifty phone lines. An hour later, three hundred law-enforcement officers positioned themselves to hit their targets. Charts displayed the location of the out-of-town agents. Times of door busts, arrests, and bookings were to be jotted in as they occurred.

At 4:40 A.M., FBI New Orleans telephoned the Miami command post: SWAT teams had sealed off the Monteleone. Yahweh Ben Yahweh was as isolated from his followers as the agents could get him. At least one bodyguard was still posted outside his suite. Some of his men had just left the hotel, bound for Houston, Yahweh Ben Yahweh's next stop.

"We're ready to go," an agent in New Orleans said.

Special agent in charge William A. Gavin, manning the Miami command post, gave the order. "Do it."

While hundreds of guests slept, lawmen swarmed into the lobby of the Monteleone. At 4:45 A.M., agent Cousins phoned room 1450. "This is special agent Herb Cousins with the FBI. I need to talk to Yahweh Ben Yahweh."

A male voice—perhaps Yahweh Ben Yahweh himself—replied, "Just a minute."

A few seconds later, Yahweh identified himself.

Cousins explained he had an arrest warrant. "We have the place surrounded. I want you to follow my instructions. Do exactly what I tell you, so no one will get hurt."

Yahweh Ben Yahweh stalled. "I have to . . . just a second." He put down the receiver and tried to notify his bodyguards, but the FBI had cut communication. He came back on the line.

"Tell your bodyguard to raise his hands and walk down to the end of the hall," Cousins said.

Yahweh relayed the instructions to the guard, then came to the telephone again. He wasn't dressed, he said. He needed a few minutes. Could he please at least put on his robe and diadem?

"No," Cousins said. "I want you to do what I say now. I want you to come out of your room, raise your hands, and walk down the hall with your hands up."

"Are you going to be there?" Yahweh asked. Evidently, he felt some relief that the arrest was being made by a black agent he had met before.

"Yes," Cousins replied. "We're concerned with everyone's safety, including your own."

"I understand," Yahweh said.

At 4:50 A.M., Cousins left his post, one floor up, and walked to the middle of the fourteenth-floor hallway.

Yahweh Ben Yahweh stepped outside in his bathrobe, his hands heavenward. He wasn't wearing his turban. His shoulder-length hair was plaited. He looked more like a survivor from Woodstock than the messiah. It was the first time an outsider had seen him without his raiments. He was just another man in a bathrobe.

He tried to hide his nervousness. "What have I been indicted for?" he asked.

"Racketeering," Cousins said. The indictment documented a pattern of terrorism: the firebombing in Delray Beach, the extortion in Opa-locka, two attempted homicides, fourteen murders, all part of the leader's management technique. Yahweh seemed stunned.

Agent Cousins cuffed him.

No one had believed it would be that easy. These were fanatics, weren't they? They had given up their messiah without a fight.

As Cousins ushered the defendant outside for the ride to the New Orleans FBI office, another agent telephoned the command post in Miami: "We've got him."

In Miami, William Gavin gave the word: "Go."

Hundreds of lawmen, in rented U-Hauls, helicopters, and airplanes, armed with pump shotguns, M-16 assault rifles, and SIG-Sauer pistols, pounced across four southern cities, swooping in on Yahweh's indicted followers. The cops wore body armor over their blue combat suits. Within seconds, voices crackled over field radios.

"We've got Woodside in custody."

"We've hit. We have James in custody."

"We've got Murphy. We're clearing."

Along Interstate 10 near Lafayette, Louisiana, two FBI agents in a Cessna spotted a white van and a bus with three suspects. They radioed Louisiana state troopers to arrest them. In Durham, Dan Israel stopped at a traffic light, where he was surrounded by dozens of gun-toting white men and a lone black agent. "Get out! Get out!" they hollered. Dan thought it was a Klan attack.

While Yahwehs were being hauled away in paddy wagons, police squad cars with flashing blue lights blocked traffic in a three-block perimeter surrounding the Temple of Love in Liberty City. Ninety-two minutes before dawn, an agent dialed the temple on his cellular phone. A woman answered.

"This is the FBI," the agent said. "We have a warrant . . ."

The woman hung up. The lawman called again. This time, no one answered.

Over a bullhorn, an agent read a message to those inside the compound to come out with their hands up. No one surrendered.

In the back of their minds, the lawmen saw a silent army of fanatics waiting behind the door with machetes, guns, and clubs. They imagined men, women, and even children ready to die for their beliefs, rushing at them in a mass of white robes, shouting, "Praise Yahweh!"

Or worse, they were too late. Yahweh's followers could already have heard their God had fallen. They'd gulped the purple Flavor-Aid, just as they had done in Jonestown, Guyana.

The lead agent gave a hand signal. A ten-man FBI arrest team sprinted across the temple's parking lot. They pounded on a metal-grated door. The Yahwehs refused to open up.

Smashing glass and metal with a modern-day battering ram, the lawmen stormed the compound.

"Everybody on the floor!"

Other raiders searched motor coaches and sedans parked in front of the temple.

There was no army, just fifteen terrified Hebrews, mostly women and children, who thought the Last Days had begun. Some wept uncontrollably as the lawmen pulled them outside, shotguns to their heads. Women were ordered to hit the ground and to remove their holy headdresses.

The cops fanned through the cavernous building, searching for suspects and evidence. No guns, no knives. If a weapons cache had ever existed, it didn't anymore. Huddled in a back closet, praying, was Brother Job, Yahweh Ben Yahweh's loyal barber. Smoke-colored glasses hid Job's tears.

Less than a half hour after Operation Jericho began, twelve suspects were safely in handcuffs, without one shot fired. A thirteenth, Sister Judith, aka Linda Gaines, was sleeping soundly in an upscale high-rise on West Peachtree Street, Atlanta. Judith was there to check on renovations at the Barclay Hotel, a former Playboy Club that the Yahwehs were transforming into downtown's "cleanest, most hospitable and most convenient address."

The agents decided to let her sleep. At 6:30 A.M., as she headed to her Lincoln town car, they grabbed her.

It had all come off beautifully, a public relations victory. It was almost the first thing in a long time, in a very flawed case, that the authorities could boast about. But it could have just as easily been a disaster. Security had been a leaky bucket at best. Not only had the TV and print media been tipped to the FBI sweep, but evidently so had Yahweh Ben Yahweh. In a trash dumpster outside the temple, agents found a handwritten note: "The investigation is coming to a close and arrest may be imminent. . . . Praise Yahweh."

Two hours before the government formally announced the indictment, Ellis Rubin called a press conference at his office to denounce the "grandstand" raid. Yahweh Ben Yahweh, the attorney said, could never get a fair trial in Miami because of bad publicity. Rubin charged that the indictment, which he'd expected for months, had been delayed by acting U.S. attorney Dexter Lehtinen until after election day. Allegedly, Lehtinen didn't want to jeopardize the re-election prospects of his wife, GOP congresswoman Ileana Ros-Lehtinen.

By early afternoon, a nationwide press was on for four followers who had escaped the federal dragnet. Eventually they would be caught, but not without a little help from Yahweh Ben Yahweh. Heeding a command for their surrender from his jail cell, two indicted disciples would turn themselves in, one in front of TV cameras on courthouse steps.

While his followers swept up broken glass and shooed away reporters, Yahweh Ben Yahweh politely completed the booking forms at the New Orleans field office. An agent joked about getting God on film with a good set of fingerprints. Yahweh kept having to use the bathroom. He asked for two phone calls. The first was to his soon-to-be-fired legal high priest, Ellis Rubin. The second was to his new legal high priest, former U.S. district judge Alcee Hastings. The ex-judge, just a year younger than Yahweh, strongly believed that American justice was biased, bent, and retooled to slap down black leaders who grew too powerful. The FBI had once accused Hastings, Florida's first black federal judge, of conspiring to shake down two hoodlums for $150,000 in exchange for reducing their sentences. A jury acquitted him, but the U.S. Congress, believing he had lied under oath, impeached him on essentially the same charges. Hastings was still fighting his impeachment and angling for a political comeback when he got Yahweh's telephone call.

By Wednesday afternoon, the messiah had changed into his robe and turban. Handcuffed, he was transported to the modern, stark white federal courthouse in New Orleans for his first appearance. For the first time in a decade, maybe in his life, he was speechless. "On the advice of counsel, I stand mute," Yahweh said softly. Two days later, at a second hearing, he would admit that, yes, his biological name was Hulon Mitchell, Jr., earthly father of four, grandfather of twenty-six.

"Do you understand you have effectively eliminated the need for the government to establish your identity?" U.S. magistrate Ivan Lemelle asked.

"Yes, I do," he replied, but "my legal name is Yahweh Ben Yahweh."

"All right, then, Mr. Ben Yahweh, if you admit that, you will be ordered to Miami."

As Yahweh languished in a parish jail, waiting for a U.S. marshal's flight to Miami, his indicted followers stood alone in court. Dressed in T-shirts, shorts, and sweat suits, they cracked knuckles, smiled, and stared blankly during arraignments. Many had no ties to the community, no relatives to support them, no steady jobs, no property, just a few hundred dollars to their names. And now, Yahweh Ben Yahweh planned to leave them without lawyers. The disciples seemed baffled by the charges against them. Brother Job wouldn't answer to his slave name. "I am a Hebrew Israelite," he told the magistrate. "I don't swear."

As word of Yahweh's arrest spread through the streets, Miami did not riot, rise, or even stir faintly. "Get 'em all!" a woman living across the street from the temple said. "They took our money!"

266

Tenants of the Dirt Road apartments celebrated. "Mom, they got him!" the eleven-year-old daughter of Brenda Daniels cried. "They finally got him!" Barbara Malone Goolsby, the legal services lawyer representing the tenants, wondered out loud if Mayor Suarez would finally take back Yahweh's keys to the city.

The mayor and other civic leaders took a dive for cover, making weak pleas of ignorance and lashing out at the criminal justice system for refusing to warn them they were coddling a terrorist. Despite newspaper stories linking the temple to unsolved homicides, despite TV images of the siege at Opa-locka, despite a federal judge's order declaring the Temple of Love Inc. a racketeering enterprise, the politicians swore they didn't know. They thought Yahweh Ben Yahweh was a model citizen. "It was my impression . . . that Yahweh Ben Yahweh did not currently face criminal investigation of any sort," Mayor Suarez said in a brief written statement. "Obviously, I was wrong."

In New Orleans, the indictment all but erased Mary Dupree's hope that her son was still alive. Her husband, Lartius, had died of a heart attack three weeks before, unaware of the forthcoming indictment.

And in Enid, Oklahoma, the people just went about their business of harvesting wheat and drilling for oil. The easiest thing to do was to say nothing, to forget that Yahweh Ben Yahweh had once been one of them. Hulon and Pearl Olive Mitchell told reporters congregating in their front yard that they fully supported the brilliant son who had fallen away from them, the protective boy who had always seen to it that the younger kids got home for dinner in time. They packed their bags for Miami to attend Junior's pretrial detention hearing. For three hours, they waited with 150 of Yahweh's followers to win a seat in the small courtroom. There they listened quietly as Richard Scruggs depicted their number one child as a maximum thug. "He preaches unabashed hate and violence," the prosecutor said.

U.S. magistrate Linnea R. Johnson ordered Yahweh Ben Yahweh held without bond, declaring him a danger to the community.

Pearl Olive told friends in her velvety voice that Junior was getting railroaded. The Reverend Hulon Mitchell, still preaching to two congregations at age seventy-six, knew from the Bible that everyone failed, except for Jesus. A sinner was saved through grace, not words. "We have our faith," Senior said as he and Pearl left the hearing for a waiting limousine. "We have our faith."

36

The criminal justice system, once it finally got the Yahwehs behind bars, was determined to wage war against them on every front: no bond, no furloughs for religious feasts, no white robes, no special diet. To counter what they saw as a trumped-up, "wicked and diabolical plot" to take out yet another American black leader, the messiah's propaganda group put the finishing touches on a sophisticated nationwide smear campaign. The People for Truth collected petitions with thousands of signatures and mass-mailed open letters to the world reporting on the "Persecution of Yahweh Ben Yahweh." Their God, they warned, was preparing to remove the mark of divine protection from "the wicked seed of Cain"—all those seeking a death sentence for him.

The way they'd been arrested and detained in a "terrorist guerrilla attack on innocent women and children" proved they'd already been tried and convicted. The selection of U.S. district judge Norman C. Roettger, Jr., to preside over the case simply confirmed their view. A hunter and mountain climber with a handlebar mustache, the judge looked a little like Teddy Roosevelt in a cloak. Appointed to the bench by Richard Nixon, Roettger had a reputation as an eccentric, hanging judge. He once refused to give jail time to a mercenary plotting against Nicaragua's Sandinista government, depicting the defendant as a patriot simply doing the American thing.

In one pretrial skirmish, the judge requested that the Yahweh defendants use their slave names in court. "I can't keep them straight," he said.

Sister Judith's court-appointed lawyer tried to explain that the common last name Israel was a tenet of the Hebrew Israelite religion, a "part of their lifestyle change."

Roettger wasn't moved. "Being on trial is a lifestyle change," he snapped.

Adding to their belief that they were being persecuted was the warlike assault by the U.S. attorney's office. Though the decision to indict had been made, the federal grand jury, which had already heard from hundreds of witnesses, kept up its investigation of Yahweh Ben Yahweh long after the arrests. The jury listened to testimony about more homicides and temple drug ties. A team of FBI and IRS agents pored through bank records, trying to find the money source that fed cash to Yahweh's terror game. Eventually, the grand jury would return a superseding indictment naming two additional followers and a fifteenth homicide victim, seventy-year-old Harold Barnett.

Backed by a task force of federal and local lawmen, Richard Scruggs and Trudy Novicki continued to visit crime scenes. They ordered charts and diagrams drawn up for the jury and crisscrossed the country to find new witnesses and reinterview old ones. Scruggs, who never before owned a gun, was issued a .357 by the FBI, which believed his life had been threatened. Never before had the prosecutor who brought down spies experienced a case with such a morass of lies, memory evasions, half-truths, and so many people so afraid to tell the truth. As he traveled from California to Oklahoma to Georgia searching for people to stand up in federal court, Scruggs quickly discovered he couldn't just go barging into houses, flashing his Justice credentials and demanding a statement. Witnesses scrambled for cover when they heard the law was in town. Some felt guilty. Others had locked the memories in a grave inside their heads. Yet others didn't want to admit their faith and lose their jobs. "I am halfway in between retirement," said Willie Swift, the ex-Hebrew who had confessed to helping dispose of Leonard Dupree's body. "I am living my life and I want to be left alone."

Hebrew witnesses saw nothing in it for them. "Why should I help?" one man told Scruggs. "You can't make the charges stick."

Hoping to penetrate the secrecy that the white lawmen had difficulty cracking, the FBI had assigned a second black case agent before the indictment. Easygoing, in his twenties, Rickey O'Donald sometimes found he had a tougher time talking to the Yahwehs than the white lawmen. "You're doing the devil's work," one told him.

To knock down walls dividing persecuted and prosecutor, Scruggs studied the secret language of the sect. He prepared his own sermons to get people to open up. Sometimes he acknowledged their worldview of a conspiracy; other times he made appeals to the heavens. "God wants you to testify," he told one witness.

Poverty and the seeming random violence of their daily lives added to the reluctance of some witnesses. In a crumbling housing project in another state, Scruggs had tracked down Neesie Broussard, the Opa-locka tenant whose brother had been shot to death. Her small checks from the tenants' court victory, totaling $1,475, came by mail, but they hadn't paid for much of a life. The sadness and fear she had felt since the day the Yahwehs killed Rudy still pierced every moment of her life. Neesie's family had moved to get away from the Yahwehs, but she still thought they were watching her. She'd already testified openly three times. Why did they need her again? In spite of her anxiety, Neesie agreed to help. She thought it was important for people to know what her family had been through.

Some witnesses had wanted to know if they could hide their identities, maybe with a mask, if they testified. Like Neesie Broussard, Patricia Albert was willing to use her name. She was the girl from Oklahoma who grew up in the Temple of Love. After leaving in January 1989, she'd talked out her "trauma" with her parents and sister. Yahweh's sister, Jean Solomon, had led the lawmen to Pat's family, and when the FBI finally caught up with her, she was no longer a child but a mother, struggling to raise two small girls, both born in the temple. Pat had a minimum-wage job at a fast-food restaurant and a small place in North Miami, where she lived with the kids and her parents. She cleaned house, did chores, and slowly learned to trust people again.

The story of her childhood seemed like a distant memory now. Despite Yahweh's personal warning to her mother that God would take revenge, Pat told Scruggs and FBI agent O'Donald about the brutality she had witnessed. Once she remembered seeing what she thought was a human head wrapped in a towel. She talked about her own abuse. Even after her marriage to Michael Mathis in 1985, even after the couple had their first child, Yahweh Ben Yahweh, Pat told the FBI, had cajoled her into sex. She recounted a lovemaking session, four days after her daughter's birth, that caused damage to her stitches.

Pat revealed these long-held secrets with a simple clarity and matter-of-factness that stunned Richard Scruggs. He thought she was one of the strongest, most sincere people he'd met, and he wanted her to understand what to expect in the courtroom. Her private life would be open to microscopic examination; defense lawyers were paid to make her look like the criminal, not the injured party. Pat agreed to testify anyway. "I'm not afraid of Yahweh Ben Yahweh," she told the prosecutor. "I've seen him with his pants off."

Pat encouraged her stepfather, Jeffrey Glover, to testify. Rumors had long circulated in Enid that Jeffrey was dead. He did nothing to correct them. He was scared for himself and his children. After learning about his daughter's abuse, he was so angry that he could have killed Yahweh Ben Yahweh. Jeffrey told his story before the grand jury, confessing to a role in the Delray Beach firebombing. He explained the way he'd been drawn in by Yahweh's magnetic appeal. "Black people were being used," he said and wept. "They were coming in and giving their all and thinking they were getting somewhere, and then once you're drained, you don't have anything. When you leave, you won't have nothing. . . . You're standing out in the cold with nothing." Realizing Jeffrey's remorse, Scruggs gave him immunity.

As the government rounded up defectors, the lawmen joked that Richard Scruggs was the new Yahweh Ben Yahweh, responsible for protecting the flock, maintaining morale, dress-rehearsing them for trial, and fielding their requests for guns, bodyguards, escorts, new names, social service help, friends, money, and reassurances. Eventually, he would recommend thirty collaborators, including Patricia and her family, to the federal witness protection program, believed to be more than in any case in U.S. history.

A main goal of the Yahweh defense was to find out who these

people were. Who was on the government's 172-person witness list? Who would they incriminate? Would people show up at the trial from nowhere? The team of young but aggressive court-appointed lawyers refused to roll over without a fight. They hired private investigators to corral witnesses loyal to Yahweh while seeking to neutralize those who'd defected to the government side. For safety reasons, Judge Roettger ruled that names of witnesses didn't have to be disclosed until shortly before they took the stand. The one-sided discovery procedures favored the government.

Having trouble disputing the government's allegations, the defense lawyers took the legal offensive. In court motions filling more than a dozen large file folders, some three inches thick, they put the government on trial for its alleged misconduct. They argued that the indictment itself was unconstitutional because the U.S. Congress had never intended the racketeering statutes to prosecute a religion. They tried to prevent, by all lawful means, the whole truth from coming out, arguing that evidence was unconstitutional, improperly obtained, or too prejudicial. They asked that their clients' cases be tried separately, demanded the removal of the trial judge, and requested a change in venue to Washington, D.C., or another place with more potential black jurors. Most of the motions were denied.

Just west of Dade County's Metrozoo, at the forty-eight-acre Metropolitan Correctional Center, the suspected death angels accused the U.S. prison system of "cruel and unusual punishment." They got sick from hunger and griped about the "prejudiced" judge, their white lawyers, and the medical care. Not making much use of the prison's tennis and squash courts, they complained instead of headaches, abscessed teeth, and delirium. Ahinadab Israel, accused of supervising the Delray Beach firebombing and the disposal of Leonard Dupree's body, began howling in a cell one day, suffering hallucinations, he said, brought on by his prison ordeal.

The epidemic spread to the women's prison, where Sister Judith, the lone woman caught in the sweep, claimed she suffered stroke symptoms. She sat in solitary, writing a diary and grieving for her three children, all estranged, all government collaborators. Inmates called her Mom, but for Judith it was small comfort. "It's not a good life.

"My boys," she'd say, "are afraid of me."

They visited her, trying to explain why they'd turned against the Hebrews. They still loved their mother. It wasn't Judith they wanted behind bars. It was Yahweh Ben Yahweh. The boys begged her to testify about the homicide of the karate expert. How could she deny it happened? Wasn't she angry that Yahweh Ben Yahweh had abused Lydia?

Sister Judith simply couldn't believe he'd raped her daughter. Lydia, almost twenty years old, had always been closer to her mother than the boys. After telling prosecutor Novicki about the abuse, Lydia felt relieved. Yet she was torn about testifying because she knew what she had to say would invite disbelief and ridicule. She knew she would never see her mother again. Lydia sent a note, asking for a final meeting. Judith refused to see her daughter. Lydia went into the witness protection program, and tried to start life over.

The justice system itself put pressure on Judith and other defendants to plead guilty. Judge Roettger told them in court one day that pretrial guilty pleas would save the taxpayers time and legal fees. (The defense lawyers were making sixty dollars an hour in court and forty dollars out of court.) But only two defendants would turn against their messiah. Twenty-four-year-old Michael Mathis, the Hebrew married to Patricia Albert, had lied to a grand jury about his role in the firebombing that burned a baby. Pat and her family persuaded him that living a "masquerade" wasn't worth it. "I was facing twenty years staying behind a lie and I was not going to do that," Michael explained. "I thought I would tell the truth and be set free." Scruggs gave him a deal. Michael would serve less than six months in prison and a halfway house, in exchange for his testimony against Yahweh and former friends.

Twenty-nine-year-old Ricky Woodside would serve about thirty months. He told his indicted blood brother he didn't have a chance against what he thought would be an all-white jury. Ricky pleaded guilty to two racketeering conspiracy acts: the murder of Aston Green and the attempted murder of Eric Burke. He also pleaded guilty to a state charge of second-degree murder.

The remaining defendants became more unified than ever before. Whenever they were moved to court for hearings, they were shackled together at the waist. Putting their whole faith in Yahweh Ben Yahweh, they listened to him preach by the prison pond. This was all divine prophecy, he told them, the price they paid for being holy. His followers rubbed his back and fanned him. They carried his cafeteria tray and gave him food off their plates. As best they could, they tried to protect and project his image.

Yahweh Ben Yahweh didn't just sit around in prison waiting for his trial to happen. The former law student helped craft his defense and even considered personally grilling his accusers. He pecked out missives to his disciples, passed messages to them by telephone and by mail, and counseled them during lengthy visits. His voice, rumbling through a speaker, reached his followers and the world via conference calls from his prison cellblock to Yahweh University. He said he'd been thrown into the lion's den for refusing to give up his faith. His joint heirs to the kingdom of God were being made to suffer the scourge of prison, to remove their holy raiments, and to come before the civil authorities with no witnesses against them, just as Christ had been made to suffer almost two thousand years before.

His quarters, he said, were freezing. His bladder was weak. He coughed blood. They denied him a daily bath. They refused to give him emery boards and toenail clippers. The guards roughly cuffed his hands behind his back each time they herded him to the shower. The prison authorities wouldn't even pay forty-five cents for a writing tablet. And the food was laden with MSG. "Prison officials have attempted to deceive me by putting 'K' on my takeout plate," Yahweh Ben Yahweh told his supporters. "But when compared to the 'unkosher' meals of the other inmates, my meals are identical to theirs. . . . I have been given plates after pork has been taken off of them. If it were not for some inmates occasionally giving me an apple, lettuce and tomato salad, and oranges, I would soon be hospitalized for malnutrition and starvation."

Why was it, Yahweh asked, that he wasn't entitled to the same high status accorded his prison buddy, the ousted Panamanian dictator Manuel Noriega? Noriega lived in a three-room dictator's suite, built at taxpayers' expense and equipped with private shower, color TV, and computers. He got unlimited supplies of Oreo cookies and strolled the prison grounds in his military uniform. All Yahweh got were "worn, ragged" garments.

The trial was delayed to air the legal moves and countermoves. The more time that passed, the stonier the Hebrews got, the more reluctant the government witnesses became. As the trial date approached, prosecutors found themselves on the defensive from different directions. Scruggs was forced to call his kingpin defendant Yahweh Ben Yahweh after Alcee Hastings produced court documents showing a legal name change. Over the government's objections, Judge Roettger ruled that the son of God was too poor to pay for his defense. The prison bent to the Yahwehs' food demands, though the guards who found candy bars and peanuts in the inmates' cells suspected they were making up their diet as they went along.

Roettger, under pressure from the ACLU, began to lean over backward to accommodate the defendants. Fearing he'd be overruled by a higher court, the judge reversed himself and said the defendants could wear white robes to the trial if they so chose. Better that, Roettger said, than to have them all appear in court in prison khakis. The judge, though, stuck to his ruling that spectators were not to enter the courtroom in white robes. A gallery of white, he said, would seem as intimidating as sheet-wearing KKK members.

By the end of 1991, the seesaw battle of the United States of America vs. God, the son of God, was careening toward a climax. Everyone whose lives had crossed paths with Miami's messiah prepared for the first public hearing. After years of secrecy, murder, fear, and oppression, it was a collision waiting to happen: damaged religious zealots, injured ex-disciples, and grieving relatives of the homicide victims all demanding justice.

37

It was not the only show in town. General Noriega, the Panamanian strongman, was on trial for dealing dope in Miami. William Kennedy Smith, an heir to the Kennedy throne, was on trial for rape in West Palm Beach. Aileen Wuornos, the nation's first female serial killer, was on trial for murdering I-95 motorists in De Land, Florida. The defendants all claimed to be innocent. But only in the sterile, four-story federal courthouse in Fort Lauderdale did the defendant claim to be divine.

"They're gonna tie him to the cross," said a middle-aged white man with a ponytail, silver cowboy boots, and a black cowboy hat. He came to court every day, just to watch what would be one of the strangest, most violent, most overwhelming trials in the history of American courtroom dramas.

In courtroom B, a wood-paneled, blue-carpeted sanctum on the second floor, God, the son of God, fifteen disciples, nineteen lawyers, and dozens of marshals, FBI agents, county deputies, and Bible-toting observers began a five-month spectacle that would be at once ugly and horrifying and—in the end—more notable for what didn't happen than what did. The Yahweh trial would set a new American standard for smoke-and-mirrors sideshows.

Richard Scruggs argued repeatedly that the jury be allowed to hear forty hours of the messiah's fist-pounding tirades and to read dozens of his angry articles. The prosecutor sought to link Yahweh's violent rhetoric to his followers' violent deeds, to show the jury the defendants had been conditioned to commit murder. He wanted to introduce the teachings to corroborate witnesses' statements that Yahweh had given followers orders to commit crimes.

Quoting from a Yahweh pamphlet, Scruggs said, " 'Yahweh hath also prepared for the wicked white man the instruments of death; Yahweh ordaineth his arrows against the white persecutors.

Sydney P. Freedberg

Behold, the wicked white man travaileth with iniquity, and hath conceived mischief, and brought forth falsehood. He made a pit, and digged it, and is fallen into the ditch which he made. The white man's mischief shall return upon his head and violent dealing shall come down upon his skull,' and then there is a biblical reference."

Scruggs waved the article "White Prison Guards Attack Hebrew" in the air. "Judge, I am no biblical scholar but that is not in the Bible. . . . Under the arguments made, then Yahweh Ben Yahweh could say, 'Go kill a white devil, Psalms 7:14 through 16,' and that would be inadmissible because it has to do with religion. That is ridiculous. . . . The fact that this defendant tosses in biblical references does not shield him."

But Alcee Hastings said his client was simply exercising his First Amendment rights to interpret the Bible as he saw it. Yahweh's statements might be the words of a political-religious zealot, but no matter how controversial his opinions, the Constitution protected them.

Roettger agreed. He refused to let the jury hear most of the articles and tapes, except for small portions he deemed relevant. What's more, the government needed to prove more than that Yahweh Ben Yahweh created a climate of violence among his followers. It wasn't enough to show that his words might have incited disciples to commit murder or arson. People could say some very bad things in life that might be unethical but that were simply not illegal. To prove Yahweh Ben Yahweh guilty of racketeering, the government had to prove its theory that he had given a follower a specific order to kill.

On Thursday, January 2, 1992, Judge Roettger stepped onto the bench to begin the task of finding twelve fair-minded people to answer that question. Underneath his robe, lawyers spotted a handgun strapped to his ankle. Lawmen packing guns and mace positioned themselves around the courthouse.

Yahweh Ben Yahweh blew kisses to his followers.

Sixty potential jurors walked past a gaggle of reporters and twenty-five of Yahweh's devotees, a few chanting "Praise Yahweh!"

Prospective panelists filled out a sixteen-page questionnaire on topics ranging from brainwashing to racism to spiritual devotion. Nine potential jurors, including a woman with a copy of *Gone With the Wind*, said they couldn't be fair.

"I don't like religion because they try to control people in the name of God," an unemployed carpenter explained.

"Strange cult," someone else said.

"I get severe migraines when put under pressure," a Delta Airlines employee explained.

"I'm not in agreement with the KKK or the Yahwehs or Satan worshipers," said a man whose son followed the Maharishi Mahesh Yogi.

A software engineer summed it up this way: "The man is a hoax."

Even the selected jurors would trade jokes in the privacy of the jury room. Maybe they should all dress in turbans too. How about if they all wore red one day? One white juror felt a black man—a Yahweh?—was stalking her and jotting down her tag number in the parking lot.

Hastings set the defense tone by accusing the prosecutors of racial bias after they rejected two of six prospective black jurors. Trudy Novicki, the State of Florida's designee assisting in the federal prosecution, explained the decision had nothing to do with race. The excused jurors had Yahweh connections. (One young hospital employee was related to Yahweh by marriage. Another prospect had worked with Sister Judith at Florida Power & Light. The judge excused a third potential black juror who admitted that a relative was a former Yahweh in hiding.)

Finally, Roettger swore a jury: a tax collector, an executive secretary, an electrician, a poker player, a fraud analyst, a bank clerk, a bookkeeper, a court clerk, a retired Western Union employee, an office manager, a prospective law student, a former principal.

Nine whites. Three blacks. Nine women. Three men. Eleven non-Hispanics. One Hispanic.

It took almost as long to seat the Yahwehs. Defense lawyers

didn't want their clients to sit next to Yahweh Ben Yahweh, so as not to appear too cozy with him. But the angelic-looking defendants all wanted to sit next to him. Sister Judith, to no one's surprise, won the honor. "We'll sit together," she told her lawyer. "We've always been together."

Yahweh and Judith had seat pads to cushion the wooden benches. His was a patchwork design; hers was paisley. The jurors chuckled that they needed a seating chart to separate one white robe from another. "We really don't have one made up," Roettger told them. "I think it is best that you do that in your own way."

Over the defense's objection, Roettger did allow the jurors to take notes, and during Richard Scruggs's opening statement, they scribbled furiously in their steno pads. They moaned as the prosecutor laid out the way Yahweh Ben Yahweh had led his "so-called religion" in a "parade of horribles," a perverted version of the three Rs. "I'm talking about retribution, retaliation, and revenge," he said. Defense lawyers rose to their feet and demanded a mistrial, calling Scruggs's remarks inflammatory and prejudicial. They thought the case was over before it began.

Roettger denied the motion, and Hastings surprised everyone by declining to present an opening argument. Yahweh Ben Yahweh evidently had decided to choreograph the show. He wanted to keep his defense secret, not only from the prosecutors but from the other defendants on trial.

The government's first witness was thirty-one-year-old Lloyd Clark, the outspoken defector whose leads had helped build the massive indictment. Two federal marshals escorted him to the witness stand. Defense lawyers promptly took swipes at his loud blue jacket, emblazoned in gold with the words "Power, Freedom, and Honor."

Lloyd was nervous as he told his story, but he told it. For three days, he described how he drifted with Yahweh's violent hate/love doctrine. His independent thoughts and will were broken by long hours of sweatshop work with little sleep and little food. "I saw my own children starving," he testified. "I was beaten. He had sex with almost every woman in the temple, including my wife."

Lloyd depicted himself as a perpetrator and a victim, a willing participant and a captive. He beat people, he stole, he would have killed, if asked. "I would have done anything," Lloyd said, "for Yahweh."

After getting free of Yahweh, the handsome Lloyd had embraced the material world. He'd refused to enter the witness protection program but he rode around with a Glock strapped to his ribcage. For a while, he made a good living as a male stripper. Under cross-examination, the Yahweh lawyers tried to paint him as shallow, showy, insincere, a man rejected by his Yahweh family and motivated by revenge. One defense attorney asked him if he had a personal vendetta against Yahweh Ben Yahweh. Of course, Lloyd replied. "I wanted to kill him for what he did."

Yahweh Ben Yahweh sat immobile in court, jotting notes on pink paper. He watched expressionless as the prosecution paraded one Judas after another. Three witnesses said he masterminded the firebombing. Four witnesses placed him in the room where the karate expert's killing occurred. The prosecutors showed blown-up photos of corpses with footprints, stab wounds, and gunshot punctures. The body of one victim was so decomposed that Scruggs couldn't bear to show the pictures.

Yahweh lawyers jumped up like marionettes, objecting to the photos. Their sole purpose, the defense said, was to get the jurors enraged, and that clearly was part of the government's strategy. A translator for a visiting judge from the former Soviet Union, who dropped by to watch the proceedings, got sick and had to leave the courtroom.

More than a dozen ex-Hebrews, with heads bowed, described what they heard, saw, and experienced. Many seemed bruised, psychologically lost, and scarred. The most important government witnesses, criminally culpable themselves, had plea-bargained in exchange for their testimony. Ricky Woodside had a series of explanations for his past inconsistent statements concerning Aston Green's beheading. At the trial, he insisted he had heard only the chopping sound of a machete pounding Aston's flesh, never saw the blade, never wielded it once.

Michael Mathis, the Delray Beach firebomber, still seemed to believe Yahweh was more than a man. With his chin resting on his left hand, Michael told the jury he covered up his arson role partly out of guilt and shame and partly out of fear. Michael said he'd seen a parade of judges and police chiefs rally around the messiah. "Who knows what the outcome may have been by me saying anything?" Michael testified. "I knew if I said anything that the consequences may have been unkosher."

One by one, the Yahweh lawyers put the defector-collaborators on trial. The attorneys grilled them on religious beliefs and the meaning of Bible Scriptures. They asked about changing memories and secret meetings. They wanted to turn the focus from their clients by portraying the rebels as womanizers, drug dealers, cheaters, and liars, men and women motivated by fantasy and jealousy. They were "spiritually wicked sons and daughters of perdition" in an unholy conspiracy with prosecutors Scruggs and Novicki.

But three women made unshakable government witnesses. About three weeks into the trial, Jean Mitchell Solomon took the stand, offering anguished testimony against her brother. What happened was so horrible that she sobbed as she told about it nine years later. Never once looking at him, she said she stood a yard away from Yahweh as his followers beat the karate man beyond recognition. They watched him die, slowly. "Oh, God," she said, her voice cracking. "They beat his tongue out. They had beat his eyes out. . . . They crushed his whole body."

Judge Roettger had to halt the proceedings so Jean could compose herself. If she was so upset, a defense lawyer asked, why had she beaten the body too? Why had she stayed for so many years after the mass murder? Out of love, out of fear, it was so complicated it was hard to explain. She still loved her brother; she still called him Yahweh Ben Yahweh.

The next Monday Mildred Banks finally got her day in court. Memories from more than a decade before came flooding to the surface as she told the jury about the ambush that made her a widow. Moses Israel had labeled her and Mishael blasphemers, she testified.

She described the attack and her desperate search for help after Moses' assassins shot her and slit her throat. A scarf covered her scar. The defense attorneys waited for the government to ask her to remove it so the jurors could see the wound. But the prosecutors did not ask. They respected Mildred's privacy and didn't want to stoop to exploitation. She left the stand with her dignity intact and without a single hole punched in her story. The weakness in her testimony, though, was that she had never seen the faces of her hooded assailants.

Five weeks later, Patricia Albert, the former Sherah Israel, took the stand. Though "a little" nervous and confused about dates of long-ago events, Pat held firm in her testimony about the role of Yahweh Ben Yahweh and follower Aher in the Opa-locka apartment killings. In a soft voice, she testified about "death angels" and gave Yahweh's explanation for the random murders of eight white vagrants: just "some crackers" losing their ears, nose, and fingers to avenge the deaths of black people. Pat was willing to talk about something else that had happened to her, something very private and painful.

Scruggs had wanted to introduce her testimony on sexual coercion to show how Yahweh Ben Yahweh used rape as a tactic to spread terror and ensure his control. But Roettger ruled evidence about Yahweh's abuse of women and girls, no matter how "colorful and juicy," irrelevant, inflammatory, inadmissible.

Although sex was off-limits, the jurors heard plenty of mind-numbing testimony about murder, arson, polygamy, slave labor, brainwashing, and starvation diets. The prosecutors had managed to paint the Temple of Love as a citadel of harsh discipline and violence, led by a crude and perhaps demonic man. But could they prove that Yahweh ordered murder?

"There's a lot of smoke but no fire," the cowboy with the ponytail announced one morning.

Every day before court, Yahweh's disciples gathered on the long, stiff-backed benches to discuss the latest in the "ungodly trial of genocide." One of Yahweh's biological daughters talked about a "malicious plot to starve" the Hebrews to death in prison. Another spectator said, "The world's not ready for a spiritual man."

A crazy lady, as Alcee Hastings called her, babbled about the breastplate of righteousness. "I'm trying to relate to the human race," the woman said. "I'm dwelling in my physical body but we have an astral body, a spiritual body, and a mental body, too!"

Inside Courtroom B, the observers watched, listened, rocked, nodded, and waved to Yahweh. "Love you," one woman whispered to her messiah. Another breast-fed her infant. A defendant thumbed through a copy of Machiavelli's *The Prince*.

The prosecutors tried to overcome years of law-enforcement ineptitude—investigators who'd lost physical evidence, witnesses who knew what was going on but who wouldn't say—with one imposing witness of questionable credibility: the lord high executioner of the Nation, Bobby Rozier.

When he walked into the courtroom, four marshals stood like a shield between him and the defendants. Bobby wore a three hundred-dollar suit, paid for by the government, and a spiked ponytail. In prison, the tall, muscly ex-football player had been busy pumping iron, studying French, reading about the Christian Crusades, and seething over the government's refusal to give him more early-release credits.

Cocky, even making wisecracks, he began to recount his six murders for Yahweh Ben Yahweh. A seventh man, Bobby told the jury, he stabbed on his own, on a hot summer afternoon. He'd heard a crowd roaring at the Orange Bowl and stopped to get a look at the football game. A Spanish-speaking man kept following him.

"I ended up killing him, throwing him into the water," Bobby said, without a trace of remorse. Amid gasps, he told the jury he would have killed more people, if only given the chance. "I felt power," he said. "I felt in control."

Once, Bobby testified, a rejoicing Yahweh Ben Yahweh gave him and another warrior the day off after they showed him a devil's ear. They celebrated by going to see the movie *Aliens*.

But during days of blistering cross-examination, the defense severely undercut Bobby's whole story by showing he had lied about parts of it. He hadn't personally seen Yahweh cut off someone's head, as he previously swore. Hammering on the lectern, defense lawyers took turns portraying him as a "lying dirtball," a sociopath, the biggest devil ever to walk into an American courtroom. This was a thug who cut the deal of the century, betraying his friends to avoid Florida's electric chair. The lawyers turned into a wolf pack. Attorney Wendell Graham even attacked Bobby's sexuality. "You never noticed any guys looking at you sweetlike?" Graham asked.

"They're like vultures trying to take pieces from me," Bobby thought, as he stepped from the witness stand. The defense strategy had crystallized: Blame as many murders as possible on Bobby.

It was hardly swift and sure justice. Judge Roettger was usually late to court, and even took a vacation during the trial. His personal stenographer cleaned up the length of court breaks on the official transcript, making some of them shorter than they actually were. "Stormin' Norman's rules of evidence," the attorneys chuckled.

During the course of the trial, two lawyers were burglarized and a third was pistol-whipped after gassing his car. Ahinadab Israel, in ankle chains and a straitjacket, went nuts, writhing, muttering obscenities, and bellowing "Yahweh, take me!" He wrestled with marshals and had to be removed from the courtroom. The trial was postponed so psychiatrists could evaluate Ahinadab. They disagreed about whether he was faking it, and Ahinadab ended up watching much of the trial from a holding cell on closed-circuit TV.

In the strangest and saddest sidelight, Scruggs's longtime secretary, Pamela Crumpler, was murdered. She had been attending the Yahweh trial daily and had her paperwork and a bag of groceries in her arms when three black men surprised her on her front porch. Investigators decided it was just a random, botched Miami robbery, having nothing to do with the Yahweh case. Scruggs, who had never had such a loyal friend, would always wonder. He and Novicki went under twenty-four-hour guard at a secret location, protected by rifle-wielding marshals.

Two weeks after the secretary's murder, a train ran over a young government witness who had testified about the Delray Beach fire-bombing. Yahweh Ben Yahweh buttonholed Scruggs during a court break. "Richard," he said, "you don't think I did that one, too, do you?"

The whole scene boggled the mind. During breaks, Alcee Hastings chomped on hot dogs and did a little political glad-handing. It sure beat what was going on in the courtroom, he admitted. Hastings seemed angry with Yahweh, though the former judge wouldn't say why. The other lawyers speculated that the son of God stiffed him of promised legal fees. Much of the action took place out of the jury's earshot, in crowded sidebar conferences at the judge's bench or in his chambers, where Roettger kept a stuffed moose head on a table. "This was better entertainment than you could find in a lot of comedy theaters," the judge said during one private conference. Because of all the delays and interruptions, the jurors were as annoyed as "wet hens," as Roettger put it.

The carnival atmosphere played right into the hands of the defense, which aimed at sabotaging and hamstringing the prosecution and making it look racist, biased, and fabricated through the endless delays and a chorus of objections.

After about eight weeks and sixty witnesses, the prosecution rested, putting on only half the number of witnesses planned. Roettger seemed in a hurry to get the case over with. He kept cautioning the prosecutors about repetitious testimony. He was becoming increasingly annoyed that the entire Yahweh matter—a murder case that should have been handled locally by Dade County state attorney Reno—was in a federal court. Picking up on the defense attorneys' constant refrain, the judge began to ask, "Why are we here?"

Then the prosecution suffered a major blow when Roettger unexpectedly threw out one of three counts, cutting Yahweh Ben Yahweh's possible maximum sentence to forty years. The judge said the government hadn't proved that Yahweh forcibly evicted the tenants during the 1986 Opa-locka apartment takeover. He agreed with Alcee Hastings's argument that the threat at the apartment complex was a "figment of the imagination of the tenants."

"Murder," Hastings said, "is not extortion."

Scruggs, incredulous, insisted that another federal judge, in the tenants' civil case, held the temple guilty of extortion. "Denied!" Roettger bellowed.

Defense lawyers were as startled as the prosecutors by the judge's ruling. "He never ceases to amaze me," said defense attorney Paul McKenna. His client, Sister Judith, had been charged with extortion too. "You never know what he's going to do."

Yahweh Ben Yahweh knew. "Yahweh intervened in count three and Yahweh will intervene in counts one and two," the son of God told a reporter, as he braced himself for the start of the defense case. "Praise Yahweh."

38

The defense case was a simple blanket denial, a well-executed, legal shell game. "B & B," one courthouse observer called it. "If you can't dazzle them with brilliance, then baffle them with bullshit." Although the Yahwehs were on trial together, they took turns presenting separate cases. Yahweh would go last. The followers' lawyers, warned by their clients not to cross Yahweh, suspected he planned to cross them. The best guess was that he would subtly do in some of his indicted co-defendants, claiming they were freelancing. Thus, he would distance himself from their criminal acts the way he had distanced himself from killer Bobby Rozier.

Sister Judith wouldn't take the stand, and her attorney tried to set her apart from the men. There were "cruel, ruthless, cold-blooded, calculated murderers" in the Temple of Love, attorney Paul McKenna admitted, but not Judith. He told the jury she was a "peaceful person who abhors violence."

The men blamed the homicides on other Yahwehs, dead Yahwehs, non-Yahwehs, or Bobby Rozier. Their lawyers depicted the victims as crazy druggies who deserved what they got. One attorney argued that even if Yahweh Ben Yahweh walked around the temple with an ear, the body part didn't have her client's name on it.

Absalom Israel, a small, handsome man with high cheekbones and a clean-cut appearance, was one of three defendants who wore dead clothes to court. He wanted to be known by his slave name, Ardmore Canton III. Besides a white-devil murder, the government had accused Ardmore/Absalom of the Delray Beach firebombing. His attorney claimed a pure case of mistaken identity. Absalom was on trial, but it was Aushalom who really did it . . . or maybe another Absalom. The lawyer for another defendant, Ahaz (accused of acting as a lookout at Carlton Carey's murder), said Ahab might have done it, or Araz or Ahab or Anab or Anihab. The Yahwehs had started

288

to run out of biblical names as their membership swelled, and had to double up on some names.

Of all the crimes in the indictment, the defense had the most trouble explaining the Dupree homicide—and how so many people had it burned into their brains that they beat a young man into a red mass. The lawyers argued Leonard was "a phantom," he wasn't dead, or if he was dead, their clients weren't there when it happened. The problem was they couldn't agree on one story, so somebody had to be lying.

Six suspected death angels took the stand. All described themselves as peaceful people. Brother Amri, the onetime utility cable splicer, charged in several homicides, testified he'd been an Eagle Scout, an all-Florida running back and offensive lineman, and a member of the United Way. Brother Dan, accused of gunning down Carlton Carey, confessed to polygamy but not to homicide. During his direct examination, Dan was emotionless, sounding almost as if he was on autopilot. During Scruggs's cross-examination, Dan became downright hostile. His cold demeanor was in stark contrast to the friendly Mikael, once known as Maurice Woodside. A Romeo-like jazz singer whose voice was a blend of Nat King Cole and Johnny Mathis, he was accused of striking the karate expert with a stick. His brother, Ricky, had also implicated him in the attack on Eric Burke. On the stand, Mikael was so hyperkinetic that courtroom spectators couldn't quit chuckling. He quoted love scriptures as if reciting from a mail-order catalog. "I am like a sheep, that's what I am," Mikael told the jury. "I'm not a warrior."

Aher Israel, charged with four murders, had the biggest smile and one of the more severe memory lapses. He took the stand on Saint Patrick's Day. The judge was wearing a green carnation. The bespectacled Aher, the former Carl Perry, wore a dark blue suit and a little ponytail.

"I would never kill anyone for any reason," he testified. "I am against that. I am a builder. I like to see things come up, not go down."

Aher claimed to be with his wife, Aleeza, who was supposedly having a baby when the killings at the Opa-locka apartments occurred. But under cross-examination, Scruggs chipped away at the alibi. The prosecutor asked Aher to describe the child's birth. Though Aher said he was with his wife during the delivery, he didn't know if she had seen a doctor, how long she was in labor, or who, if anyone, cut the umbilical cord.

"Did you deliver the baby?" Scruggs asked.

"No," Aher replied.

"Did she deliver the baby?"

Aher didn't say.

"Nobody delivered the baby?" Scruggs persisted.

"Yes," Aher said. "Someone delivered the baby."

"Who was that?"

"The baby delivered the baby. The baby came out."

"This baby just popped out . . . ?"

Aher, who left Miami shortly after the killings, said the prosecutor would have to ask Aleeza. "I was not pregnant."

As the needle of credibility swung back and forth, the defense tried to unravel the government's carefully woven argument with a parade of Hebrew witnesses eager to show their loving side. The mother of the Nation of Yahweh, age eighty-four, testified she'd never been starved. She drew smiles and laughter when she gave her weight: 154 pounds. A Harvard-educated doctor talked about the divine nature of every human being and offered an emotional account of his conversion to the Hebrew faith. An old man said he'd never been forced to give up his house; on the contrary, a loving and generous Yahweh Ben Yahweh insisted he keep it. A historian told the jury about non-mainstream black religious movements. And a few white businesspeople, including a daft stewardess who became known among the prosecutors as Sister Bimbo, praised Yahweh for cleaning up the slums.

Two defenses were especially energetic. Enoch Israel, accused of Aston Green's beheading, didn't take the stand, but his lawyer, Chris Mancini, put on witnesses to show that his client was the "fall guy." Turning into a prosecutor, Mancini argued that Ricky Woodside and Lloyd Clark had constructed a series of lies to minimize their involvement in the decapitation. They wanted to protect themselves and one of the real killers, Ricky's older brother, Mikael.

Hoseah Isaac's lawyer, Thomas Buscaglia, presented an alibi the government had trouble dissecting: Several witnesses testified that Hoseah, a short, skinny man, was driving a Yahweh tour bus when the white vagrant he allegedly murdered was killed.

Aided by lively defenses, the prosecution's case against the followers was getting lost in a haze of confusion, race, religion, politics, fear, the charisma of lawyers, outright weirdness, and a parade of paid government informants. Though Yahweh lawyers privately conceded most of their clients were probably guilty, their strategy was to make it difficult for the jurors to form any mental picture of the killings—to blur or erase the possibilities about what happened—even, in the end, to make them uncertain that *anything* happened. Three lawyers presented no cases at all. Why defend yourself against something that may not actually have occurred? The prosecution's case was crippled a little more when, during a conference with the attorneys one Monday, Judge Roettger blurted out, "I think it's very likely that some of the defendants in this case are going to be acquitted." His comment, to the prosecutors' dismay, was headlined in the morning papers and probably read by some of the unsequestered jurors.

The case against Yahweh Ben Yahweh always had been stronger than the case against his disciples. When the spotlight turned on him, Alcee Hastings still sensed trouble. Despite the rank and file's optimism, Hastings had been "put out" by some of the followers' evasive and rambling performances on the stand. Jurors, he noticed, had stopped taking notes. An older Hungarian man on the panel seemed especially unsympathetic.

Calling Yahweh to the stand was risky, but not calling him could prove fatal. No matter what the ex-judge thought, Yahweh stubbornly insisted on testifying. He knew he'd have to craft his best sermon for twelve unbelievers. On Tuesday, April 21, 1992, Hastings's announcement that his client planned to testify sent a buzz through the courthouse corridors. A young prosecutor joked with Richard Scruggs about what would happen when God, the son of God, raised his right hand. Would he swear to tell the truth "So help me . . . me"?

Hastings, by this time, made little secret of his distaste for his client. Despite the ex-judge's criminal problem, Hastings had a reputation as a warm, compassionate man. Both prosecutors and defense attorneys liked him and applauded his momentous human rights rulings from the federal bench. A tireless advocate for society's powerless, he possessed a certain majesty when he articulated the ideals of equality. Yahweh Ben Yahweh was hardly Alcee Hastings's ideal. He left the direct examination to co-counsel Wende Rush. She was a Yahweh business associate who'd been called to coordinate the Nation's defense and spew the party line.

Amid a low cheer in the packed courtroom, Yahweh ascended to the stand, affirmed to tell the truth, and settled into the witness chair. He wiped his glasses, pulled the microphone close, and folded his hands. He played to the gallery as he gave his name and occupation for the record.

"Full name is Yod-Heh-Vav-Heh Bet-Noon Sofeet Yod-Heh-Vav-Heh. English translation, Yahweh Ben Yahweh. My occupation: I am the grand master of the celestial lodge, architect of the universe, I am the blessed and only potentate, founder of the Nation of Yod-Heh-Vav-Heh, true holiness and righteousness."

He sounded lucid, confident, charming. He took no blame for anything. He didn't order killings, he didn't know anything about beatings or forced marriages, he never abused anyone. He never silenced the children with threats of God's wrath. He opposed hate, never deprived his followers of food or sleep, and didn't know—didn't even care—about temple finances. The temple was a great democracy where his followers made the decisions, not him. Any violence he preached about, such as death to blasphemers, came strictly from the Bible. How could he be blamed if a few naughty people had misinterpreted the Word of God?

"I've heard testimony that is shocking to me where individuals

292

pretending to be my followers admit to participating in murders,"
Yahweh said. "Any soul that did those things because they did it
for Yahweh, I consider it unfortunate. . . . Those victims, it's a very
heinous thing to happen. I feel very bad about it. Also, the families
have had to suffer."

Faint sniffles could be heard in the courtroom. Women took out
handkerchiefs and dabbed their moist eyes.

Yahweh Ben Yahweh had built a wall of plausible deniability,
painting himself as a misunderstood spiritualist, persecuted by the
government for teaching Luke 19:27: "But those mine enemies,
which would not that I should reign over them, bring hither and
slay them before me."

The direct examination took forty-two minutes. Richard
Scruggs's cross-examination took more than two days. In a low-key,
deceptively timid style, the prosecutor began by trying to shred
Yahweh's religious facade. Scruggs asked him to go into a little detail
about his past lives as Junior Mitchell, Airman Mitchell, Hulon X,
Brother Love, Father Michel, Moses Israel, Yahshua the messiah—
all before he became the son of God and God himself.

"You were working your way up?" Scruggs scoffed.

"Sly remark," Yahweh Ben Yahweh rejoined. "It certainly was
not something I worked my way up to." He insisted it was a spiritual
niche he'd been seeking, not a scam. "It was something that happened, a metamorphosis."

Yahweh testified that during his Brother Love days, he studied
religion. "Were you the son of God yet?" Scruggs asked.

"I have been the son of God all the time, but I didn't know it."

The prosecutor, armed with more information than Yahweh
allowed, forced him to say Brother Love had done a little betting on
the side.

"Where did you get the money to gamble at the dog track?"
Scruggs asked.

"Objection," Wende Rush said.

"Sustained," the judge mumbled.

The prosecutor also had hotel bills and photographs suggesting that Yahweh had cavorted with Sister Judith's daughter at a fancy Miami Beach resort. "You recall running up big bills at the Hotel Alexander?"

Yahweh couldn't remember. "I find it amazing that you would ask me to recall specifics on 1981" or even earlier, he told Scruggs. "I can't recall what I ate last month on any day and I don't believe you can."

"You're not omnipotent?" the prosecutor snapped.

The spectators jeered. Defense attorneys shouted a new round of objections and demands for mistrial.

With all of Yahweh's vagueness about his past incarnations, Scruggs was painting a picture of a cheap swindler, and possibly a pimp, who didn't give a damn about his followers and thought he was above criminal prosecution.

"If I had such powers," Yahweh said, breaking into a wide grin, "I wouldn't be here."

The courtroom burst into loud laughter.

As Yahweh prepared to take the stand on day two, he cornered Scruggs. "Richard, can I tell you something off the record?"

"No," Scruggs replied. "There's nothing off the record."

"Come on," Yahweh persisted. "Off the record?"

Scruggs finally agreed. "OK. What is it?"

"I just wanted you to know you're really a good prosecutor."

"Off the record?" Scruggs replied. "You're a slick son of a bitch."

Yahweh flashed a smile. But over the next two days, his gentle demeanor turned icy as Scruggs pored over the details of real killings, real beatings, real people. At one point, he flaunted a grisly autopsy photo of the beheaded Aston Green. "Is that one of the enemies who was killed?"

Yahweh glanced away. He didn't recognize that person.

"Do you recall a young man being brought to the temple who was, for lack of a better term, a karate expert?" Scruggs asked.

"No," Yahweh replied. "I don't remember the hundreds and thousands of people who come . . . it just becomes a sea of faces."

"Is it not, in fact, true, sir, that you directed your sister and everyone else in that room to hit the bloody body of that man with a stick?"

"No such incident took place in my presence, so how could I possibly direct anyone to do anything?"

"Is it in fact true that your death angels were the ones who committed the acts against Carlton Carey?"

"I did not have death angels," Yahweh said. "I do not have death angels. That is a matter between almighty God . . . and He does whatever He wills."

Did he remember preaching that God had caused firebombs to rain down on Delray Beach?

"Not on that neighborhood," Yahweh Ben Yahweh said, "but certainly on two neighborhoods, and they were Sodom and Gomorrah." He blamed the arson on renegades, "Robert Rozier and his boys," who acted "individually, of their own will."

What about when his followers raised their hands and vowed they'd kill for him? "They were lying," Yahweh explained. "Blasphemers are being killed all over the planet every minute of the day. . . . I have nothing to do with it as his son."

Yahweh became angry. It was almost as if he were staging a confrontation with an abstract enemy.

The prosecutor asked about the secret brotherhood and an initiation rite in which a sword was placed at a follower's head. Didn't it show that he, not God, had power over life and death? "The fact that you asked me a question like that," Yahweh said, "indicates that you are unenlightened and profane."

The courtroom spectators shuddered. Two government witnesses privately warned Scruggs that the very question had marked him for death.

Yahweh repeatedly looked over to his lawyers for reassurance. He accused the government of quoting his preachments out of context. He compared his life to Jesus Christ's.

Scruggs asked, "Is that what I'm doing, persecuting you?"

"Of course you are," Yahweh replied, elaborating later: "He

was born and he didn't show forth any sign of his mission until he was age twelve, when he went with his parents to the synagogue and thereupon he asked some questions of the priests that they were unable to answer. In fact, his parents were returning home and discovered he was not with them and they returned back to the synagogue and found him still asking questions of the priests and they were astonished they could not answer his questions. From that point, from age twelve until age thirty, an eighteen-year period, you have no history of Christ, but this is the period wherein he studied, wherein he increased in wisdom, knowledge, and understanding of both his mission and who he was."

Yahweh talked faster and faster. He ticked off more words, more Bible interpretations. As his testimony dragged on, jurors rolled their eyes in disbelief, and in boredom. A chunky woman juror with a bouffant hairdo coughed, then spilled a cup of water on her dress during one of Yahweh's lengthy answers. "I hope I didn't cause that," he said.

For all his cleverness and unequivocal denials, defense attorneys whispered during court breaks that Yahweh was tightening the noose around his neck. "He's convicting himself," one lawyer said. The danger now was that Yahweh's performance would bring down every one of his co-defendants. Even Alcee Hastings admitted that his client was "running his mouth an awful lot."

Yahweh Ben Yahweh's voice became strained. He tried to re-assure the jury he was the prince of peace. His only goal, he said, was to rescue sixty million blacks in America, "the lost sheep of Israel." His fiery words had been "a call to action for my people to wake up to the knowledge of their history, culture, language, names, land, nationality." A call to "get off welfare and food stamps and become self-sufficient and independent and stop being a tax burden on America."

In his final hours on the stand, Yahweh Ben Yahweh read passages from the Books of Leviticus, Deuteronomy, Isaiah, Daniel, Luke, and Revelation. Interruption was unthinkable. He stared down, rubbed his forehead, pulled in his lower lip. He was tired, determined not to break down. He began discussing the Christian spirituals of his childhood, hymns like "Steal Away to Jesus," sung by homesick African slaves in the cotton fields of the South. He gulped and held back tears. There'd always been something to singing, suffering, and soul that made "an emotional connection," he explained. "If I could hear my mother pray again."

Yahweh blew his nose. For a few seconds, he couldn't go on. A woman spectator placed her face in her hands and quietly cried.

After more than ninety witnesses and eight weeks of testimony, the defense rested. The government presented a few rebuttal witnesses, but they blurred the truth more than they clarified it. Yahweh's predicted day of liberation, April 30, 1992, came and went, and then the racial undertones that had always been present grew more complicated.

The Los Angeles riots sent reverberations through the Fort Lauderdale courtroom. Radio and TV stations wondered about the effect of the Los Angeles rage on the Yahweh trial. The unsequestered jurors became aware of the verdict in the beating of the motorist Rodney King and the wrenching national debate over race and justice that followed. There had never been a hint that a guilty verdict in the Yahweh case could set off racial violence. In fact, an overwhelming majority of black south Floridians scarcely noticed Yahweh's existence or dismissed him as an out-and-out crackpot. Even so, defense attorneys asked for special instructions to the jury. Judge Roettger expressed concern. He hoped that a prescheduled, two-week recess would insulate the jury from any riot influence.

On Thursday, May 14, 1992, when the trial resumed for closing arguments, there wasn't much to say. For months, every point had been made and remade. Jurors had dozed off, and defendants, too, had to keep from falling asleep.

Prosecutor Novicki, a tall, statuesque woman with a sharp, sometimes harsh edge, used the larger-than-life-sized color pictures of corpses and a Yahweh sword to make her points. "Death by sword was their preferred method of execution," she told the jury. "Decapitation and ear amputation became the calling cards of the death angels."

By the end of the long trial, even the deliberate and cautious

297

United States of America was caught up in a tide of passions. No-vicki's detailed description of Aston Green's decapitation wounds was simply too much for his mother. Louretta Green, who went to the trial every day, rushed from the courtroom in tears.

"Oh, God have mercy," Mrs. Green sobbed. "Did you see what they did to my son? They should hang 'em. They're gonna kill again."

For nineteen hours, Yahweh lawyers referred to Martin Luther, Thomas Jefferson, Ben Franklin, Ralph Emerson, Jack Nicholson, Émile Zola, and the Books of Genesis and Proverbs. They cracked jokes, cursed mildly, recited nursery rhymes, and referred to *Hawaii Five-O*, *The Silence of the Lambs*, *Perry Mason*, *Columbo*, and *Murder, She Wrote*. They appealed to emotions and prejudices, nipping away at the edges of the government case. But their arguments boiled down to what attorney Thomas Buscaglia called the three *R*s: "race, religion, and Robert Rozier."

The Los Angeles riot had given Richard Gagliano, attorney for Mikael Israel, the opportunity to exploit race and fear in his closing statement. "Right now, the world is watching you, especially since what is going on in L.A.," Gagliano told the jury. "The jury system is failing. When you look at what happened in Los Angeles, that jury was wrong. Those people were guilty. The jury system is on trial here."

Gagliano's remarks were so inflammatory that even some of his defense colleagues demanded a mistrial. But after all the time invested, after millions of public dollars spent, after what Roettger called one of the most unmanageable, "horrendous" trials he'd ever seen, starting over was the last thing on his mind.

Yahweh Ben Yahweh had wanted to address the jury again, but Roettger didn't think that was a very good idea either. The closing argument fell to Alcee Hastings, who gave the most inspired performance his colleagues ever witnessed.

Shifting from preacher to salesman to comedian, Hastings moved quickly and lightly across the courtroom. He sought to evoke racial and religious guilt as he likened Yahweh Ben Yahweh to a Gandhi-esque figure. Fingers pointing, arms waving, the ex-judge told the jury that the government had targeted his client because he preached he was the son of God. They targeted him because he was guiding the lame-minded black men of America to salvation.

"Is he being persecuted because his teachings cause the blind black men of America to see that white people caused at least some of their troubles?" Hastings asked.

"He is guilty of preaching. He is guilty of teaching. He is guilty of cleanliness. He is guilty of caring. . . . He is guilty of sharing, guilty of wearing a diadem. He is guilty of having scriptural knowledge. He's guilty of loving people. He's guilty of sisterhood and, yes, brotherhood. . . . He's guilty of saying that he's the son of God. But he ain't guilty of racketeering murder, and they have not proven it."

The federal RICO statutes, Hastings argued, were intended to bring down Mafia dons. "They didn't say a damn thing about anybody's religion. . . . Why is the religion on trial?"

Alcee Hastings held the attention of the jury and the spectators in one clenched fist.

Richard Scruggs never believed in histrionics; trials, he thought, were supposed to be clearinghouses for the truth, won by facts and trial preparation. In his final, unemotional argument, he asked the jury to look through the defense's red herrings and phony alibis. He said the Yahwehs had lied to protect their messiah. Seeking to restore the credibility of government witnesses, he admitted Bobby Rozier was a bad man. "That's why Yahweh liked him," Scruggs said in a slight southern drawl. Any inconsistencies in the testimony of other witnesses weren't intentional falsehoods, he insisted. They were simple mistakes caused by the passage of time.

"Yahweh Ben Gandhi," Scruggs scoffed. "He sees a world of enemies and preaches violence against those enemies."

39

After a decade of investigation and denial, 19 months of court battles, about 16 weeks and 14,000 pages of trial testimony, three burned-out copy machines, 160 witnesses, 260 pieces of evidence, and 100 mistrial motions, the search for truth in the life and times of Yahweh Ben Yahweh seemed destined to end in yet one more transformation for Miami's messiah.

Freedom.

The jurors, who kept getting sick during the trial, seemed incapable of coming to a decision, any decision. "Half those people," juror Janet Hansen told Judge Roettger, "I don't think are too bright anyway."

Hansen, a divorced secretary, was among four jurors who threw the trial into turmoil by staging a mini-mutiny before the deliberations were to begin. They offered a litany of explanations for wanting off the case. European vacations. Weddings. Graduations. Law school.

"Absentee ballot?" one asked.

Hansen claimed that another juror had sexually harassed her. Though she didn't think the government proved its case beyond a reasonable doubt, she told the judge during a private conference that she was having trouble sleeping because of the bloody photographs. She dreamed her mother was stabbed. "I'm scared," she said. Yahweh Ben Yahweh's followers could stalk her. When she left her house to carry out the garbage, she looked over her shoulder. "I don't know that many black people." She started to cry.

With fear, frustration, and anger threatening to invade the deliberations, Roettger summoned the lawyers. "I've never had anything blow up in my face like this in my life," he said. "Suddenly, I no longer controlled the situation in any way, shape, or form."

After consulting with the attorneys, the judge decided to replace

Hansen with an alternate. The other reluctant panelists would stay. They'd be sequestered until their deliberations were over.

Roettger read the jurors forty-nine pages of baffling instructions on the workings of the federal racketeering laws. To find Yahweh guilty of racketeering, they had to agree with the prosecutors' contention that he played a role in two crimes listed in the indictment or that he had agreed two crimes would occur. To convict on a conspiracy charge, they had to find only that a defendant agreed at least two of those crimes would be committed. In his final instruction, the judge took the unusual step of reminding them—even militant atheists among them—to put aside their biases. They were there to decide guilt or innocence, not questions of religion or racial justice. "The majority of the jury is not the same race as the defendants," Roettger counseled. "If you have any biases in that area, rise above them." Then he sent them out to consider the facts.

It was Saturday, May 23, 1992, 12:30 P.M. The jury had lunch, then started arguing, politely at first. Should they go to church on Sunday? Was seven-time killer Bobby Rozier telling the truth? Was Yahweh a misunderstood messiah? A deluded lunatic? Or a cold-blooded liar? What was reasonable doubt? Did guilty mean they had to agree on at least two acts in the indictment or was one enough?

Then the jurors started complaining about one another. The majority nonsmokers were upset with the minority smokers. The nonsmokers couldn't breathe. If they wanted to smoke, they should go outside to the courtyard!

Just an hour or so after lunch, the young jury forewoman, a pretty law school clerk named Elissa Miller, sent Roettger a note: They were divided. Some had reasonable doubt.

On Sunday, some jurors attended church. Then they deliberated for five hours and forty-five minutes. They listened to the tape of a song about jealousy, performed by defendant Mikael. Back at the hotel where they were sequestered, they did jigsaw puzzles and played poker and Scrabble. One man read Tom Clancy novels. By Monday, the deliberations were in chaos. Some of the jurors refused to talk, and forewoman Miller, nicknamed Miss Perfect during the trial, sent five handwritten notes to the judge, each gloomier than the previous one. Hung. Stuck. At a standstill.

One woman lay on the floor in a fetal position, crying, and an out-and-out yelling match erupted over a factual issue. "Knock it off!" another panelist hollered. "It's enough!"

A black woman juror, who'd said on her jury questionnaire that she felt victimized by racial discrimination, kept refusing to convict Yahweh Ben Yahweh of anything, never really explaining her reasons.

On Tuesday, jurors were still hopelessly confused. They didn't understand the judge's instructions. Juries rarely understood RICO instructions. Even lawyers didn't understand RICO instructions.

Nonsmokers were inclined to convict. Smokers were inclined not to convict. They asked the judge if they could forego deliberations on individual crimes if they believed the defendants were guilty as a group. "Please help us!" the forewoman wrote. "If we do not clear up this misunderstanding, we are stuck!"

Roettger tried to streamline the instructions. He told the jury to ignore a sentence that required them to decide whether the sixteen defendants had joined "a plan on one occasion" to commit illegal acts named in the indictment. They had to reach a verdict on each count as it applied to each defendant. "Please continue to deliberate."

They were tired and desperate. They were sick of U.S. marshals following them, and now a juror was concerned she'd miss her grandson's wedding in June. Another woman got angry with the forewoman because the juror wanted to send her own notes to the judge. And she wanted a six-pack of beer.

On Wednesday, May 27, 1992, at 9:15 A.M., Elissa Miller wrote, "I never expected this and I am scared."

The judge again ordered the jurors to bear down. He scoffed at demands for a mistrial, prompting more complaints from defense attorneys. They argued that Roettger was holding the jurors hostage, coercing them into reaching a verdict at any cost.

Thirty hours passed. Wednesday morning, they horse-traded

for a few hours, and then, at about 1 P.M., as Richard Scruggs was walking on the beach in Fort Lauderdale, near the secret condo where he had been living since the trial began, his beeper went off. There were verdicts.

"We got 'em all," Scruggs thought.

As he drove to court, paramilitary equipment rolled down the street. Federal SWAT teams took up positions around the courthouse, alongside dozens of local and state police snipers. An agent with an assault rifle hung from the roof of a nearby bank. "Fear of the unknown," as one lawman put it, had prompted some of the strictest security measures the courthouse had ever seen. Authorities wanted to flex their muscles, ensure community safety, and quell violence should any flare.

Courtroom B was as tight as a violin string as everyone waited for Judge Roettger to arrive. The defendants prayed. The lawyers reminisced about five months in trial. Two had gotten married and two were getting divorced. One attorney fought the AIDS virus, and another had lost his father. Five defense lawyers were undergoing IRS audits, and one was under investigation for grand theft. Glenn Feldman, the lawyer with AIDS, had remarked during the trial that he was having nightmares about the case.

"Bill for them," another attorney told him.

Alcee Hastings had gone through what he called "decomposition." But now, as he waited for the verdicts, he felt somewhat optimistic, not only because of his successful closing argument but because of his improving political prospects. He'd announced plans to run for Congress in a new, predominantly black district encompassing parts of Broward and Palm Beach counties.

An hour passed. Two hours. Where was Stormin' Norman? Maybe he was "feeding corn to the chickens." It was a Yahweh expression for catching a victim off-guard. Or maybe Roettger's secretary needed a little time to brush his honor's mustache.

Finally the judge arrived, and somehow, somewhere in the fog, the twelve people lost in the judicial wilderness came stumbling out into the sunshine with decisions.

Sydney P. Freedberg

They acquitted seven disciples (Mikael, Absalom, Jesse Obed, Abiri, Isaiah Solomon, Hezion, and Hoseah Isaac). The jury deadlocked on the fate of two (Enoch and Aher). In a minor judicial faux pas, they messed up the verdict form on Brother Job, acquitting him of a crime he'd never been charged with. After reading all the verdicts, they excused themselves to go back to the jury room for a quick deliberation about him.

Job, Amri, Dan, Ahinadab, Sister Judith, and Ahaz—whose name, ironically, had surfaced only eleven times during the entire trial—were all convicted of conspiracy.

None of the defendants was convicted of the substantive racketeering count that would have tied them to specific murders. The jury acquitted several defendants of the charge, and declared itself hung on the racketeering accusation against Sister Judith.

As for Yahweh Ben Yahweh, the jury found him guilty of conspiracy but was deadlocked on the substantive racketeering charge. As the clerk read the brokered verdicts, Yahweh didn't flinch. One of his co-defendants burst into tears.

Judge Roettger ordered the two Yahwehs whose cases had ended in mistrial freed, released on their recognizance. The outcomes at first shocked, then disappointed Richard Scruggs, who couldn't believe the jury hadn't returned more guilty verdicts. "What the hell happened?" he asked himself. He watched in disbelief as the acquitted Hebrews began to collect their belongings. A band of killers, the prosecutor thought, was about to hit the street.

Dazed by their sudden deliverance, the disciples filed past a nonchalant Yahweh Ben Yahweh, kissing him on the back of his right hand or on his lips.

But before they could leave, prosecutor Novicki turned to Detective Rex Remley. The State of Florida had decided to recharge some of the men with murder one. "Arrest them," she said.

Operation Jericho, Florida style, was now about to begin. The lawmen rounded up the disciples, herded them to a holding cell near the courtroom, and slapped arrest affidavits on Yahweh Ben Yahweh and another convicted disciple, plus four Hebrews the jury hadn't

304

convicted. Aher Israel's moment of jubilation turned to anger when he was rearrested for killing Rudy Broussard and Pudley Brown. Aher's lawyer, Charles White, called it "outrageous." Though the federal racketeering case had never precluded Florida murder indictments, the notion of recharging acquitted defendants rubbed some defense attorneys the wrong way.

Yahweh Ben Yahweh, now facing three first-degree murder indictments, said nothing as the marshals accompanied him back to prison. He left the press conferences to his freed disciples, who hugged, kissed, and, for the first time publicly, talked on the courthouse steps. "Yahweh is God and his son will be vindicated!" said Isaiah Solomon, acquitted of killing a white devil.

The Yahweh lawyers hailed the verdicts as a defense victory. Attorney Thomas Buscaglia laughed that thousands of hours of prayer had an effect on the outcome.

Hastings said the prosecution had suffered a major blow. "And it ain't over yet!" he gloated. Mikael, whose brother had testified against him, called his acquittal a prophecy, but his lawyer, Richard Gagliano, credited something else: "Dumb luck. I guess they liked his music."

Richard Scruggs had never felt worse in his life. As the sun went down, the prosecutor left the courthouse for a gin and tonic, passing a sniper team posted outside. He couldn't stop second-guessing himself. Had he overcharged the case? Had the stronger homicides gotten lost in the weaker ones? Or was this simply a case where the jury system had broken down?

In the next few days, traumatized jurors tried to explain verdicts that seemed to defy logic. They denied that fear, race, or religion had entered the deliberations. They admitted they were overwhelmed by the massive trial, the number of defendants, the complexities of the racketeering laws, and the facts of each case. "There was so much testimony that details of each incident tended to get overlooked," one panelist said.

Jurors believed Yahweh Ben Yahweh played a role in planning the arson at Delray Beach and one or two homicides. The eight so-called white-devil murders, while Yahweh might have ordered them, were not proved by the government. The jurors would not convict on the word of an admitted serial killer. "There was reasonable doubt," forewoman Miller said. In the end, the stories of Bobby Rozier and Yahweh Ben Yahweh were irreconcilable and would be forever, unless one of them owned up to perjury.

It would take the Yahweh jurors months to recuperate from their ordeal. They had dreams about the defendants, the photographs of mutilated bodies, and the graphic testimony about murders.

But if the case was stressful for jurors, it was doubly so for Yahweh's accusers. They scurried back into hiding after the verdicts, scattered soldiers who had fought the same war and now carried the same scars. The best that could be said about Jean Solomon's experience was that it was over. Slowly, the reality set in that her testimony had convicted her brother. She returned to Oklahoma, took a job as a motel housekeeper, and guarded the secret of her past. Her heart was weak, her blood pressure high. Battered by lawyers and pressured by cops, Jean told her family she was sorry she had testified. Despite her remorse, she still got icy stares from the other Mitchells, for none of them would ever accept that Junior was guilty.

Lloyd Clark, the unofficial spokesman for victims and survivors nationwide, was determined to forgive and forget. After the trial, he ditched his gun, sipped ice tea in the California sunshine, and put his feelings on paper. His elation wouldn't last. Fanatics were still out there in dead clothes, and Lloyd could never tell what the next twist in the road might bring. With a new state homicide trial ahead, Lloyd was forced to enter the witness protection program after years of resistance. He took his new wife, Cristina, with him, but he lost his two Yahweh children. Though the kids still had unhappy memories of life in the Temple of Love, they returned to their mother, who, Lloyd suspected, remained a secret devotee of Yahweh Ben Yahweh.

The experience had left Lloyd improved in some ways, bitter in others. For years, he had tried to overcome the lawmen's apathy, and then at the trial defense attorneys treated him as though he was black on the outside and white on the inside. "Color," Lloyd had come to realize, "don't mean a damn thing."

Lloyd would always be proud of the work he had done in getting Yahweh behind bars. But for Eric Burke, the hothead defector who started it all, justice delayed would mean justice denied. Eleven years before, Eric had gone into hiding after the botched attempt on his life and the murders of his defector friends. In a crumbling neighborhood in southwest Atlanta, he fixed cars, shooed away hooligans and pimps, and hoped Hebrew killers would never find him.

Eric survived the Yahwehs, but he couldn't survive the streets. On a partly cloudy afternoon in February 1988, he was fatally shot in the chest after an argument with a neighborhood thug. Eric was fifty years old.

In the spring of 1992, more than four years after Eric Burke's death, state attorney Janet Reno's office announced it would seek the death penalty against Yahweh Ben Yahweh.

40

....

Uriah David Israel, national ambassador of the Nation of Yahweh, picked up the reins of the steadily unraveling empire. In modest ways, he offered himself as a substitute for Yahweh Ben Yahweh. A bespectacled former banker, Uriah David searched for ways to rebuild Yahweh's base. He did national tours and spread the teachings on a TV show, "From Poverty to Riches," broadcast on cable channels in south Florida and major metropolitan areas. The differences between the two men were hard to miss. Yahweh had always been bombastic and unrestrained. Uriah David was soft-spoken and modest. He admitted he could never replace "the architect of the universe," whose heroic standing was sure to be enhanced by his trial. Uriah David vowed that the Nation of Yahweh would thrive and grow as never before.

According to the Bible, the persecuted would flee to another city; and a handful of Yahweh's die-hard supporters packed their bags for downtown Atlanta. There, Uriah David managed the group's eleven-story Barclay Hotel on Luckie Street. Smiling waitresses in the hotel's Celebrity Café answered questions about the menu—chicken, waffles, and stewed greens—with a "Yes, sir" or a "No, sir."

In the limbo months between the verdict and sentencing, the Hebrews kept up their studies and discussed prophetic Bible passages. There was no doubt Yahweh's angels would come to punish the foolishness of mankind. God would pull the heavens backward until the messiah was set free. Ever since the FBI had swooped down on Yahweh Ben Yahweh, his followers had been clipping news reports about world disasters: fifteen thousand earthquakes, eighteen typhoons, two heat waves, three mud slides, three droughts, seventy-three tornadoes, a major cholera epidemic, assorted UFO sightings, a frog pestilence, a major river changing course, burgeoning homelessness, unemployment, and global recession.

The manacled messiah himself kept a tally of cataclysmic events on a yellow pad, and during an interview with *Penthouse* magazine, he prophesied, "My incarceration equals plagues in both America and the world. . . . Death and destruction, war and threats of war. . . . You can't persecute the son of God and expect to be blessed. . . . You can't hold Yahweh Ben Yahweh and think you are going to come out of a recession. Unless America faces up to the fact— unless the world faces up to the fact—this is the Judgment Day."

In August 1992, six convicted followers returned to the federal courthouse in Fort Lauderdale to face their own judgment days. Showing no shred of remorse, they railed against the legal system and the apostates who had framed them. Brother Job pleaded with Judge Roettger to assign him to the same federal pen as his messiah. "He can't see too good," Job said. "Maybe we can tie each other's shoes."

Sister Judith had stayed quiet throughout the ordeal, still the mystery figure, the repository of all the sect's secrets, financial and otherwise. At her sentencing, her elderly parents pleaded for leniency, and Judith read from a handwritten script. She'd lived by the Bible and always taught her three kids to lead a moral and righteous life. Now the government had stolen them. Prosecutors turned them into "secret agents," terrifying them into testifying against her. "They truly poisoned my children," she said.

Judith's eyes filled with tears. It reminded her of Nazi Germany—the lawmen, Nazi soldiers. "I was horrified by the prosecution version of me," she told Judge Roettger. "We are not guilty."

Prosecutor Trudy Novicki called her a liar. "The government didn't take Judith Israel's children from her. It was Judith Israel that cut her children off. . . . She was the second in command. She was there in 1979, before there was a Yahweh Ben Yahweh, when there was only a Brother Love . . . just a Linda Gaines. She cared about power beyond caring about her own family. She cares about only one person: Yahweh Ben Yahweh."

Novicki told Judge Roettger about the abuse of Judith's daughter. Her mother had been so blinded by love for Yahweh that she'd called Lydia a liar. Roettger hadn't allowed Lydia's testimony at the trial, and now he was glad he hadn't. Judith, he said, would never be paroled. One by one, the judge called their crimes "shocking" and "brutal." He sentenced the followers to hard time—from fifteen to sixteen and a half years—away from their fallen idol.

Yahweh Ben Yahweh's lawyers fought a delaying action, getting a sentence postponement even as their client fended off a series of new challenges. He feuded with Alcee Hastings, accusing the former judge of "ineffective counsel." He demanded a new lawyer for his upcoming murder trials. There was a test of wills with new saviors rising from obscurity to do battle with Yahweh Ben Yahweh. In Los Angeles, a man named Prophet Yahweh popped up in a black robe and a black turban. "The true Yahweh is opening the door for me," he proclaimed. "Even if Hulon Mitchell, Junior, gets life, he will continue to live in the minds of my people. The true Yahweh knows this, and he has chosen me to be the brother that he is going to use to destroy Hulon Mitchell's teachings from off the face of the planet Earth!"

The Los Angeles Yahweh would soon be forgotten, but Yahweh Ben Yahweh began to taste more fame. Despite his conviction, the Yahwehs still had an audience, especially in the black media, and they kept playing to that audience. With the trial, their message had spread from the *London Observer* to a Seattle radio station. The Barclay Hotel, with its bargain-basement prices and distinctive white Yahweh flag, was becoming a bit of a tourist attraction.

As the hour of Yahweh's sentencing drew near, his supporters' conversations with God flowed, as the prophet Amos put it, like a mighty river. Then, on a Monday in August 1992, Hurricane Andrew's 180-mile-an-hour winds slammed into the Metropolitan Correctional Center, where Yahweh Ben Yahweh lay behind bars. The hurricane ripped off the roof, knocked down a twenty-foot cyclone fence, and tore apart the prison walls. The rubble zone stretched for miles. Homes and lives were left a tortured mess, whole streets, concrete and all, disappeared, and the trees—the stately royal palms and the hundred-year-old banyans—were smashed to splinters.

But thirty miles north of the prison, the tidy, two-story Yahweh resort villas stood unharmed, sparkling in the Miami sunshine. And Yahweh Ben Yahweh was safe. Before the landfall, he'd been loaded on a U.S. marshal's plane under tight security. He spent a few nights at a Cracker prison in northern Florida, and eleven days after Andrew, he returned to the Fort Lauderdale courthouse for sentencing. It was a hot and sticky Friday afternoon. The pewlike benches of Courtroom B were filled with one hundred perspiring and teary-eyed followers. Yahweh looked old and frail. Worry lines streaked his face. He was forty pounds lighter than he once had been. He rubbed his luminous eyes and turned to scan the faces of his followers. He stepped to the podium to speak. He'd misplaced his glasses during the hurricane. He said he hadn't had a chance to read the government's presentence investigation report. He would appreciate a postponement.

Judge Roettger was unmoved. Another delay was out of the question. The courtroom spectators waited for a spellbinding sermon from the messiah, but with murder trials ahead, with anything he said now likely to bite him in the ass later, Yahweh Ben Yahweh didn't speak. He didn't have to. Judgment was God's and punishment was in his hands. "I leave it in the hands of Yahweh and you," he told Judge Roettger.

Alcee Hastings rose to defend his client, condemning the "inveterate liars" who'd testified at the trial. But there was no fire in his belly. Disillusioned, on the verge of withdrawing from Yahweh's case, Hastings was just going through the motions.

He left the passion to Richard Scruggs, who pleaded for the maximum term. The prosecutor labeled Yahweh a megalomaniac con man who'd deluded the criminal justice system over a twenty-year span. "Think about the destruction of this one man," he implored.

Yahweh Ben Yahweh had exploited very ordinary people, using race and religion as a shield to amass power, money, women, even children. He didn't understand the harm, the hurt, the trauma, the humiliation, and the scars that he inflicted on so many people.

"Perhaps the United States of America has never seen anything

311

like it," Scruggs told Judge Roettger. "My only regret is that I can stand here and plead for only twenty years. That's not enough."

Not enough for Alphonso Bonaby, whose children still had nightmares of seeing their house in flames.

Not enough for Mildred Banks, who lost her husband, her faith, and her health. She lived with a seam on her neck and a bullet that obstructed blood flow to the brain.

Not enough for Lydia Gaines, who felt isolated and confused in the witness protection program after years of abuse, rape, and abandonment.

Not enough for Mildred Kelley, Ray's widow, or Michelle Dupree, Leonard's sister, or Pinkey Benebee, age seventy-two, retired nurse with sixty-three grandchildren, Big Man's mother. "He shook your hand by sunrise," Mrs. Benebee would say of Yahweh Ben Yahweh, "and murdered you by night."

The courtroom was still for a good thirty seconds. Yahweh was subdued. Reporters seated in the jury box fidgeted with their pads and whispered that twenty years was a fait accompli. Two Yahweh jurors watching the sentencing for "therapy" sat quietly in the fifth row. Across the aisle a man in a blue ski cap underlined a passage from the Bible with a yellow marker. A woman blew a kiss, but the messiah appeared not to notice.

Finally, it was Judge Roettger's turn to speak. Finally, a federal judge would say what nobody in power had dared say for a decade. The length of the sentence didn't matter. It was moral certitude that was needed now: soothing words to the victims, thanks to the witnesses who came forward, a message from the justice system that hate and bigotry would not be tolerated. Finally, someone in authority would pass judgment on what happens when religion goes too far, when blind faith leads to conspiracy and murder.

Roettger wiped his mustache and avoided Yahweh's glare. His nasal, southern drawl sinking to a murmur, he began. He mumbled something about evidence of horrendous crimes, but it was hard to hear his exact words. Non-Hebrew spectators waited for the judge to tremble with outrage over the destruction Hulon Mitchell wrought.

They waited for him to say Mitchell should feel lucky he was being locked up for only twenty years. He should have gotten life or Florida's death penalty.

But Roettger didn't say any of that. He said Yahweh deserved some reward for good deeds. "The Nation of Yahweh under the leadership of this defendant . . . tried to be a good citizen," he said. "They literally cleaned up the community."

The courtroom went silent. Richard Scruggs was stunned. After complimenting the convicted felon, Judge Roettger reduced Yahweh's already reduced sentence to eighteen years. "I hope you will be a force for good in our community and nation," he said.

"Thank you," Yahweh Ben Yahweh replied. "I and my followers will do that."

Three months later, Yahweh Ben Yahweh beat a murder rap. After losing one death row case against him, state attorney Reno dropped charges in two other homicides. There would be no prosecutions of at least nineteen Yahweh-connected murders and disappearances in Miami and elsewhere, and not a single case of Yahweh child abuse would be prosecuted. Prosecutors explained that the charges were too dated; the details were too vague; the statute of limitations had run out; the victims were too fragile; Yahweh Ben Yahweh was already behind bars.

The U.S. attorney's office declined to retry Yahweh on the racketeering charge that had ended in a hung jury. The FBI was unable to trace the mysterious source of the Nation of Yahweh's wealth. And at no time did the justice system hint at the possibility of political corruption or address the bureaucratic neglect that had allowed terrorism in Miami to go unchecked.

On the street, people never understood what had happened. The case simply fueled a belief that the criminals held the upper hand in Miami, that the justice system couldn't even put away killers who sliced up people in public. For about a year after the Yahwehs disappeared from the headlines, the Temple of Love became a place to hide in the shadows and smoke crack. Like much of Yahweh Ben Yahweh's Miami kingdom of white palaces—the real estate, the grocery stores, the promises to clean up the ghetto—it became home to rats, burned tires (so the homeless could keep warm), and ghosts. The temple's neighbors threw rocks at it and trashed it, picking it clean of everything of value, including the copper wiring.

As time went on, civic leaders who once paid homage to Yahweh preferred to think that what happened in the Magic City in the 1980s—the killings, the young bodies crushed, stabbed, shot—never really happened at all. Instead, they advertised Miami as a paradise of hope and promise, with its richness of multicultural flavor, the sweet aroma of citrus trees, the with-it restaurants and shops in trendy South Beach, the sunbeams changing the bay water's color with each sparkle, from blue to green to gray, like Brother Love's eyes.

Like other politicians who kept quiet about him, Janet Reno landed on her feet. She experienced a metamorphosis into a tough crime fighter and went to Washington to become the nation's top cop. Her first major bad guy: an apparition of Yahweh Ben Yahweh. In defending her decision to storm David Koresh's Branch Davidian compound, U.S. Attorney General Reno cited reports that the children of Mount Carmel had been hostages of a madman, hit with wooden paddles and forced into sex. Ironically, in all her years as Dade County state attorney, she had never publicly expressed concern about the children of the Temple of Love. It was Richard Scruggs, named to a top post at the Justice Department, who assessed Reno's handling of the ill-fated raid in Waco, Texas. His 348-page report contradicted his boss on key points, including her justification for the assault. In an interview, Scruggs said the unprosecuted allegations of child abuse in the Yahweh case were "many times more serious" than in the Branch Davidian affair.

Bit by bit, Yahweh's followers staged a comeback. They broadcast their message on cable television, flooded Congress and the Bureau of Prisons with "proof" of the messiah's persecution, and in the spring of 1994 stepped up their attack in a series of court appeals. They demanded a new trial, claiming the government was hiding evidence of Yahweh Ben Yahweh's innocence. Bobby Rozier, they said, had told a jailhouse lawyer he intended to lie against the son of God from the witness stand.

Some people just assumed that the guilty verdict against Yahweh would be totally annulled one day—owing to a legal quirk or, as he had always predicted, divine intervention. Barring appeals, Yahweh will serve two thirds of his sentence. With credit for time served since his arrest, he will get out in about 2001, by which time he will be sixty-six years old.

At this writing, he remains behind the stone walls of the old maximum-security Big House in Lewisburg, Pennsylvania. He has called his incarceration a "learning experience . . . an opportunity of correction that I might be perfect in everything I do."

His prison keepers have said he has transformed himself into a model inmate with no trouble coping with the routine of prison life. Wearing fresh khaki shirts, he is entitled to fourteen cents an hour waxing floors and toting trash alongside an assortment of Colombian drug lords and Mafia dons. Lewisburg is a tranquil Amish town of seven thousand, and it is hard to imagine a place farther removed from the world of his fiery oratory. In Miami, the roar of his sermons, the buzz of his temple presses are not heard anymore. But for the people who still love him—the people he once called blind and deaf niggers, walking, dead zombies, and lords of the trash pile—his deeds live in words inscribed in their hearts.

"Remember, I have the key to go from poverty to riches! When the morning comes, we'll be ruling the earth! When the morning comes, we'll have the victory! Won't that be a glad day? Won't that be a glad time?"

Source Notes

....

The formal reporting for *Brother Love* started in October 1986, when I covered the Opa-locka homicides as a reporter for the *Miami Herald*. The book is based largely on 25,000 pages of official records, including grand jury proceedings, FBI reports, and investigative narratives not normally available to outside scrutiny.

I have also conducted more than 200 interviews and reviewed more than 300 newspaper accounts, magazine articles, and voluminous additional material. Since their court appeals have not been exhausted, Yahweh's incarcerated followers were cautioned by temple counsel not to speak with me. Yahweh Ben Yahweh, though I have met him in the course of my reporting for the *Herald*, declined through his attorneys to be interviewed for this book.

In the narrative of events, some dialogue and quotations attributed to Yahweh come from named temple informants. Many of his lengthier monologues are extracted from forty hours of his taped temple sermons. Some of the recordings were obtained from the Dade County state attorney's office under Florida's public records laws, and others were made available by former Hebrews or purchased from the Yahweh organization. The tape recordings include the following:

Feast of Tabernacles 9/83
Memorial Blowing of Trumpets
Genesis 1:2—The Earth Was Without Form and Void: Parts 1 and 2
Dry Bones 5/22/85
Dry Bones Ezekiel 37, #18
Preparing for Rulership: Nos. 5, 6, 7, 8, and 9
Law Concerning Parents and Children (9/18/85; 10/23/85;
     10/30/85; 11/6/85; 12/2/85)
Untitled tape of speech in Philadelphia
Untitled tape dated 5/29/85
Untitled tape dated 10/9/85
Untitled tape dated 10/16/85

Source Notes

Untitled tape dated 3/19/86
Our True History: Parts 1, 2, 3, and 4
Laws of Inheritance
Hebrew Language: Parts 1 and 2
To Live Forever—Be Charitable: Parts 1, 2, and 3
Franchise OPS: Nos. 1 and 2
Day of Atonement 1989: Parts 1, 2, and 3
Be Aware: Parts 2 and 4

In addition to the audiotapes, I have reviewed videotapes of Yahweh Ben Yahweh appearing at a class in the temple and a rally in Miami. I have also relied on transcripts of Yahweh Ben Yahweh's testimony outlined below:

1967: trial testimony by Hulon Shah in Superior Court of Fulton County—*State of Georgia v. Grady XXX Rogers.*

1967: trial testimony by Hulon Shah in the Superior Court of Fulton County—*State of Georgia v. Carlton X Woods.*

1987: deposition by Yahweh Ben Yahweh in U.S. District Court, Southern District of Florida—*Jane Doe No. 1. et al. v. Temple of Love Inc.*

1988: deposition by Yahweh Ben Yahweh in Circuit Court of the 11th Judicial Circuit for Dade County—*State of Florida v. Robert Rozier, Jr.*

1989: trial testimony by Yahweh Ben Yahweh in *Jane Doe v. Temple of Love.*

1991: bail appeal by Yahweh Ben Yahweh in U.S. District Court, Southern District of Florida—*United States of America v. Hulon Mitchell, Jr., aka Yahweh Ben Yahweh et al.*

1992: trial testimony by Yahweh Ben Yahweh in *U.S. v. Mitchell et al.*

Articles and books written under Yahweh's various incarnations also provided essential information. The writings, many undated, are as follows:

Mitchell, Hulon, Jr. "Theories of Capital and Capitalism," a thesis submitted to the faculty of Atlanta University in partial fulfillment of the requirements for the degree of Master of Arts. Atlanta: August 1964.

Modern Christian Church flyer for "Father Michel (The King)."

Modern Christian Church brochure for first anniversary celebration, June 29, 1969.

Yahweh Ben Yahweh. "If I Had Five Minutes with the Pope," *Miami Herald*, September 10, 1987.

Books and articles published by the Temple of Love include: *The Holy*

Bible (The Way It Looked Before the White Man Changed It); You Are Not a Nigger! Our True History, the World's Best-Kept Secret: Yahweh God of Gods; The Mighty Black Man; Yahweh Judges America; Let My People Go; 100 Years of Lynchings; Divine Dietary Laws for Hebrew Israelites; From Poverty to Riches: The Works of Yahweh Ben Yahweh; "A Plan to Destroy the Obsolete People (So-Called Negroes)"; "Concentration Camps for Blacks"; "Don't Murder Your Baby"; "Teach Your Children Yahweh's Laws"; "We Must Educate Our Own Children"; "The Hebrew Israelite Program of Self-Development"; "Blacks Must Buy Silver and Gold Quick"; "What Is the Black Man's Law Concerning Justice?" "We Must Unite at All Cost"; "We Must Defend Ourselves Against Assault, Rape, Murder and Injustice"; "Re: Vicious Harassment by White Fireman"; "Yahweh's Hypocrites Are Warned"; Hebrew Israelite University Summer/Winter Catalogue 1982–1983; "White People Are Open Vicious Haters of the Black Man"; "Yahweh's Judgment on America"; "Yahweh Tours America"; "Celebrate the Black Man's Holidays"; "Come Feast with Yahweh at the Feast of Weeks"; "Black Leadership & Yahweh"; "Yahweh Says Never Again"; "White America, the Wicked Terrorist"; *O.C.L. Yahweh YBY*; "Yahweh—Politics and Morals"; "Yahweh Gives Us Warning"; "America Terrorizes Yahweh's Hebrew Israelites"; "White Americans Are Kidnappers and Terrorists"; "White America Tortures Yahweh Followers"; "White America the Wicked Terrorist"; "White Prison Guards Attack Hebrew"; "Yahweh Is Not for Cowards"; "Yahweh Demands Separation"; "White America Murders Blacks Daily"; "Yahweh Kills Blasphemers"; "Whites Shoot Yahweh Follower"; "Yahweh Says Never Again"; "The Wicked Seek to Destroy Followers of Yahweh"; "Open Letter to the World: The *Miami Times* Attempts to Defame Yahweh Ben Yahweh and the Nation of Yahweh"; *On the Ocean; The Exciting World of Yahweh*; Job's Beauty Supply Grand Opening; "Open Letter to the World: Miami Harassment of Yahweh University"; *Yahweh Ben Yahweh, Miami Arena.*

Articles and pamphlets published by The People for Truth: "Now Is the Judgment of This World: The Prince of This World Shall Be Cast Down"; "Open Letter to the World: We Must Support Yahweh Ben Yahweh"; "Miami Witnesses 20-Year Reunion of Yahweh Ben Yahweh and Louis Farrakhan"; "The Persecution of Yahweh Ben Yahweh"; "U.S. Government Persecutes Yahweh Ben Yahweh in Jail"; "U.S. Government Continues Pretrial Persecution of Yahweh Ben Yahweh"; "U.S. Government Conspires to Deny Yahweh Ben Yahweh Bond"; "The Pretrial Persecution of Yahweh Ben Yahweh Continues"; "Strange Explosions Kill Yahweh

Source Notes

••

Child"; "Prejudiced Judge in Yahweh's Trial Asked to Step Down"; "Stop the Double Standard in the Yahwehs' Trial"; "U.S. Government Systematically Starves Yahweh Followers"; "Yahweh Case Evidence Distorted"; "Federal Judge Roettger Stacks Jury Against Yahweh"; *A Background Report on the Persecution and Inquisition of Yahweh Ben Yahweh and the Nation of Yahweh*; "The Crucifixion of Yahweh Ben Yahweh"; "Judge Roettger Changes Venue to Guarantee Yahweh Conviction"; "Malnutrition Drives One Member Insane"; "Yahweh Uses Nature to Retaliate Against America's Persecution of Yahweh Ben Yahweh."

Another important source was the daily reporting in the *Miami Herald* and the *Enid News and Eagle*. I would like to cite in particular the work of Edna Buchanan, Donna Gehrke, Mark Kriegel, Joe Oglesby, Susan Sachs, Charles Strouse, and Andres Viglucci. For research and library assistance, I want to thank Liz Donovan and Cristina Vazquez in Miami; Michael Mudd in Norman, Oklahoma; Jeff Osterkamp in Lakeland, Florida; Michael M. Cassell in Atlanta; Mary Katherine Huffman of the Oklahoma Historical Society; Rick Sayre of Phillips University's Zollars Memorial Library; Diane C. Hunter of the *Atlanta Journal-Constitution* library; Stephen Goldfarb of the Atlanta Public Library, and Minnie Clayton of Special Collections at Atlanta University Center, Robert W. Woodruff Library. Sincere thanks also to the records custodians at the Dade County state attorney's office, who quickly responded to my Public Records Act requests, and to Thomas Buscaglia, Dennis Kainen, Steve Kassner, and Albert Levin, who allowed me access to thousands of pages of federal documents.

Lastly, I owe an enormous debt to Rick Bragg, Tsitsi Wakhisi, Meg Laughlin, Willy Fernandez, Mark Seibel, Rick Ovelmen, Bill Cooke, and Alexandra Ozols. They graciously listened, read portions of the manuscript, and offered friendship, love, and professional assistance when I needed it.

Following are additional sources of information in greater detail:

Part I: Autumn of Terror

••

INTERVIEWS: Edna Buchanan; Ruben Burke; Bobby Cheetam; Lloyd Clark; Joe Davis; Lewis Dunehoo; Marvin Dunn; Louretta Green; Barbara Howard; John King; Carl Masztal; Joe Oglesby; Ulises Ordunez; Ron Polk; Steve Roadruck; Richard Scruggs; Al Singleton; J. J. Trimble; James Walker; Charles Wetli; Tommy Williams.

SWORN STATEMENTS: Mildred Banks; Eric Burke; Carlton Carey.

DEPOSITIONS: Barbara Barker; Lottie Pierre; Earl Scrivens.

320

Source Notes

GRAND-JURY TESTIMONY: Richard Davis; Milton Johnson; Ricardo Woodside.

COURT TESTIMONY: Paul Addison; Virginia Addison; Mildred Banks; William Bass; William Bevan; Fred Carter; Lloyd Clark; Ronald Cooksley; Herb Cousins; Joe Davis; William Hanlon; R. Hart; Neal Haskell; Raymond Mayhew; Gurbachan Soni; Charles Triana; Walter Walkington; Charles Wetli; Timothy Wiseman; Ricardo Woodside.

REPORTS OF FBI INTERVIEWS: Mildred Banks; Eric Burke; Maurice Willacy; Ricardo Woodside.

POLICE REPORTS: W. R. Baker; D. S. Ballard; R. Cooksley; R. Diers; A. Fernandez; J. King; R. Mayhew; S. Parr; J. Reschetar; S. Roadruck; T. D. Surman; C. Triana; W. Walkington; T. Williams; T. Wiseman.

MISCELLANEOUS DOCUMENTS: Eric Burke's death certificate; Burke's rap sheets and felony complaints; probation report by Keith Camp; arrest forms on Aston Green; Green's funeral service obituary; autopsy reports of Green and Carlton Carey; crime-scene photos and sketches; Mildred Banks's hospital records.

PUBLICATIONS:

Buchanan, Edna. "Hooded Gunmen Attack Dropouts of Sect," *Miami Herald*, November 16, 1981.

Oglesby, Joe. "A Hebrew Israelite Defector Talks," *Miami Herald*, December 17, 1981.

Porter, Bruce, and Marvin Dunn. *The Miami Riot of 1980* (Lexington, Mass.: Lexington Books, 1984).

Szymkowiak, Ken. "Former Black Israelites in Hiding; Leader Denies Sect Role in Killings," *Miami News*, November 17, 1981.

Wetli, Charles, and Rafael Martinez. "Brujeria: Manifestations of Palo Mayombe in South Florida," *Journal of Florida Medical Examiners*, August 1983.

Wetli, Charles, and Rafael Martinez. "Tattoos of the Marielitos," *American Journal of Forensic Medicine and Pathology*, 1989.

Wetli, Charles, and Rafael Martinez. "Santeria: A Magico-Religious System of Afro-Cuban Origin," *American Journal of Social Psychiatry*, Summer 1982.

Part II: Divine Calling

INTERVIEWS: Taalib Ahmad; Dorice Allen; Jamil el-Amin; Charlie Bailey; Ralph Ballard; Nathaniel Barnes; Hubert W. Blackwell; Summum

Source Notes

Bonum-Udoko; Margaret Buvinger; Jeannie Mae Cheadle; Nodie Mae Chiles; Joe Clytus; Art Cox; Evelyn Dixon; R. T. Garland; Virginia Garrison; James L. Green; McCree Harris; David Heath; Donald F. Heath; Hattie McCoy Hightower; Herb Hildabrand; Mark Hutchison; Thomas Jarrett; Beatrice Jech; Robert W. Jech; J. L. Jordan; Ed Jorden; Bobby Kinard; Floydean Kratzer; Clara Luper; Lillie Merthie; H. G. McBrayer; Paul McKenna; Henry Mitchell; Jefferson Mitchell; Marvin Mitchell; Ramona Mitchell; Roberta Montgomery; Mae Doss Moore; Billy and Irene Mucker; Carolyn Mulherin; C. J. Neal; Clayton Nolen; Steve Norton; Ibraham Pasha; E. Patterson; Eugene Pitts; Phil Porter; Maureen Priebe; Carrie Roseberry; Jim Sandefur; Darreyl F. Scott; A. C. Searles; Alfred (Spring) Shannon; G. J. Sharpe; Charles Sherrod; Lewis Slaton; Janice Smith; T. J. Smith, Sr.; Kenneth Sorey; Al Stewart; David Thomson; Willie Thompson; Effie Turner; Harriet Walton; Leroy Watson; Amanda White; Patricia Williams; R. P. Reneir Woodley III; Sam Wright; Leonora Yarborough.

SWORN STATEMENTS: Tawana Hill; Anthony Solomon.

DEPOSITIONS: Carter Cornelius.

GRAND JURY TESTIMONY: Freddie Gaines; Kelly Gaines; Jeffrey Glover; Lawrence Lee; Anthony Solomon; Jean Solomon.

COURT TESTIMONY: Paul George; Jeffrey Glover; Judith Israel; Lawrence Lee; Oscar Merthie; Anthony Solomon; Jean Solomon.

REPORTS OF FBI INTERVIEWS: Patricia Albert; Anthony Solomon; Jean Solomon.

POLICE REPORTS: J. King; M. M. Mayfield–W. J. Moss; D. Pritchett–L. Melvin; R. Remley.

MISCELLANEOUS DOCUMENTS: Enid and Kingfisher city directories and telephone books; Kingfisher County school enumeration records; marriage license, McClain County clerk's office; marriage license, Kingfisher County clerk's office; school records from McClain County, Kingfisher County, and Garfield County; Kingfisher County assessment roll records; deed and mortgage in Kingfisher County clerk's office; Garfield County property records; information reply from the Military Personnel Records Center, Saint Louis, Missouri; letter from Department of the Air Force, Air Training Command, Randolph AFB Texas; Phillips University transcript for Hulon Mitchell, Jr.; Phillips University course catalogue; Oklahoma University registrar's office; Oklahoma University course catalogue; Oklahoma University student-faculty phone book; 1961 Sooner yearbook; Atlanta city directories; Atlanta University course catalogue; Modern Christian Church incorporation papers; Fulton County estate files of Billy S. Jones; Fulton County property records; Garfield County District Court criminal and civil complaints, petitions, and decrees; Fulton County Superior Court files—Lucious Boyce and Virginia Garrison et al.; Linda Gaines's divorce file; Dade County state attorney's files–Herman Sands; handwritten diary, Patricia Albert; Orlando city directories.

PUBLICATIONS:

Atlanta Constitution. "White Baptist Church Sold to Atlanta's Muslims," February 24, 1965.

Atlanta Constitution. "Five Muslims Indicted in Police Attacks," March 11, 1967.

Atlanta Daily World. "Apprehend 3rd Man in Jone Murder Case," June 17, 1969.

Atlanta Journal. "Smyrnan Tells How Muslims Got Land," February 21, 1965.

Atlanta Journal. "Agreement Halts Muslim Temple Sale," June 4, 1968.

Atlanta Journal. "One Hunted in Gunfight with 'Prophet,' " May 26, 1969.

Black Chronicle. "Cultist Linked to Enid," November 15, 1990.

Brown, Phil. "Negroes Pack Enid Lunch Counter," *Enid Daily Eagle,* August 27, 1958.

Carson, Clayborne. *In Struggle: SNCC and the Black Awakening of the 1960s* (Cambridge, Mass: Harvard University Press, 1981).

Carson, Clayborne, David J. Garrow, Vincent Harding, and Darlene Clark Hine, eds. *Eyes on the Prize: America's Civil Rights Years, A Reader and Guide* (New York: Penguin Books, 1987).

Castleman, Jack. "Grand Jury Given Testimony about Death of Negro Child; Father Denies Sons Tossed Fire Bombs; Rev. Mitchell Due to Tell Jury Sons Were Not in Town," *Enid Daily Eagle,* June 12, 1968.

———. "Grand Jury Hears Final Witness in DA's Probe," *Enid Daily Eagle,* June 14, 1968.

Church Of God In Christ Official Manual (Memphis: Church Of God In Christ World Headquarters Inc., 1973).

Crawford, Anne. "A Black Muslim Tells Their Story on WQXI," *Atlanta Constitution,* April 22, 1963.

Enid Daily Eagle. "Negroes Break up Conference by Merchants," August 28, 1958.

Enid Daily Eagle. "Cafe Operators Pick Group to Talk with Enid Negroes," August 29, 1958.

Source Notes

Enid News and Eagle. "Enid Minister Is Found Innocent of Creating Disturbance Charge," September 7, 1972.

Freedberg, Sydney. "Leader Talks Peace and Power," *Miami Herald,* July 8, 1990.

Gaines, Orville. "Furious Shoot-out Kills 'Father Jone,' " *Atlanta Journal,* May 24, 1969.

Hendrickson, Kenneth E., Jr., ed. *Hard Times in Oklahoma: The Depression Years* (Oklahoma City: Oklahoma Historical Society, 1983).

Hutchison, Mark. "Professors Saw Sect Leader as Bright Student," *Daily Oklahoman,* November 9, 1990.

———. Mark. "Black Sect Leader Visited Enid, Stirred Tension, Source Says," *Saturday Oklahoman and Times,* November 10, 1990.

Kingfisher Free Press, October 1935.

Kingfisher Times, October 1935.

Lawson, Steven F. *Running for Freedom: Civil Rights and Black Politics in America since 1941* (New York: McGraw-Hill, Inc., 1991).

Luper, Clara. *Behold the Walls* (Oklahoma City: Jim Wire, 1979).

McCartney, Keeler. "Five Black Muslims Charged after Melee in Streets," *Atlanta Constitution,* March 7, 1967.

Melton, J. Gordon. *Encyclopedic Handbook of Cults in America* (New York and London: Garland Publishing, Inc., 1986).

Melton, J. Gordon. *Encyclopedia of American Religions,* 3d ed. (Detroit: Gale Research, Inc., 1989).

Mitchell, Chloe. "An Experimental Study Using Pictorial Paired Associates to Compare Learning Rates of Normal Negro and White Children." UMI Dissertation Information Service, 1992.

Morgan, H. Wayne, and Anne Hodges Morgan. *Oklahoma: A History* (New York: W.W. Norton & Co., 1984).

Payne, Wardell J., ed. *Directory of African-American Religious Bodies* (Washington, D.C.: Howard University Press).

Perry, Harmon. "2nd Suspect Dead in Prophet Slaying," *Atlanta Journal and Constitution,* May 25, 1969.

The Phillipian (1958–1960).

Rosicrucian Manual. (San Jose: Rosicrucian Press, 1938).

Sachs, Susan. "Cult's Self-Styled Messiah Inspires Discipline, Fear," *Miami Herald,* December 8, 1985.

Smith, Reuben. "Muslim Trial in Assault Starts Today," *Atlanta Constitution,* April 4, 1967.

———. "Muslim Convicted in Assault," *Atlanta Constitution,* April 6, 1967.

Thomas, Keith L. "Sect Apparently Has Substantial Membership Here," *Atlanta Constitution,* December 26, 1986.

Time. "Destiny Rides Again," October 11, 1982.

The WPA Guide to 1930s Oklahoma, compiled by the Writers' Program of the WPA in the State of Oklahoma (Lawrence, Kansas: University of Kansas Press, 1986).

Files titled "Afro-American" and "Leona Mitchell" in the Library Resources Division, Oklahoma Historical Society.

Files titled "Rev. Hulon Mitchell, Sr.," "Byron Mitchell," and "Hulon Mitchell, Jr.," *Enid News and Eagle* morgue.

Files titled "Black Muslims" and "Negroes-Boycott," *Atlanta Journal-Constitution* morgue.

Part III: Heaven on Earth

INTERVIEWS: Anne Marie Adker; Taalib Ahmad; George Ailsworth; Dwayne Aldous; Danny Alvarez; Guy Anderson; James Angleton; Curtis Atkinson; Dora Bain; Dorothy Baker; Michael Band; Jay Barnhart; Ruben Betancourt; Ferdinand Bigard; Angelo Bitsis; Oliver Boorde; Danny Borrego; Robert Brand; Paul Brassard; Jinx Broussard; Gerald Campbell; Pablo Canton; Ringo Cayard; Lloyd Clark; Jimmy Cleveland; Allan Cooper; Herb Cousins; Brenda Daniels; Bill Davis; Frank Davis; Marvin Davis; Katherine Deans; Ralph DeLoach; Dave DeMaio; Victor De Yurre; Marvin Dunn; Lartius Dupree; Mary Dupree; Jean Eckes; T. Willard Fair; Robert Fallon; Glenn Feldman; Jim Freeman; Arnold Gellman; Marla Gibbs; Artie Gigantino; Michelle Dupree Green; Frank Hancock; Michael Higgs; Jessie Hill; Tom Hillstrom; Rick Holton; Don Horn; Barbara Howard; Yosiah Israel; Dennis Kainen; Steve Kassner; Rosario Kennedy; Jerrold Knee; Marvin Kornberg; Mark Kriegel; David Lazarus; Ellen Leesfield; Al Levin; Brad Liston; Walter Livingstone; Ed Lopez; Charles Mahan; Chris Mancini; Meky Manresa; Raul Masvidal; Vince McGhee; Paul McKenna; Matilda McKenzie; Alex Michaels; Ed Moore; Judith Moss; Katrina Murphy; Derwin Norwood; Gertrude Novicki; Rickey O'Donald; Joe Oglesby; Eric O'Neal; John Pell; Stephen Plotnick; Ron Polk; Gary Proctor; Edwin Ratiner; Rex Remley; Ann Richter; David Rivero; Antonio Rodriguez; Noel Roy; Robert Rozier, Jr.; Ellis Rubin; Earl Sanders; Penny Schwam; Richard Scruggs;

Source Notes

Jim Sewell; Charles Sherwood; James Smith; Sky Smith; Xavier Suarez; Art Teitelbaum; Bert Traud; Gene Upshaw; Raoul Vinneau; Jeffrey Weinkle; Frank Wesolowski; Charles White; Mike White; Richard White; Larry Preston Williams; Geoff Wong; Mike Wright.

SWORN STATEMENTS: Mildred Banks; Raymond M. Broussard; Steven Brown; Eric Burke; Carlton Carey; Sherry Crist; M. Hudson; Tawana Hill; G. C. Jones; Ellen McDuffy; S. Pitts; Herman Sands; Charles Saunders; Sharon Saunders; Anthony Solomon.

DEPOSITIONS: Danny Borrego; Kasha Briggs; Denise Broussard; Steven Brown; John Butchko; Lloyd Clark; Carter Cornelius; Abishag Israel; Adah Israel; Judith Israel; Nahum Israel; Obadiah Israel; Ock Ephrim Israel; Solomon Israel; Yoel Israel; David Kosloske; James Littlejohn; Phyllis Philpot; Gerald Reichardt; Rex Remley; Wilbert Rolle; Karen Strawder; Robert Taaffe.

GRAND JURY TESTIMONY: Robert Brand; Greg Cannon; Lloyd Clark; Richard Davis; Freddie Gaines; Kelly Gaines; Jeffrey Glover; Craig Hartmann; Milton Johnson; Lawrence Lee; Ricardo Melendez; Danielle Mitchell; Rickey O'Donald; Robert Rozier, Jr.; Sharon Saunders; Anthony Solomon; Jean Solomon; Karen Strawder; Willie Swift; Ricardo Woodside; Richmond Young.

PRETRIAL TESTIMONY: Richard Besser; John Challenor; Arnold Gellman; Yavin Israel; David Lazarus; Brenda Moore; Charles Saunders.

COURT TESTIMONY: Patricia Albert; Myrna Allen; Angela Anderson; David Anderson; Blondell Anthony; Robert Beasley, Jr.; Alphonso Bonaby; Alton Bonaby; Robert Brand; Kasha Briggs; Patricia Brinson; Denise Broussard; Dorothy Brown; Glenn Brown; Teresa Butler; Robert Bux; George Campbell; Lloyd Clark; Myra Conyers; Emily Crawford; Eunice Crawford; Sherry Crist; Brenda Daniels; Alfreda Davis; Donald Dupree; Barbara Duvall; Richard Ecott; Linda Efford; Constance Foster; Freddie Gaines; Bobby Gay; Jeffrey Glover; Dexter Grant; Gail Guynn; Karen Guzman; Samuel Hall; Ruth Hamm; Reginald Haring; Rose Haring; Craig Hartmann; Catherine Hendrix; Abishag Israel; Adah Israel; Aleeza Israel; Job Israel; Judith Israel; Lavon Israel; Michael Israel; Sher-Jahahub Israel; Veronica James; Robert Kennington; Lawrence Lee; Angela Leonard; Arthur Lester; Walter Lightburn; George Lopez; Michael Mathis; Nadine McIntyre; Broderick McKinney; Martina Mish; Roger Mittleman; C. Newbold; Deborah Palmer; Carl Perry; Marvin Pitts; Amtullah Raheem; Valerie Rao; Floyd Reeves; John Riley; Sylvia Romans; Robert Rozier, Jr.; Arnaldo Salamero; Robert Sarnow; Elenora Smith; James Smith; Ronald Smith; Sherry Smith; Anthony Solomon; Jean Solomon; Carla Stokes; Willie Swift; Robert Watkins; Gregory Wertz; Annette Jackson Williams; Sharon Wilson; Maurice Woodside; Ricardo Woodside; William Young.

REPORTS OF FBI INTERVIEWS: Patricia Albert; Eric Burke; Greg Cannon; Lloyd Clark; Barbara Coleman; John Foster; Charlzetta Glover; Jeffrey Glover; V. A. Harris; Lawrence Lee; Michael Mathis; Ellen McDuffy; Orlando Milligan; Danielle Mitchell; Rufus Pace, Jr.; Marvin Pitts; S. Pitts; Robert Rozier, Jr.; Charles Saunders; Sharon Saunders; Anthony Solomon; Jean Solomon; Gwendolyn Stevenson; Karen Strawder; Willie Swift; Maurice Willacy; Ricardo Woodside.

REPORTS OF POLICE INTERVIEWS: Vurney Burke; Lydia Gaines; Robert Hall; Richard Ingraham; Erroline Milligan; Willie Morrison; Arnold Odom; William Robinson; Robert Rozier, Jr.; Herman Sands; Leo Solomon; Vonzell Solomon; Carroll Williams; Ricardo Woodside.

POLICE REPORTS: S. Andress; W. R. Baker; D. S. Ballard; C. Barnett; A. Betancourt; D. Borrego; S. Bowman; R. Brand; E. Brillant; J. Butchko; R. Cooksley; J. O. Crawford; C. Duncan; R. Ecott; R. W. Evans; M. Fisten; P. Francisco; R. Garcia; J. M. Geller; D. Gilbert; R. Hart; C. Hartmann; D. Jones; R. Kennington; J. King; D. Kosloske; R. Mayhew; W. D. Merritt; D. Morales; J. Murias; A. Oliva; R. Ortiz; L. Parker; S. Parr; W. Petrovich; G. Reichardt; R. Remley; S. Roadruck; B. Roberson; A. Rodriguez; T. Romagni; L. Sanchez; J. Smith; R. Smith; R. Taaffe.

MISCELLANEOUS DOCUMENTS: Patricia Albert's handwritten diary; Lloyd Clark's unpublished manuscript; arrest records of Robert Beasley, Jr., Richard Ingraham, John Foster, Rufus Pace, Sr., James Louis Mack, Anthony Murphy, Ricardo Woodside, Dexter Leon Grant, Carl Douglas Perry, Robert Rozier, Jr., Anthony Solomon, Freddie Gaines, and Kelly Gaines; Dade County state attorney's files—Herman Sands; Florida secretary of state incorporation papers for Temple of Love Inc., Genesis Food Co-op Inc., Exodus Housing Co-op Inc., and Israelite Education Association Inc.; Dade County property records; firsthand observations of Temple of Love and Yahweh University; Fire Safety Bureau inspection report, dated July 24, 1981, and subsequent "memo to file," dated August 5, 1981; U.S. Army records—John Foster; National Climatic Data Center records; Yahweh's bus schedule; promotional brochure for Ethnic Gold Hair Care Products and confidential distributor's price list; Robert Rozier's transcripts—Cordova High School and UC Berkeley; UC Berkeley—Blue & Gold yearbook; Berkeley player profiles and sports information questionnaire; Rozier's student conduct files; Florida Department of Corrections report—Rozier; affidavit—

Source Notes

Alfred Perry; medical records—Leonard Dupree; letter from Chaplain Joseph F. Hunt dated January 18, 1984, and Moses Israel's reply, dated January 25, 1984; home study report by Jo Ann Stovall concerning Wilbert Rolle's children; public school records for ex-Hebrew children; drawings by eleven-year-old ex-Hebrew boy; Queens County (N.Y.) district attorney's records—Yesher Israel et al.; Delray Beach paramedic rescue reports; Yahweh Ben Yahweh's letter to Alphonso Bonaby and Marvin Hendrix, dated May 22, 1986; Florida Bureau of Fire and Arson laboratory-analysis reports; FBI laboratory-analysis report; American International Container invoices and corresponding delivery receipts; Lady Godiva Corp. invoices; FBI report of Lloyd Clark's polygraph; autopsy reports of Aston Green, Carlton Carey, Harold Barnett, Glendell Fowler, Kurt Doerr, Clair Walters, James Myers, Luis Llerena, Lyle Austin Bellinger, Raymond Kelley, Cecil Branch, Harry Byers, Reinaldo Echevarria, Rudolph Broussard, Anthony Brown, and Willie Livingston; police reports for victims Daniel Evans, Robert Henderson, Attilio Scalo, Ricardo McGee, Michael Mahaven, Nina De Salone Kelley, Carlos Alonso, Thomas Robinson, and Elizabeth Schwark; crime-scene photographs and sketches; memo of "ear" task force meeting dated October 3, 1986; police laboratory-analysis report dated December 23, 1986; closeout memo from Dade County state attorney's office dated February 13, 1987; TV footage of Opa-locka takeover: copies of identification cards belonging to Walter Lightburn; letter to Tonyaa Weathersbee from Yahweh Ben Yahweh, dated May 7, 1986; Opa-locka paramedic rescue summaries; federal and Dade County court files—Opa-locka; letter to Florida Attorney General Bob Butterworth, from Barbara Malone, dated July 20, 1987; letter to Barbara Malone from David K. Miller, chief counsel, Florida attorney general's office, dated July 27, 1987; letter to Assistant State Attorney Katherine Fernandez Rundle from Barbara Malone, dated September 15, 1987; firsthand observation of the Yahweh hotels, supermarkets, and other businesses; Oklahoma Department of Corrections report—Anthony Solomon; Rozier's proffer, dated March 7, 1988; Rozier's plea agreement dated March 23, 1988; Dade County state attorney's files—Willie Livingston; City of Miami "Overtown Ventures" file; City of Miami inspection reports and interoffice memo—Yahweh University; correspondence between Judith Israel and Fire Inspector C. E. Davis; City of Opa-locka Police Department internal review, dated April 25, 1988; Florida Department Health and Rehabilitative Services school inspection report, dated May 30, 1990; anonymous letter, postmarked July 12, 1990, signed "speaking for the innocent."

Source Notes

PUBLICATIONS:

Anti-Defamation League of B'nai B'rith. "The Black Hebrew Israelites," 1987.

———. "The Yahwehs: Violence and Anti-Semitism in a 'Black Hebrew' Sect," 1991.

Askari, Emilia. "Singer Changes His Tune for Yahwehs," *Miami Herald*, August 13, 1987.

Associated Press. "9 in Sect Held in Child Abuse," *New York Times*, April 6, 1986.

———. "Black Sect Holds 'Open House,' " *Los Angeles Sentinel*, December 4, 1986.

———. "Pipe-Bomb Explosion Near Synagogue Stirs Anti-Semitism," *Fort Lauderdale Sun-Sentinel*, May 7, 1988.

Bond, Charles. "Message of Black Self-Help in Miami Is Hard to Ignore," *Palm Beach Post*, October 14, 1990.

Buchanan, Edna. "Man Is Stabbed, Left to Die on Boulevard," *Miami Herald*, July 21, 1986.

———. "Missing Ears Link Murders, Cops Say," *Miami Herald*, October 3, 1986.

Cheakalos, Christina. "Yahwehs Excommunicate Member Held in Murder," *Miami Herald*, June 11, 1987.

Colon, Yves. "Man Arrested in Stabbings of Two Workers," *Miami Herald*, April 25, 1984.

Daily Californian, 1976–1977.

Dewar, Heather. "Woman Who Fled Yahwehs Is Threatened," *Miami Herald*, August 18, 1989.

Evans, Christine. "Former Yahweh Who Killed 4 Gets 22 Years in Plea Bargain," *Miami Herald*, June 8, 1988.

———. "Temple of Fear," *Miami Herald*, February 24, 1991.

Fair, T. Willard. "Me, Yahweh Ben Yahweh—and Racism," *Miami Times*, May 24, 1990.

———. "Looking at Yahweh through Others' Eyes," *Miami Times*, July 19, 1990.

Fiedler, Tom, and Sydney Freedberg, "After Slow Start, Yahwehs Developed Clout in Politics," *Miami Herald*, December 23, 1990.

Florida Intelligence Unit report, Organized Crime Committee. "Black Hebrew Israelites (Yahwehs) in Florida," November 6, 1984.

Freedberg, Sydney, and Mark Kriegel. "Yahweh Member Charged in Killings," *Miami Herald*, October 31, 1986.

Source Notes

....

Freedberg, Sydney. "Community Relations Board Chief Criticizes Cops in Yahweh Case," *Miami Herald*, November 1, 1986.

Freedberg, Sydney, and Steve Rothaus. "Opa-locka: Pleas for Help Never Taped," *Miami Herald*, November 4, 1986.

———. "Police Tape Fails to Record Bomb Threat," *Miami Herald*, November 5, 1986.

Freedberg, Sydney. "Fear, Neglect Let Yahwehs Take Over Slum," *Miami Herald*, November 9, 1986.

———. "Yahwehs Open Temple to Press; Deny Comparisons to Jonestown," *Miami Herald*, November 26, 1986.

———. "Yahweh Robert Rozier Led Many Lives," *Miami Herald*, November 27, 1986.

———. "Yahweh Testifies in Crime Probe; Prosecutors Seek Sect's 'Lamb's Book,' " *Miami Herald*, May 4, 1990.

———. "Yahweh Dazzles a Business Crowd; Says Probe Based on 'Army of Liars,' " *Miami Herald*, May 26, 1990.

———. "Yahwehs Get Warning for Violations at School," *Miami Herald*, June 15, 1990.

———. "Leader Talks Peace and Power," *Miami Herald*, July 8, 1990.

———. "Murder in the Temple of Love?" *Miami Herald*, July 8, 1990.

———. "State Probes Long-Held Claims of Child Abuse in Yahweh Sect," *Miami Herald*, November 9, 1990.

Freedberg, Sydney, and Donna Gehrke. "From Idealists to 'Death Angels'?" *Miami Herald*, December 31, 1990.

Froomkin, Dan. "Yahwehs Set Family Values for Reopened Motel," *Miami Herald*, August 4, 1987.

Gehrke, Donna. "Unlikely Meeting Ended in Death," *Miami Herald*, December 4, 1990.

Getter, Lisa. "Suarez Wins; Carollo Out; Broad Base of Support Aids Mayor," *Miami Herald*, November 11, 1987.

Gibbs, Lisa. "Yahwehs Try to Calm Chamber Fears," *Miami Herald*, October 22, 1987.

———. "Education According to Yahweh," *Miami Herald*, February 4, 1988.

Goldfarb, Carl. "City Concessions Helped Gary Set up Deal with Yahwehs," *Miami Herald*, May 13, 1990.

Hicks, Desiree F., "Front Door to Miami Spruced Up," *Miami Herald*, May 17, 1987.

Kriegel, Mark. "Landlords Offer Drug Houses to City," *Miami Herald,* October 18, 1986.

———. "Landlords Want Out; Tenants Fear for Future," *Miami Herald,* October 26, 1986.

———. "Yahwehs Take Over Opa-locka Apartments," *Miami Herald,* October 29, 1986.

———. "Cop: I Was Told to Lie about Yahweh Case," *Miami Herald,* April 2, 1987.

———. "Firebombing's Victims Still Suspect Sect," *Miami Herald,* May 16, 1988.

Lawrence, David, Jr. " 'I Apologize'—It's Not So Hard to Say," *Miami Herald,* August 12, 1990.

Lee, Felicia. "Yahweh Sect Gains New Respect, Friends," *Miami Herald,* May 16, 1988.

———. "Yahwehs Buy Seaside Motel," *Miami Herald,* May 23, 1988.

Longa, Lyda. "Sect's Service Center Saves More Than Souls," *Fort Lauderdale Sun-Sentinel,* December 3, 1989.

May, Patrick. "Sect Steadily Buying Dade Properties," *Miami Herald,* June 28, 1987.

———. "Yahwehs Denied Tax Breaks on Several Properties," *Miami Herald,* July 4, 1987.

———. "Leader of Yahwehs Shows off His Sect's Latest Acquisition," *Miami Herald,* July 12, 1987.

McQueen, Mike. "Grand Jury Scrutinizing Yahweh Sect's Finances," *Miami Herald,* June 26, 1990.

Miami Herald. "Surroundings Different But Cornbread Is Great," October 28, 1982.

Miami Times. October 30, 1986.

Miami Times. "Spreading Larceny," November 13, 1986.

Mooney, Carolyn. "Yahweh Sect Moves into Hallandale," *Miami Herald,* December 12, 1984.

Oglesby, Joe. "Sect Attacks White Man's 'Fairy Tale,' " *Miami Herald,* July 13, 1981.

———. "Hebrew Israelite Leader Keeps His Past a Secret," *Miami Herald,* July 13, 1981.

New Jersey Afro-American. "15 Arrests Made in Police Raid of Hebrew Israelite Temples," April 12, 1986.

New York Times. "Boy Scout Recruiter, Sect Member Held in Child Abuse Case," April 12, 1986.

Source Notes

••

Philbin, Walt. "Sect May Have Overpowered Karate Champ," *Times-Picayune*, November 10, 1990.

Prater, Constance. "A Part of Me Gone Astray: A Yahweh Hitman? No, Not My Old Friend," *Miami Herald*, November 25, 1990.

Ramos, Ronnie. "Blank Cop Tapes Blamed on Human Error," *Miami Herald*, January 7, 1987.

———. "Shelter Will Be Stadium Again Soon," *Miami Herald*, January 5, 1989.

Rubin, Ellis. "Sect Treated Unfairly, Lawyer Contends," *Miami Herald*, July 8, 1990.

Sachs, Susan. "Cult's Self-Styled Messiah Inspires Discipline, Fear," *Miami Herald*, December 8, 1985.

———. "Police Stepping up Probes in Wake of Yahweh Arrest," *Miami Herald*, November 1, 1986.

ShopTalk. "Two Sensational Miami Soft Waves," September 1990.

Smith, Stephen. "Yahwehs Buy Motel on Biscayne," *Miami Herald*, February 22, 1987.

———. "Community Welcomes Yahwehs as 'Godsend,' " *Miami Herald*, March 8, 1987.

Smothers, Ronald. "Social Worker's Judgment Faulted in Abuse Case," *New York Times*, April 8, 1986.

Strouse, Charles. "Open for Business: Yahwehs Start Overtown Market," *Miami Herald*, April 15, 1990.

Strouse, Charles, and Sydney Freedberg. "Yahwehs Turn Cult Image to Economic Clout," *Miami Herald*, May 13, 1990.

Tomb, Geoffrey. "Yahwehs, Tenants Wait It Out at Opa-locka Complex," *Miami Herald*, October 30, 1986.

Uhler, David. "Fired Deputy Checked on Other Yahwehs," *Fort Lauderdale Sun-Sentinel*, November 5, 1986.

Wallace, Richard. "Yahwehs Told to Stay Away from Apartments," *Miami Herald*, November 7, 1986.

Viglucci, Andres, and Charles Strouse. "Sect Money Shrouded in Mystery," *Miami Herald*, November 18, 1990.

Viglucci, Andres, and Sydney Freedberg. "U.S. Investigates Financial Deals by Yahweh Cult," *Miami Herald*, December 3, 1990.

Voboril, Mary. "Black Hebrews Say in Leaflet Police Plotting to Kill Them," *Miami Herald*, November 19, 1981.

White, Dale. "Religious Sect Leaves Calling Card for Mayors," *St. Petersburg Times*, December 13, 1984.

Source Notes

Young, April. "Ben Yahweh Speaks Out against Violence," *Miami Times*, June 25, 1987.

TV reports: CBS News, West 57th, Yahweh Ben Yahweh"; Expose, January 13, 1991, "Yahwehs."

Part IV: Operation Jericho

INTERVIEWS: Perry Anderson; Pinkey Benebee; Don Blocker; Thomas Buscaglia; Lloyd Clark; Herb Cousins; Chuck Davis; Mary Dupree; Glenn Feldman; Richard Gagliano; William Gavin; Wendell Graham; Louretta Green; Kathy Hamilton; Alcee Hastings; Volney Hayes; Barbara Howard; Aleeza Israel; Julian Jackson; Dennis Kainen; Steve Kassner; Albert Levin; Chris Mancini; Edwin McCausland; Ray McGhee; Paul McKenna; Donna Mest; Paul Miller; Denise Murphy; Gilbert Myers; Gertrude Novicki; Rickey O'Donald; Howard Pohl; Rex Remley; Robert Rozier, Jr.; Ellis Rubin; Wende Rush; Marcia Sandler; Penny Schwam; Richard Scruggs; Fred Taylor; Charles White; Prophet Yahweh.

COURT TESTIMONY: Robert Beasley, Jr.; Carl Blake; George Campbell; Fred Carter; Barbara Coleman; Barry Crown; Pierre De Jean; Jesse Diopaec; Constance Foster; Paul George; Gail Guynn; Hatti Hunter; Job Israel; Judith Israel; Lavon Israel; William Carlton King; Arthur Lester; Walter Lightburn; George Lopez; Aubrey Maloney; Michael Mathis; Broderick McKinney; Lloyd Miller; Carl Murray; Carl Perry; Amtullah Raheem; Rudy Shears; Thomas Simmons; Estella Williams; Maurice Woodside; Ricardo Woodside; William Young.

POLICE REPORTS: M. Bryant; P. Rothert.

MISCELLANEOUS DOCUMENTS: FBI press release 11/7/90; U.S. Department of Justice news release 11/7/90; authorized in-cell belonging list/Metropolitan Correctional Center; detainee request from Walter Lightburn to Broward County Jail; plea agreements for Ricardo Woodside and Michael Mathis; letter of immunity to Jeffrey Glover; court files and transcripts of proceedings in case no. 90–868, volumes 1 through 69; jurors' notes; Georgia Secretary of State incorporation papers; Fulton County Clerk of Superior Court deed index; personal notes of trial by Glenn Feldman; letters from Prophet Yahweh, 8306 Wilshire Blvd., Beverly Hills, CA; Dade Circuit Court case file nos. 92-018643, 92-018644, and 92-018645; letter from Tami Willis, production assistant, BET, dated November 12, 1991; letter to Sydney Freedberg from Yahweh Ben Yahweh, dated April 16, 1993.

Source Notes

PUBLICATIONS:

Associated Press. "Yahweh Defended by His Brother," *Enid News and Eagle*, May 30, 1992.

———. "Yahweh Followers Say Verdict Won't Kill Sect," *Orlando Sentinel*, May 30, 1992.

Cannizaro, Steve, and Walt Philbin. "Miami Sect Leader Accused of Ordering 'White Devils' Killed," *Times-Picayune*, November 8, 1990.

Cox, Art. "Father Says Son Is Innocent," *Enid News and Eagle*, November 8, 1990.

Due, Tananarive. "Miami, Followers Honor Yahweh at Arena Speech," *Miami Herald*, October 8, 1990.

Edwards, Allen. "Father Professes Son's Innocence," *Enid News and Eagle*, January 2, 1992.

Epstein, Gail. "Yahweh Murder Charges Dropped," *Miami Herald*, December 19, 1992.

Fonzi, Gaeton. "Yahweh Ben Yahweh: 'This Is the Judgment Day,' " *Penthouse*, February 1992.

Freedberg, Sydney. "Yahweh Sect Leader, 16 Followers Indicted," *Miami Herald*, November 8, 1990.

———. "Families Learned Details from Media," *Miami Herald*, November 14, 1990.

Freedberg, Sydney, and Christine Evans. "Politics, Religion Slowed Probe of Sect," *Miami Herald*, November 16, 1990.

Freedberg, Sydney. "Deaths and Disappearances under Investigation," *Miami Herald*, July 8, 1990.

Gehrke, Donna. "Two Disciples Turn Themselves In; Yahweh Called for Surrender from Jail," *Miami Herald*, November 17, 1990.

———. "Prosecution: Tapes Prove Yahweh Ordered Killings," *Miami Herald*, November 21, 1990.

Gehrke, Donna, and Sydney Freedberg. "Yahwehs Suspected in More Murders," *Miami Herald*, December 16, 1990.

Gehrke, Donna. "Grand Jury Probes Yahweh Sect Drug Connections," *Miami Herald*, May 7, 1991.

———. "Yahweh Family Ties Break as Sister, Son Testify against Brother, Mom," *Miami Herald*, January 25, 1992.

———. "Yahweh Witnesses Detail Sect's Rules about Diet, Sex," *Miami Herald*, February 16, 1992.

———. "Yahweh Defense Begins Today," *Miami Herald*, March 10, 1992.

————. "1 of 3 Charges Dropped against Yahweh," *Miami Herald*, March 11, 1992.

————. "Yahweh's Message Delivered on Cable TV Show," *Miami Herald*, April 3, 1992.

————. "Mother of Alleged Yahweh Victim Has Outburst during Graphic Closing," *Miami Herald*, May 15, 1992.

————. "Yahweh Trial Nearing Its End," *Miami Herald*, May 14, 1992.

————. "Yahweh Jurors Doubted Star Witness," *Miami Herald*, May 29, 1992.

————. "Publicity Helped Group Spread Its Message," *Miami Herald*, May 28, 1992.

Goldfarb, Carl. "Attorney: Rescind Yahweh Proclamation," *Miami Herald*, November 13, 1990.

Harrison, Carlos. "Predawn Arrest in New Orleans Triggers Seven-State FBI Sweep," *Miami Herald*, November 8, 1990.

————. "Yahweh Follower a Suspect in 4-Year-Old Rape, Murder," *Miami Herald*, November 20, 1990.

Lyons, David. "We're Going to Do This Again," *Miami Herald*, May 30, 1992.

Muhammad, Richard. "Government Plot Behind Yahweh Arrest: Attorney," *Final Call*, September 9, 1991.

Ocker, Lisa. "Juror: Race and Religion Not Factors," *Fort Lauderdale Sun-Sentinel*, May 28, 1992.

————. "Followers Say Faith Strong Despite Trial, Convictions," *Fort Lauderdale Sun-Sentinel*, May 29, 1992.

Richey, Warren. "Jurors to Remain Despite Jokes About Yahweh Trial," *Fort Lauderdale Sun-Sentinel*, January 7, 1992.

————. "Star Witness's Explosive Testimony Rejected in Yahweh Case, Juror Says," *Fort Lauderdale Sun-Sentinel*, May 29, 1992.

Swarns, Rachel. "Yahweh: No Grudges," *Miami Herald*, November 30, 1991.

Williams, Ernestine. "Yahweh Summation Graphic; Gruesome Emotions Run High in Broward Courtroom," *Palm Beach Post*, May 15, 1992.

————. "Jury Convicts Yahweh of Conspiracy," *Palm Beach Post*, May 28, 1992.

Yanez, Luisa. "Mutilated Victim's Mom Decries Verdict's Delay," *Fort Lauderdale Sun-Sentinel*, May 28, 1992.